English Grammar Workbook

FOR

DUMMIES®

by Geraldine Woods

WILEY

Wiley Publishing, Inc.

English Grammar Workbook For Dummies®

Published by
Wiley Publishing, Inc.
111 River St.
Hoboken, NJ 07030-5774
www.wiley.com

Copyright © 2006 by Wiley Publishing, Inc., Indianapolis, Indiana

Published simultaneously in Canada

For general information on our other products and services, please contact our Customer Care Department within the U.S. at 800-762-2974, outside the U.S. at 317-572-3993, or fax 317-572-4002.

For technical support, please visit www.wiley.com/techsupport.

Wiley also publishes its books in a variety of electronic formats. Some content that appears in print may not be available in electronic books.

Library of Congress Control Number is available from the publisher.

ISBN-13: 978-0-7645-9932-3

ISBN-10: 0-7645-9932-1

Manufactured in the United States of America

10 9 8 7 6 5

1B/SQ/QU/QW/IN

WILEY

About the Author

Geraldine Woods began her education when teachers still supplied ink wells to their students. She credits her 35-year career as an English teacher to a set of ultra-strict nuns armed with thick grammar books. She lives in New York City, where with great difficulty she refrains from correcting signs containing messages such as "Bagel's for sale." She is the author of more than 40 books, including *English Grammar For Dummies, Research Papers For Dummies, College Admission Essays For Dummies,* and *The SAT I Reasoning Test For Dummies.*

Dedication

For the students who labor (and occasionally smile) in the grammar portion of my English classes.

Author's Acknowledgments

I owe thanks to my colleagues at the Horace Mann School, who are always willing to discuss the finer points of grammar. I appreciate the work of Kristin DeMint, Sarah Faulkner, and Neil Johnson, editors whose attention and intelligence guided my writing. I also appreciate the efforts of Lisa Queen, my agent, and of Roxanne Cerda and Kathy Cox, Wiley acquisitions editors.

Publisher's Acknowledgments

We're proud of this book; please send us your comments through our Dummies online registration form located at www.dummies.com/register/.

Some of the people who helped bring this book to market include the following:

Acquisitions, Editorial, and Media Development

Project Editor: Kristin DeMint

Acquisitions Editor: Kathleen M. Cox

Copy Editors: Sarah Faulkner, E. Neil Johnson

Editorial Program Coordinator: Hanna K. Scott

Technical Editor: Sue Williams, PhD

Senior Editorial Manager: Jennifer Ehrlich

Editorial Assistant: Nadine Bell

Cover Photos: © Getty Images

Cartoons: Rich Tennant (www.the5thwave.com)

Composition Services

Project Coordinator: Adrienne Martinez

Layout and Graphics: Denny Hager, Stephanie D. Jumper, Lynsey Osborn, Melanee Prendergast, Heather Ryan

Proofreaders: Leeann Harney, Jessica Kramer, Henry Lazarek, Joe Niesen, Dwight Ramsey

Indexer: Joan Griffitts

Special Help
Michelle Hacker

Publishing and Editorial for Consumer Dummies

Diane Graves Steele, Vice President and Publisher, Consumer Dummies

Joyce Pepple, Acquisitions Director, Consumer Dummies

Kristin A. Cocks, Product Development Director, Consumer Dummies

Michael Spring, Vice President and Publisher, Travel

Kelly Regan, Editorial Director, Travel

Publishing for Technology Dummies

Andy Cummings, Vice President and Publisher, Dummies Technology/General User

Composition Services

Gerry Fahey, Vice President of Production Services

Debbie Stailey, Director of Composition Services

Contents at a Glance

Table of Contents

Introduction

Good grammar pays. No, I'm not making a sentimental statement about the importance of a job well done or the satisfaction of learning for learning's sake, though I believe in both of those values. I'm talking about cold, hard cash, the kind you fold and put into your wallet. Don't believe me? Fine. Try this little test: The next time you go to the movies, tear yourself away from the story for a moment and concentrate on the dialogue. Chances are the characters who have fancy jobs or piles of dough sound different from those who don't. I'm not making a value judgment here; I'm just describing reality. Proper English, either written or spoken, tends to be associated with the upper social or economic classes. Tuning up your grammar muscles doesn't guarantee your entry into the Bill Gates income tax bracket, but poor grammar may make it much harder to fight your way in.

Another payoff of good grammar is better grades and an edge in college admissions. Teachers have always looked more favorably on nicely written sentences, and grammar has recently become an additional hurdle that applicants must jump over or stumble through when they sit for the SAT or the ACT, the two most important standardized tests for the college bound.

The good news is that you don't have to spend a lifetime improving your English. Ten minutes here, ten minutes there, and before you know it, your grammar muscles will be toned to fighting strength. This book is the equivalent of a health-club membership for your writing and speaking skills. Like a good health club, it doesn't waste your time with lectures on the physiology of flat abs. Instead, it sends you right to the mat and sets you up with the exercises that actually do the job.

About This Book

English Grammar Workbook For Dummies doesn't concentrate on what we English teachers (yes, I confess I am one) call *descriptive grammar* — the kind where you circle all the nouns and draw little triangles around the prepositions. A closely guarded English-teacher secret is that you don't need to know any of that terminology (well, hardly any) to master grammar. Instead, *English Grammar Workbook For Dummies* concentrates on *functional grammar* — what goes where in real-life speech and writing.

Each chapter begins with a quick explanation of the rules (don't smoke, don't stick your chewing gum on the bedpost, be sure your sentence is complete, and so forth). Okay, I'm kidding about the smoking and the chewing gum, but you get the idea. I start off telling you what's right and wrong in standard English usage. Next, I provide an example and then hit you with ten or so quick questions. Just to make sure you know that I'm not wasting your time, in every chapter I give you a sample from real-life English (with a fairly absurd situation, just to keep your funny bone tingling), so you can see how proper grammar actually aids communication.

After filling in the blanks, you can check your answers at the end of the chapter. In *English Grammar Workbook For Dummies,* I also tell you why a particular choice is correct, not just for the sake of learning a set of rules but rather to help you make the right decision the next time — when you're deciding between *their* and *they're* or *went* and *had gone,* for example.

As the author of *English Grammar For Dummies* (Wiley) and a grammar teacher for more decades than I care to count (let's just say that I had an inkwell in my first classroom), I believe that if you truly get the logic of grammar — and most rules do rest upon a logical basis — you'll be a better, more precise communicator.

English Grammar Workbook For Dummies offers a special welcome to readers for whom English is a second language. You've probably picked up quite a bit of vocabulary and basic grammar already. *English Grammar Workbook For Dummies* lets you practice the little things — the best word choice for a particular sentence, the proper way to create a plural, and so forth. This book moves you beyond comprehension to mastery.

Finally, because standardized college entrance exams are now a permanent part of the landscape, I've taken special care to provide examples that mirror those horrible tests. If you're facing the SAT or the ACT in the near future, don't despair. Everything the grammar-testing gurus expect you to know is in this book.

Conventions Used in This Book

To make your practice as easy as possible, I've used some conventions throughout this book so that from chapter to chapter or section to section you're not wondering what the heck is going on. Here are a few to note:

- ✔ At the end of each chapter is the "Answers" section, which covers all the exercises in that chapter. You can find the answers by thumbing through the book until you come to the pages with the gray trim on the outside edge.

- ✔ The last exercise in each chapter is comprehensive, so you can check your mastery of the material in that chapter and sharpen your editing skills. You can find the comprehensive answers and explanations in the "Answers" section. The callout numbers pointing to the corrections in the exercise correspond with the numbered explanations in the text. I also provide an appendix devoted entirely to providing comprehensive practice with the grammar skills you develop as you consult *English Grammar For Dummies* and as you complete the exercises throughout this workbook.

What You're Not to Read

I promise you that I've kept the grammar jargon to a minimum in this workbook, but I must admit that I have included a couple of terms from schoolbook land. If you stumble upon a definition, run away as fast as you can and try the sample question instead. If you can get the point without learning the grammatical term, you win a gold star. Likewise, feel free to skip the explanation of any question that you get right, unless of course you want to gloat. In that case read the explanation while crowing, "I knew that."

Foolish Assumptions

In writing the *English Grammar Workbook For Dummies,* I'm assuming that you fall into one or more of these categories:

- ✔ You know some English but want to improve your skills.
- ✔ You aspire to a better job.

- You want higher grades or SAT/ACT scores.
- You feel a bit insecure about your language skills and want to communicate with more confidence.
- You're still learning to speak and write English fluently.

I've made two more global assumptions about you, the reader. First, you have a busy life with very little time to waste on unnecessary frills. With this important fact in mind, I've tried to keep the explanations in this book clear, simple, and *short,* so you can get right to it and practice away. I've left the fancy grammar terms — *gerunds, indicative mood, copulative verb,* and the like — by the wayside, where, in my humble opinion, they belong. I don't want to clutter up your brain; I just want to give you what you need to know to speak and write in standard English. For the total, complete, and occasionally humorous explanations, pick up a copy of the companion book, *English Grammar For Dummies,* also written by yours truly (and published by Wiley).

Second, I assume that you hate boring, schoolbook style. You'd prefer not to yawn as you read. No problem! I too glaze over when faced with sentences like "The administrative council approved the new water-purification project outlined in by-law 78-451 by a margin of three votes to two." To keep you awake, I've used my somewhat insane imagination to create amusing sentences that will (I hope) make you smile or even laugh from time to time.

How This Book Is Organized

Life gets harder as you go along, doesn't it? So too *English Grammar Workbook For Dummies.* Parts I and II concentrate on the basics — plopping the right verbs into each sentence, forming singulars and plurals, creating complete sentences, and so on. Part III moves up a notch to the pickier stuff, not exactly world record but definitely the state-champ level. In Parts III and IV, you get to try your hand at the most annoying problems presented by pronouns (those pesky little words such as *I, me, theirs, whomever,* and others), advanced verb problems, and comparisons (*different than? different from?* find out here!). Part V is totally practical, polishing up your writing style and explaining some common word traps into which you may fall. Now for more detail.

Part I: Laying Out the Concrete Slab: Grammar Basics

In this part I take you through the basic building blocks — *verbs* (words that express action or state of being) and *subjects* (who or what you're talking about) — with a quick side trip into pronouns (*I, he, her,* and the like). I show you how to create a complete sentence. In this part you practice choosing the correct verb tense in straightforward sentences and find out all you need to know about singular and plural forms.

Part II: Mastering Mechanics

This part's devoted to two little things — punctuation and capital letters — that can make or break your writing. If you're not sure whether to head *North* or *north* or if you want to know where a comma belongs, this part's for you.

Part III: The Pickier Points of Correct Verb and Pronoun Use

Paging *who* and *whom,* not to mention *I* and *me.* This part tackles all the fun stuff associated with pronouns, including the reason why (for all practical intents and purposes) *everyone* can't eat *their* lunch. Part III also solves your time problems, making you decipher the shades of difference in verb tense *(wrote? had written?)* and voice (not *alto* or *soprano,* but *active* or *passive*).

Part IV: All You Need to Know about Descriptions and Comparisons

Part IV doesn't tackle which stock is a bad investment (and which is even worse), but it puts you through your paces in selecting the best descriptive words *(good? well?).* Part IV also weeds out illogical or vague comparisons.

Part V: Writing with Style

In Part V, the wind sprints and stretches are over, and it's time to compete with world-class writers. The toughest grammatical situations, plus exercises that address fluidity and variety, face you here. I also throw in some misunderstood words *(healthful* and *healthy,* to name just two) and let you practice proper usage in this part.

Part VI: The Part of Tens

Here you find ten ways that people trying to be super-correct end up being super-wrong and ten errors that can kill your career (or grade).

Icons Used in This Book

Icons are the cute little drawings that attract your gaze and alert you to key points, pitfalls, and other groovy things. In *English Grammar Workbook For Dummies,* you find these three:

I live in New York City, and I often see tourists staggering around, desperate for a resident to show them the ropes. The Tip icon is the equivalent of a resident whispering in your ear. Psst! Want the inside story that will make your life easier? Here it is!

When you're about to walk through a field riddled with land mines, it's nice to have a map. The Warning icon tells you where the traps are so you can delicately run like mad from them.

Theory doesn't go very far when you're working on grammar. You have to see the language in action, so to speak. The Practice icon alerts you to (surprise!) an example and a set of practice exercises so you can practice what I just finished preaching.

Where to Go from Here

To the refrigerator for a snack. Nope. Just kidding. Now that you know what's where, turn to the section that best meets your needs. If you're not sure what would benefit you most, take a moment to think about what bothers you. No, I'm not talking about the fact that your favorite brand of yogurt just cut two ounces from each container. I'm talking about the parts of writing or speaking that make you pause for a lengthy head scratch. Do you have trouble picking the appropriate verb tense? Is finding the right word a snap but placing a comma cause for concern? Do you go out of your way to avoid sentences with *who* because you never know when to opt for *whom*?

After you've done a little grammatical reconnaissance, select the sections of this book that meet your needs. Use the "How This Book Is Organized" section earlier in this introduction, the table of contents, and the index to find more detail about what is where. Turn to the exercises that address your issues and use the rest to line the birdcage. Of course, if you decide to read every single word I've written, you win my "favorite person of the month" award. But don't beat yourself up if you pick and choose from the selection of tune-ups.

If you aren't sure whether a particular topic is a problem, no problem! Run your eyeballs over the explanation and sample question. Try a couple of sentences and check your answers. If everything comes out okay and you understand the answers, move on. If you stub your toe, go back and do a few more until the grammar rule becomes clear.

When you understand each concept separately but have trouble putting the whole picture together, take a stab at the comprehensive exercise that ends each chapter. You have to find and correct mistakes in a short piece of lunatic writing. After you find them, check yourself.

One more thing: Don't try to do everything at once. Hit your mind with a half cup of grammar (about ten minutes or so) at a time. More will stick, and as a huge plus, you'll have time to go bowling.

Part I
Laying Out the Concrete Slab: Grammar Basics

In this part . . .

*I*f you've ever built a house — with real bricks or with kiddy blocks — you know that the whole thing is likely to fall down unless it's sitting atop a strong foundation. This part provides the stuff you need to lay the best foundation for your writing. Chapter 1 takes you through Verbology 101, explaining how to select the best verb for present, past, and future situations. In the same chapter, you find the most popular irregular verbs and everything you need to know about the ever-helpful helping verb. Chapter 2 sorts verbs into singular and plural piles and helps you match each verb to the correct subject. Then you're ready to pair pronouns and nouns (Chapter 3) and to distinguish complete from incomplete or too-long sentences (Chapter 4). Ready? I promise I won't let the roof fall on your head!

Chapter 1

Placing the Proper Verb in the Proper Place

In This Chapter

▶ Examining past, present, and future tenses

▶ Practicing the perfect tenses

▶ Navigating among irregular forms

▶ Handling helping verbs

As short as two letters and as long as several words, verbs communicate action or state of being. Plus, even without a new Rolex, they tell time. Unfortunately, that handy little time-keeping function, like the buttons on my watch, can be confusing. In this chapter, I hit you with basic time questions. No, not "You're late again *because* . . . ?" but "Which verb do I need to show what's completed, not yet begun, or going on right now?" The first section hits the basic tenses (past, present, and future) and the second hits the perfect tenses, which are anything *but* perfect. After that, you can work on irregulars and helping verbs.

Choosing among Past, Present, and Future

Verbs tell time with a quality known as tense. Before you reach for a tranquilizer, here's the lowdown on the basic tenses. You have three, and each has two forms — lo-carb and fat-free. Sorry, I mean *plain* (called by its basic time designation — present, past, or future) and *progressive* (the *-ing* form of a verb). *Progressive* places a little more emphasis on process or on action that spans a time period, and the present progressive may reach into the future. In many sentences, either plain or progressive verbs may be used interchangeably. Here's a taste of each:

✔ *Past tense* **tells what happened either at a specific, previous time or describes a pattern of behavior in the past.** (In the sentence "Diane tattooed a skull on her bulging bicep," *tattooed* is a past tense verb. In "During the Motorcycle Festival, Diane was flexing her bicep," *was flexing* is a verb in past progressive tense.)

✔ *Present tense* **tells you what's going on now at the present moment, or more generally speaking, what action is recurring.** It also touches the future. (In the sentence "Grace rides her Harley," *rides* is a present tense verb. In "Grace is always polishing her Harley" and "Grace is riding to Florida," the verbs *is polishing* and *is riding* are in present progressive tense.)

✔ *Future tense* **moves into fortune-teller land**. (The verb in "Grace will give Diane a ride around the block" is *will give*, which is in future tense. In "Grace will be bragging about her new motorcycle for months," *will be bragging* is in future progressive tense.)

Okay, time to check out a sample problem. The *infinitive* (the grandpappy of each verb family) follows every sentence. Stay in that family when you fill in the blank, choosing the correct tense. When you're finished with this sample, try the practice problems that follow.

0. Yesterday, overreacting to an itty-bitty taste of arsenic, Mike _____ his evil twin brother of murder. *(to accuse)*

A. **accused**. The clue here is *yesterday,* which tells you that you're in the past.

1. Fashion is important to David, so he always _____ the latest and most popular poaching style. *(to select)*

2. Last year's tight, slim lines _____ David, who, it must be admitted, does not have a tiny waist. *(to challenge)*

3. While David _____ new clothes, his fashion consultant is busy on the sidelines, recommending stripes and understated plaids to minimize the bulge factor. *(to buy)*

4. David hopes that the next fashion fad _____ a more mature, oval figure like his own. *(to flatter)*

5. Right now Diane _____ an article for the fashion press stating that so-tight-it-may-as-well-be-painted-on leather is best. *(to write)*

6. She once _____ a purple suede pantsuit, which clashed with her orange "I Love Motorcycles" tattoo. *(to purchase)*

7. While she _____ the pantsuit, two shoppers urged her to "go for it." *(to charge)*

8. Two days after Diane's shopping spree, Grace _____ about show-offs who "spend more time on their wardrobes than on their spark plugs." *(to mutter)*

9. However, Diane knows that Grace, as soon as she raises enough cash, _____ in a suede outfit of her own. *(to invest)*

10. David, as always, _____ in with the last word when he gave Grace and Diane the "Fashion Train Wreck of the Year" award. *(to chime)*

11. Two minutes after she received the award, Diane _____ it on a shelf next to her "Best Dressed, Considering" medal. *(to place)*

12. Every day, when I see the medal, I _____ what "considering" means. *(to wonder)*

13. Grace _____ it to me in detail yesterday. *(to explain)*

14. "We earned the medal for considering many fashion options," she _____. *(to state)*

15. David, who _____ Diane tomorrow, says that the medal acknowledges the fact that Grace is "fashion-challenged" but tries hard anyway. *(to visit)*

Shining a Light on Not-So-Perfect Tenses

The perfect tenses tack *has, have,* or *had* onto a verb. Each perfect tense — present perfect, past perfect, and future perfect — also has a progressive form, which includes an *-ing* verb. The difference between plain perfect tense and progressive perfect is subtle. The progressive perfect is a bit more immediate than the plain form and refers to something that's ongoing or takes places over a span of time. In many sentences the plain and progressive forms may be interchanged. Here's when to use the perfect tenses:

- *Present perfect* **links the past and the present**. An action or state of being began in the past and is still going on. (In the sentence "Despite numerous reports of sightings around the world, Kristin has stayed close to home," the verb *has stayed* is in present perfect tense. In "Kristin has been living within two miles of the Scottish border for the last decade," *has been living* is a present perfect progressive tense verb.)

- *Past perfect* **places one event in the past before another event in the past**. (The verb in "Mike had dumped his dirty laundry in his mother's basement long before she decided to change the front-door lock" is *had dumped,* which is in past perfect tense. In the sentence "Christy, Mike's mother, had been threatening a laundry strike for years, but the beginning of mud-wrestling season pushed her to the breaking point," *had been threatening* is a past perfect progressive tense verb.)

- *Future perfect* **implies a deadline sometime (surprise, surprise) in the future**. (In the sentence "Before sundown, David will have toasted several dozen loaves of bread," *will have toasted* is in future perfect tense. The verb in "By the time you turn on the television, *Eye on Cooking* will have been covering the toasting session for two hours, with six more to go," is *will have been covering,* which is in future perfect progressive tense.)

Practice, especially with these verbs, makes perfect, so try this example and then plunge ahead. The verb you're working on appears as an *infinitive* (the basic, no-tense form) at the end of the sentence. Change it into the correct tense and fill in the blank.

Q. Kristin _____ an acceptance speech, but the "Spy of the Year" title went to Hanna instead. *(to prepare)*

A. **had prepared**. With two events in the past, the *had* signals the prior event. The preparing of the speech took place before the awarding of the title, so *had prepared* is the form you want.

16. Mike _____ on thin ice for two hours when he heard the first crack. *(to skate)*

17. Diane _____ Mike for years about his skating habits, but he just won't listen. *(to warn)*

18. David — a delicate, sensitive soul — accompanied Mike to the pond and then to the hospital. After David _____ an hour, the doctor announced that the skater was free to go. *(to wait)*

19. After today's skating trip ends, David _____ a total of 1,232 hours for his friend and _____ countless outdated magazines in the emergency room family area. *(to wait, to read)*

20. Grace _____ to speak to Mike ever since he declared that "a little thin ice" shouldn't scare anyone. *(to refuse)*

21. Mike, in a temper, pointed out that Grace's motorcycle _____ him to the hospital even more frequently than his skates. *(to send)*

22. In an effort to make peace, Kristin _____ quietly to both combatants before they ever stop yelling at each other. *(to speak)*

23. Despite years of practice, Tim _____ success only on rare occasions, but he keeps trying to resolve his brother's conflicts anyway. *(to achieve)*

24. At times Tim's conflict-resolution technique _____ of violent finger pokes in the fighters' ribs, but he is trying to become more diplomatic. *(to consist)*

25. After Mike _____ that his brother's wisest course of action was to "butt out," Tim simply ignored him. *(to declare)*

26. We all think that Tim _____ up on conflict resolution by the time Mike turns 30. *(to give)*

27. Despite failing with Mike every time he tries to avoid a quarrel, Tim _____ interest in a diplomatic career several times over the last few weeks. *(to express)*

28. Although Mike _____ several ambassadors about his brother's career plans during his visit to the United Nations last week, no one granted Tim an interview yesterday, though he spent the day begging for "just five minutes." *(to approach)*

29. Kristin, the soul of kindness, said that before Tim makes his next career move, she _____ that "it's hard to break into this field" at least five times. *(to declare)*

30. David could help, as he _____ as an ambassador for the last seven years and won't retire until 2010. *(to serve)*

Navigating among Irregular Forms

Designed purposely to torture you, irregular verbs stray from the usual *-ed* form in the past tense. The irregularity, which doesn't entitle you to the sale price the way it does for irregular sheets or other things that are actually useful, continues in a form called the *past participle*. You don't need to know the terms; you just need to know what words replace the usual *-ed* verb configuration (*sang* and *sung* instead of *singed*, for example).

You can't memorize every possible irregular verb. If you're unsure about a particular verb, look it up in the dictionary. The definition will include the irregular form.

Here's a set of irregular problems to pickle your brain. Fill in the blanks with the correct irregular form, working from the verb indicated in parentheses. Notice that the parentheses don't, strictly speaking, contain a verb at all — just the ancestor of that particular verb family, the infinitive. Check out the following example.

0. With one leg three inches shorter than the other, Natalie seldom _____ into second base, even when the team was desperate for a base hit. *(to slide)*

A. slid. No *-ed* for this past tense! *Slid* is the irregular past form of *to slide*.

31. If you discover a piece of pottery on the floor, look for Natalie, who has _____ many vases because of her tendency to dust far too emotionally. *(to break)*

32. Once, Natalie _____ with sadness at her first glimpse of a dusty armchair. *(to shake)*

33. David, no mean duster himself, _____ a manual of daily furniture maintenance. *(to write)*

34. The manual, entitled *Dust or Die,* _____ to the top of the best-seller list. *(to rise)*

35. News reports indicated that nearly all the copies had been _____ by fanatical cleaners. *(to buy)*

36. David once dusted the fire alarm so forcefully that it went off; the firefighters weren't amused because David had _____ the fire alarm a little too often. *(to ring)*

37. The fire chief promptly _____ to speak with the mayor about David's false alarm. *(to go)*

38. The mayor has _____ an investigation into a new category of offenses, "False Dust Alarms"; almost immediately, David _____ to protest. *(to begin)*

39. "I have _____ to a new low," sighed David, as he enrolled in the local chapter of Clean Anonymous. "I hear that Natalie has _____ a new hobby. Maybe I can too." *(to sink, to find)*

40. Natalie _____ David to a fly-catching meet, and soon his interest in grime _____ the dust. *(to take, to bite)*

41. Natalie, however, became completely excited by fly catching and _____ a tapestry with a delicate fly pattern. *(to weave)*

42. David, worried about Natalie's enthusiasm for winged pests, _____ help. *(to seek)*

43. "Leave the flies," _____ David. *(to say)*

44. "Never!" Natalie declared as she _____ her coffee. *(to drink)*

45. David soon _____ up on Natalie and her new hobby. *(to give)*

Mastering the Two Most Common Irregulars: Be and Have

Two irregular verbs, *to be* and *to have,* appear more frequently than a movie star with a new film to promote. And like a movie star, they tend to cause trouble. Both change according to time and according to the person with whom they're paired. (Amazing that the movie-star comparison works on so many levels!) Because they're common, you need to be sure to master all their forms, as Table 1-1 shows.

Table 1-1	Verb Forms for the Irregular Verbs "To Be" and "To Have"		
Pronoun(s)	*Verb Form for "To Be"*	*Pronoun(s)*	*Verb Form for "To Have"*
I	am	I/you/we/they	have
you/we/they	are	it/he/she	has
it/he/she	is		
I/it/he/she	was		
you/we/they	were		

Note: The combining form of "to be" is *been,* and the past form of "to have" is *had.*

Fill in the blanks with the correct form of *to be* or *to have,* as in this example and the following exercises:

Q. Joyce the lifeguard _____ out in the sun long enough to fry her brain, but she intends to go inside soon because the Picnic Olympics is on television this evening.

A. **has been**. *Been* is the combining form used with helping verbs, such as *has.*

46. If pickling _____ necessary, I'll bring my own vinegar.

47. Who ever _____ enough cucumbers on this sort of occasion?

48. "Not me," replied Mike. "I _____ totally comfortable with the green vegetables in my refrigerator."

49. Kristin, never outdone, _____ a different idea.

50. "Grace and I _____ firmly in the anti-vegetable camp," she commented.

51. By the time she finishes the meal, Kristin _____ three trophies for carbo-loading.

52. Diane _____ Champion of the Potato Salad Competition for three years in a row, counting this year.

53. Grace _____ second thoughts about her entry choice; she now thinks that she should have picked sides instead of main dishes.

54. The soon-to-be-announced winners in each category _____ extremely pleased with the prizes this year.

55. Give me a taste because I _____ a judge.

Getting By with a Little Help from Some Other Verbs

In addition to *has, have, had,* and the *be* verbs (*am, is, are, was, were,* and so on) you can attach a few other helpers to a main verb, and in doing so, change the meaning of the sentence slightly. Helpers you need to consider hiring include:

- ✔ ***Should*** **and** ***must*** **add a sense of duty.** Notice the sense of obligation in these two sentences: "David *should* put the ice cream away before he eats the whole thing." "David *must* reduce his cholesterol, according to his doctor."

- ✔ ***Can*** **and** ***could*** **imply ability.** By the way, *could* is the past tense of *can.* Choose the tense that matches the tense of the main verb or the time period expressed in the sentence, as in these examples, "If Hanna *can* help, she will." or "Courtney *could* stray from the beaten path, depending upon the weather."

- ✔ ***May*** **and** ***might*** **add possibility to the sentence.** Strictly speaking, *might* is for past events, and *may* for present, but these days people interchange the two forms. So far the sky hasn't fallen. Check out these examples: "I *may* go to the picnic if I can find a bottle of ant-killer." "I told Courtney that she *might* want to bring some insect repellent."

- ✔ ***Would*** **usually expresses a condition or willingness.** This helper explains under what circumstances something may happen. ("I *would* have brought the mouse if I had known about the cat problem.") *Would* may also express willingness. ("He *would* bait the trap. . . .") *Would* sometimes communicates repeated past actions. ("Every Saturday he *would* go to the pet store for more mouse food.") The present tense of *would,* the helping verb *will,* may also indicate a condition in the present or future. ("I *will* go if I *can* find a free ticket.")

Now take a crack at this example and following exercises. Add a helper to the main verb. The information in parentheses after the fill-in-the-blank sentence explains what meaning the sentence should have.

Q. Steve said that he _____ consider running for Parks Commissioner, but he hasn't made his mind up yet. *(possibility)*

A. **might** or **may.** The *might* or *may* shows that Steve hasn't ruled out a run.

56. Melissa, shy as ever, said that she _____ go to the tree-cutting ceremony only if the press agreed to stay outside the forest. *(condition)*

57. Kirk, beat reporter for the local radio station, _____ not agree to any conditions, because the station manager insisted on eyewitness coverage. *(ability)*

58. Lisa, on the other hand, explained that if barred from the event she _____ rely on an interview with Steve after the event. *(possibility)*

59. Lisa knows that Steve _____ leap to fame based on the tree-cutting incident, and she doesn't want to miss an important scoop. *(ability)*

60. All good reporters _____ know that if a tree falls in the forest, the sound is heard by a wide audience only if a radio reporter is there. *(duty)*

61. Sound engineers, on the other hand, _____ skip all outdoor events if they _____ do so. *(condition, ability)*

62. On-air talent always _____ find a way to weather all hardships, including bad weather. *(ability)*

63. Some media watchers believe that reporters _____ be a bit more modest. *(duty)*

64. In response, reporters claim that the public _____ not appreciate humility if they _____ choose greater entertainment value. *(condition, ability)*

65. Steve _____ have allowed the press at the scene had he known about the fuss. *(condition)*

Calling All Overachievers: Extra Practice with Verbs

Time to sharpen all the tools in your verb kit. Read the memo in Figure 1-1, a product of my fevered brain, and correct all the verbs that have strayed from the proper path. You should find ten.

To: All Employees

From: Christy

Subject: Paper Clips

It had come to my attention that some employees will be bending paper clips nearly every day. A few copy clerks even bended an entire box. Because of my duty as your supervisor, I would remind you that paper clips have been expensive. In my ten years of superior wisdom as your boss, I always gave you a fair deal. I will have given you a fair deal in the future also, but only if you showed some responsibility. Therefore, I will begin inspecting the desks in this office this morning. By quitting time, I will have been checking every single one. If your desk contains a bent paper clip, you would find yourself out of a job.

Figure 1-1:
A sample memo with some confused verbs.

Answers to Problems on Verbs and Verb Tenses

1 **selects**. Notice the time clues? The first part of the sentence contains the word *is*, a present-tense verb, and the second part includes the word *always*. Clearly you're in the present with a recurring action.

2 **challenged**. Another time clue: *last year's* places you in the past.

3 **is buying** or **buys**. The second verb in the sentence (*is*) takes you right into the store with David, watching the unfolding action. Present progressive tense gives a sense of immediacy, so *is buying* makes sense. The plain present tense (*buys*) works nicely also.

4 **will flatter**. The key here is *next,* which puts the sentence in the future.

5 **is writing**. The time clue "right now" indicates an ongoing action, so the present progressive form *is writing* works well here.

6 **purchased**. Diane's bad taste splurge happened *once,* which means it took place in the past.

7 **was charging** or **charged**. The second part of the sentence includes the verb *urged,* which places you in the past. I like the past progressive (*was charging*) here because the word *while* takes you into the process of charging, which went on over a period of time. However, the sentence makes sense even when the process isn't emphasized, so *charged* is also an option.

8 **muttered** or **was muttering**. The clue to the past is *two days after.* The second answer gives more of a "you are there" feel, but either is correct.

9 **will invest**. The time words here, *as soon as,* tell you that the action hasn't happened yet.

10 **chimed**. If David *gave,* you're in past tense.

11 **placed**. The first verb in the sentence (*received*) is in the past tense, so you know that the action of placing the award on the shelf is also in past tense.

12 **wonder**. The time clue here is "every day," which tells you that this action is still happening at the present time and should be in present tense.

13 **explained**. The "yesterday" is a dead giveaway; go for past tense.

14 **stated**. The saga of Grace and Diane's award is in past tense, and this sentence is no exception. Even without the story context, you see the first verb (*earned*) is in past tense, which works nicely with the past-tense verb *stated.*

15 **will visit**. The time clue is "tomorrow," which places the verb in the future.

16 **had been skating** or **had skated**. You have two actions in the past — the skating and the hearing. The two hours of skating came before the hearing, so you need past perfect tense. Either the plain or the progressive form works here, so give yourself a gold star for either answer.

17 **has been warning** or **has warned**. The second half of the sentence indicates the present (*won't listen*), but you also have a hint of the past (*for years*). Present perfect is the best choice because it links past and present. I like the immediacy of progressive here (I can hear Diane's ranting), but plain present perfect also is okay.

18 **had waited** or **had been waiting**. The waiting preceded the doctor's announcement, so you should use past perfect. Progressive adds a "you are there" feel (good if you're a fan of hospital waiting rooms) but isn't necessary.

19 **will have waited, will have read**. The deadline in the sentence (the end of today's trip) is your clue for future perfect tense.

20 **has refused**. Notice the present-past link? Mike *declared* and Grace is acting now. Hence you need present perfect tense.

21 **had sent**. The pointing and the hospital-sending are at two different times in the past, with the hospital occurring first. Go for past perfect for the earlier action.

22 **will have spoken**. The future perfect needs an end point (in this sentence, the end of the yelling) before which the action occurs.

23 **has achieved**. If he *keeps trying*, you have a present-tense idea that's connected to the past *(despite years of practice and on rare occasions)*. Present perfect connects the present and past.

24 **has consisted**. This sentence has a present-tense clue *(at times)*. The sentence tells you about the past *(at times)* and the present *(is trying)*, so present perfect is the one you want.

25 **had declared**. The *after* at the beginning of the sentence is your clue that one action occurs before another. Because both are in the past, you need past perfect tense for the earlier action.

26 **will have given**. A deadline at some point in the future calls for future perfect tense.

27 **has expressed**. The sentence ties the present to the past, as you see in the time clues *failing* (which implies present) and *over the last few weeks* (which implies past). The present perfect tense is perfect for present-past links. (Sorry for the pun.)

28 **had approached**. The sentence discusses two actions in the past. Mike's action — an approach to ambassadors — took place before Tim's action — begging for "a few minutes of your time." You express the earlier of two past actions with the past perfect tense.

29 **will have declared**. A future deadline (before Tim makes his next career move) requires future perfect tense.

30 **has served**. The sentence tells you that David was and still is the ambassador. To link past and present, go for present perfect tense.

31 **broken**. The verb *to break* has two irregular forms, *broke* and *broken*.

32 **shook**. *To shake* has two irregular forms, *shook* and *shaken*.

33 **wrote**. For correct writing, use *wrote*, which is the past tense of the verb *to write*.

34 **rose**. You've probably heard that "a rose is a rose by any other name." Be sure to rise to the occasion and choose *rose* or *risen*, not *rised*.

35 **bought**. Let this verb remind you of other irregulars, including *caught, taught,* and *thought*. Here's a line to help you remember: I thought I was in trouble because I caught a cold when I taught that class of sneezing 10-year-olds, but fortunately I had bought a dozen handkerchiefs and was well prepared.

36 **rung**. The bell *rings, rang,* or *has/have/had rung*.

37   **went**. Take a memo: I *go*, I *went*, and I *have* or *had gone*.

38   **begun, began**. The plain past tense form is *began*, and the form that combines with *has, have,* or *had* is *begun*.

39   **sunk, found**. *To sink* becomes *sank* in the past tense and *has* or *have sunk* in the perfect tenses. *To find* becomes *found* in both past and present/past perfect.

40   **took, bit**. These two forms are in simple past; the perfect forms use *taken* and *bitten*.

41   **wove**. The past tense of *to weave* is *wove*.

42   **sought**. This irregular form wandered far from the original. The past tense of *to seek* is *sought*.

43   **said**. This irregular verb is the past tense of *to say*.

44   **drank**. Three forms of this verb sound like a song to accompany a beer blast: *drink, drank,* and *drunk*. The middle form, which is past tense, is the one you want here. The form that combines with *has* and *have* (in case you ever need it) is *drunk*.

45   **gave**. The verb *to give* turns into *gave* in the past tense.

46   **is**. Here you're in present tense.

47   **has**. You need a singular, present verb to match *who* in this sentence.

48   **am**. The verb *to be* changes to *am* when it's paired with *I*.

49   **has** or **had**. This answer depends on the tense. If you're speaking about a past event, choose *had*, but if you're speaking about something in the here and now, *has* is your best bet.

50   **are**. You need a plural to match *Grace and I*.

51   **will have**. The sentence speaks about the future.

52   **has been**. The sentence requires a link between past and present, so simple past won't do. You need present perfect, the bridge between those two time periods. *Has been* does the job.

53   **had**. The sentence calls for a contrast with *now,* so opt for past tense.

54   **will be**. Once more into the future!

55   **am** or **will be**. You may choose either present or future, depending upon the context.

56   **would**. The going is dependent upon the press arrangement. Thus *would* is the best choice.

57   **could**. The agreement wasn't possible, and the whole thing is in past tense, so *could* wins the prize.

58   **may** or **might**. Lisa, if she's in the mood, will cover the tree-cutting without seeing it. This possibility is expressed by the helpers *may* or *might*.

59   **can**. You need to express ability in the present tense, which *can* can do.

60   **should**. Gotta get that duty in, and *should* does the job.

61 **would, could** or **will, can**. If you're speaking in past tense, go for the first answer pair. The second set takes you into the present. Don't mix and match! If you're in one time period, don't switch without a good reason to do so.

62 **can**. Now you're firmly in present tense (clue word = *always*) and *can* adds a sense of ability.

63 **should**. When duty calls, opt for *should*.

64 **would, could** or **will, can**. The public's appreciation is conditional, and *would* expresses that fact. The second half of the sentence talks about ability, using *could*. The *would/could* pair is best for past tense, and *will/can* does the job for present. Be sure to stay only in one tense. No mixing allowed.

65 **would**. The first part of the sentence talks about a condition that is not actually happening, and *would* fills the bill.

To: All Employees

From: Christy

Subject: Paper Clips

66 It ~~had~~ **has** come to my attention that some employees ~~will be~~ **have** **67**

been bending paper clips nearly every day. A few copy clerks even

68 ~~bended~~ **bent** an entire box. Because of my duty as your supervisor, I

69 ~~would~~ **should** remind you that paper clips ~~have been~~ **are** expensive. In **70**

my ten years of superior wisdom as your boss, I always ~~gave~~ **have** **71**

given you a fair deal. I will ~~have given~~ **give** you a fair deal in the future

72 also, but only if you ~~showed~~ **show** some responsibility. Therefore, I will **73**

begin inspecting the desks in this office this morning. By quitting time, I

74 will have ~~been checking~~ **checked** every single one. If your desk

contains a bent paper clip, you ~~would~~ **may** find yourself out of a job. **75**

66 *Had come* is wrong because it places one action in the past before another action in the past — not the meaning expressed by this sentence. Instead, sentence one needs a verb to link past and present, and *has come* fills the bill.

67 *Will be* places the action in the future, but the memo once again seeks to establish that the bending went on in the past and continues in the present, so present perfect tense (*have been bending*) does the job.

68 *Bent* is an irregular past form. *Bended* is never correct in standard English.

69 Because you're talking about duty, *should* works nicely here. You may also select *am reminding* because the boss is in the process of reminding the employees of paper clip prices.

70 Present tense is better because the boss is concerned about current expenses.

71 The boss is bragging about fairness in the past, which continues in the present. Thus present perfect tense *(have given)* is best. **Note:** The *always* may be placed between the two words of the verb *(have always given)* if you wish.

72 *Will give* is correct; *will have given* implies a deadline.

73 The boss is talking about the present and future, not the past, so *showed* is inappropriate. Go with the present tense form, *show*.

74 No need for progressive here, because the boss wants to tell the underlings when the investigation will end, not when it will be going on.

75 You're expressing a real possibility here, so *will* or *may* works well. The helper *will* is more definite. *May* leaves a little wiggle room.

Chapter 2

Matchmaker, Make Me a Match: Pairing Subjects and Verbs Correctly

· ·

In This Chapter

▶ Forming plural nouns

▶ Pairing subject and verb forms in common sentences

▶ Dealing with difficult subjects

· ·

*I*n Grammarworld, which is located somewhere under the ground that normal people walk on, the difference between singular (the one, the only, the solitary) and plural (anywhere from two to a crowd) is a big deal. In this respect, grammar follows real life. When the obstetrician reports on the ultrasound or your date lists ex-spouses, the difference between one and more than one is a matter of considerable interest.

In this chapter I show you how to tell the difference between singular and plural nouns, pronouns, and verbs, and I get you started on pairing them up correctly in some common sentence patterns. I also help you tackle difficult subjects such as *everyone*, *somebody*, and *either* and *neither*.

When One Just Isn't Enough: Plural Nouns

When I was in elementary school, the only spell-check was the teacher's very long, very sturdy, and very often employed ruler. "Don't you know you're supposed to change the *y* to *i* and add *es*?" Miss Hammerhead would inquire just before the ruler landed (*Bam!*) on a pupil's head. Hammerhead (not her real name, or was it?) was teaching spelling, but she also was explaining how to form the plural of some *nouns,* the grammatical term for words that name people, places, things, or ideas. Here are Miss Hammerhead's lessons, minus the weaponry:

✔ **Regular plurals pick up an *s*** *(one snob/two snobs* and *a dollar/two billion dollars).*

✔ **Nouns ending in *s*, *sh*, *ch*, and *x* tack on *es* to form the plural** *(kindness/kindnesses, splash/splashes, catch/catches,* and *hex/hexes),* **unless the noun has an irregular plural.** I tell you more about irregular plurals in a minute.

✔ **Nouns ending in *ay*, *ey*, *oy*, *uy* — in other words, a vowel before *y* — simply add an *s*** *(monkey/monkeys* and *boy/boys).*

✔ **Nouns ending in *y* preceded by a consonant change the *y* to *i* and add *es*** *(butterfly/butterflies* and *mystery/mysteries).*

✔ **Irregular nouns cancel all bets: anything goes!** Sometimes the noun doesn't change at all, so the plural and singular forms are exactly the same *(fish/fish deer/deer);* other times the noun does change *(leaf/leaves* and *child/children).* When you're unsure about an irregular plural, you can check the dictionary. The definition lists the plural form for each noun.

When making the plural of a proper name — say, *Smith* — just add *s*. Don't change any letters even if the name ends with a consonant-*y* combo (*Smithy*, perhaps). Just add *s* for the *Smiths* and the *Smithys*.

Are you up for some multiplication? At the end of each sentence is a noun in parentheses. Write the plural in the blank, as in this example:

Q. Jennifer remained doubtful about the existence of flying dinner _____. *(plate)*

A. **plates**. Love those regular plurals! Just add *s*.

1. Jennifer's previous arguments have been so dramatic that her friends have frequently inquired about committing her to any of several local mental health _____. *(clinic)*

2. Jennifer, with her usual wit, refers to these establishments as _____. *(nuthouse)*

3. The town eccentric, Jennifer has several _____ of light green hair, courtesy of a bottle of dye. *(thatch)*

4. Jennifer sees her unusual hair color as a weapon in the battle of the _____. *(sex)*

5. Few people know that Jennifer, an accomplished historian and mathematician, has created a series of _____ on the Hundred Years' War. *(graph)*

6. Jennifer also knows a great deal about the role of _____ in colonial America. *(turkey)*

7. She discovered that the average colony had four turkeys — a guy who never paid his bills, an idiot who thought "Come here often?" was a good pickup line, and two _____ who plucked out their _____ to protect against witchcraft. *(woman, lash)*

8. The _____ of envy at Jennifer's scholarship were quite loud. *(sigh)*

9. A couple of professors, however, think that Jennifer's _____ are filled with bats. *(belfry)*

10. Perhaps they're right, because Jennifer has encountered quite a bit of wildlife in her bell towers, including _____, _____, and _____. *(deer, squirrel, goose)*

Isn't Love Groovy? Pairing Subjects and Verbs

To make a good match, as every computer-dating service knows, you have to pair like with like. In Grammarworld, you have to link singular subjects with singular verbs and plural subjects with plural verbs. The good news is that most of the time English verbs have only one form for both singular and plural. "I *smirk*" and "the dinosaurs *smirk*" are both correct, even though *I* is singular and *dinosaurs* is plural. You have to worry only in these few special circumstances:

✔ **Talking about someone in the present tense requires different verb forms for singular and plural.** The singular verb ends in *s,* a strange reversal of the regular nouns, where the addition of *s* creates a plural. ("He spits" and "They spit." *Spits* is singular; *spit* is plural.)

✔ **Verbs that include *does/do* or *has/have* change forms for singular and plural.** With one important exception (that I explain in a minute), singular verbs use *does* or *has*. ("Does John paint his toenails blue?" *Does paint* is a singular verb. "John has stated that his toenails are naturally blue." The verb *has stated* is singular.) Now for the exception: *I* (the one, the only, always singular pronoun) pairs with *do* and *have*. Why? I have no idea. Just to make your life more difficult, probably.

✔ **The verb *to be* changes form according to the noun or pronoun paired with it.** The singular verb forms and some matching pronouns include *I am, you are, he/she/it is, we/they are, I was, you were, he/she/it was, we/they were.*

✔ **Two subjects joined by *and* make a plural and take a plural verb.** As you discovered in kindergarten, one plus one equals two, which is a plural. ("Kristin and David plan a bank job every two years." *Kristin and David* forms a plural subject, and *plan* is a plural verb.)

✔ **Two singular subjects joined by *or* take a singular verb.** The logic here is that you're saying one *or* the other, but not both, so two singles joined by *or* don't add up to a double. ("David or his friendly branch manager is cooking the books to cover the theft." *David* is a singular subject, and so is *manager,* and each is matched with the singular verb *is cooking*.)

✔ **Ignore interrupters when matching subjects to verbs.** *Interrupters* include phrases such as "of the books" and "except for . . ." and longer expressions such as "as well as . . ." and "which takes the cake." Some interrupters *(as well as, in addition to)* appear to create a plural, but grammatically they aren't part of the subject and, like all interrupters, have no effect on the singular/plural issue. ("Kristin, as well as all her penguins, is marching to the iceberg today." The subject, *Kristin,* is singular and matched with the singular verb *is*.)

✔ *Here* and *there* **can't be subjects.** It's in their contract. In a *here* or *there* sentence, look for the subject after the verb. ("Here are five pink beans." In this sentence, *beans* is a plural subject, and *are* is a plural verb.)

✔ **The subject usually precedes the verb but may appear elsewhere.** ("Around the corner speed Kristin and David, heading for the getaway car." *Kristin and David* form a plural subject, which is matched with *speed,* a plural verb.)

Test yourself with this example. In the blank, write the correct form of the verb in parentheses.

Q. John's podiatrist _____ interested in the toenail-color issue. *(remain/remains)*

A. **remains**. The subject is singular (John has only one foot doctor!) so the verb must also be singular. The letter *s* creates a singular verb.

11. Hinting delicately that blue _____ not a natural color for nails, Nadine _____ her toes in distress. *(is/are, wriggle/wriggles)*

12. John, whose hair _____ been every color of the rainbow, says that he _____ from a toe condition. *(has/have, suffer/suffers)*

13. We _____ not buying his story. *(am/is/are)*

14. You probably _____ John because you _____ everyone the benefit of the doubt. *(believe/believes, give/gives)*

15. _____ you think that John's friends always _____ the truth? *(Does/Do, tell/tells)*

16. _____ his story fallen on disbelieving ears? *(Has/Have)*

17. No one ever _____ when John _____ avoiding reality. *(know/knows, am/is/are)*

18. He _____ sometimes created very convincing tales. *(has/have)*

19. Why _____ everyone believe him? *(does/do)*

20. I _____ completely dismayed by John's dishonest tendencies. *(was/were)*

21. There _____ six security guards in the safety deposit area. *(was/were)*

22. David, as well as such a well-known criminal mastermind as Alissa, _____ easily caught. *(was/were)*

23. His arrest on a variety of charges _____ being processed as we speak. *(is/are)*

24. There _____ a movie director and a literary agent in the crowd trying to gain access to David. *(was/were)*

25. David's offers, in addition to a serious marriage proposal, _____ a ghostwritten autobiography and a reality television show. *(includes/include)*

26. Imagine the show: Formally dressed as always, across the screen _____ David and Kristin. *(waddles/waddle)*

27. The producer of the series _____ guaranteed a hit. *(has/have)*

28. Kristin or Carrie, driven by a desire for fame and stretch limos, _____ sure to be interested in the deal. *(is/are)*

29. _____ there any hope for the law abiding citizens of this country? *(Is/Are)*

30. Stay tuned as the Justice Network, but not its partner stations, _____ hourly bulletins. *(broadcasts/broadcast)*

Taming the Brats: Difficult Subjects to Match with Verbs

Like a child who has missed a nap, some subjects delight in being difficult. Difficult though they may be, *most, all, either, each,* and other brats will, with a bit of attention, quickly turn into well-behaved subjects. Here are the rules:

> ✔ **Pronouns ending in -one, -thing, and -body (everyone, something, and anybody, for example) are singular,** even though they sometimes sound plural. ("Everyone is here." Singular subject *everyone* must be matched with the singular verb *is.*)

✔ *All, some, most, none,* and *any* **can be either singular or plural.** Subjects that can be counted are plural. ("All the ears that stick out are going to be super-glued to the scalp." The subject *all* is plural, because you can count *ears.*) A subject that is measured but not counted is singular. ("Most of my hatred for broccoli stems from an attack by a renegade vegetable salesman." The subject *most* is singular because hatred, at least metaphorically, can be measured but not counted.)

✔ *Either* **and** *neither* **alone, without** *or* **and** *nor,* **are singular.** ("Neither of my uncles has agreed to take me to the movies this afternoon." The singular subject *neither* matches the singular verb *has.*)

✔ **In** *either/or* **and** *neither/nor* **sentences, match the verb to the closest subject.** ("Either Josh or his partners are going to jail." The verb in this sentence, *are going,* is closer to *partners* than to *Josh.* Because *partners* is plural, you need a plural verb. If the sentence were reversed, the verb would be singular: "Either his partners or Josh is going to jail.")

✔ *Each* **and** *every* **are always singular, no matter what they precede.** ("Each of the five thousand computers that Elizabeth bought was on sale." "Every computer and printer in the office has been certified 'stolen' by the FBI." In these sentences the addition of *each* and *every* creates a singular subject that must be paired with a singular verb.)

Ready to relax? I don't think so. Try these problems. Underline the correct verb from each pair.

0. Neither the fire marshal nor the police officers (was/were) aware of the bowling tournament.

A. **were.** Did you use a ruler? The subject *police officers* is closer to the verb than *marshal.* Because *police officers* is plural, the verb must also be plural.

31. All the dancers in Lola's musical (is/are) required to get butterfly tattoos.

32. Either of the principal singers (has/have) enough talent to carry the musical.

33. Every orchestra seat and balcony box (is/are) sold already.

34. Why (does/do) no one understand that Lola's musical is extremely boring?

35. Most of the songs (has/have) been written already, but the out-of-town tryouts suggest that more work is needed.

36. Everyone (has/have) invested a substantial amount in *Whatever Lola Wants,* but no one (is/are) expecting a profit, despite the strong ticket sales.

37. Neither her partners nor Lola (is/are) willing to speculate on the critical reception.

38. Any of the reviews (has/have) the ability to make or break the production.

39. (Has/Have) either the director or the musicians agreed on a contract?

40. Everyone (agrees/agree) that Lola should cut the fifth song, "Why I Tattoo."

41. Lola is much more interested in tattoos than most of the members of the audience (is/are).

42. I don't understand the tattoo fixation because neither of Lola's parents (has/have) any tattoos.

43. Perhaps every one of Lola's 20 tattoos (is/are) a form of rebellion.

44. Some of the tattoos, of course, (is/are) to be covered by makeup, because Lola's character is an innocent schoolgirl.

45. However, each of the tattoos (has/have) special meaning to Lola, and she is reluctant to conceal anything.

46. "Truth," she says, "is important. All the fame in the world (is/are) not as valuable as honesty."

47. Lola talks a good line, but all her accountants (believes/believe) that she will go along with the necessary cover-up.

48. (Has/Have) someone mentioned the Tony Awards to Lola?

49. Either Lola or her producers (is/are) sure to win at least one award — if nobody else (enters/enter) the contest.

50. Every Tony and Oscar on Lola's shelf (is/are) a testament to her talent.

51. Neither of her Tony awards, however, (has/have) been polished for a long time.

52. Perhaps someone (has/have) neglected to hire a cleaning professional to spruce up Lola's house.

53. Both of Lola's brothers (is/are) in the field of furniture maintenance.

54. (Was/Were) either of her brothers called in to consult about trophy cleaning?

55. If so, perhaps either Lola's brothers or Lola herself (is/are) on the verge of a cleaner future.

56. Most of us, I should point out, (believe/believes) that Lola will never forget to shine her Oscar statuettes.

57. In fact, some of the Oscars that Lola has won (sparkles/sparkle) blindingly.

58. All of the Oscar-night attention (is/are) very appealing to Lola, who doesn't even attend the Tony ceremony, even when she's nominated.

59. Because neither Tom Cruise nor his costars (attends/attend) the Tony ceremony, Lola makes a point of being "on location" when the big night rolls around.

60. Each of the last fifteen Oscar nights, however, (is/are) an almost sacred obligation, in Lola's view.

Calling All Overachievers: Extra Practice with Hitching Subjects and Verbs

Sharpen your error-spotting skills. Tucked into the letter in Figure 2-1, written by a master criminal to his accomplice (okay, written by me, and I never even jaywalk, let alone rob banks!) are ten errors in subject-verb agreement and ten incorrect plural forms, for a total of 20 mistakes. Cross out each incorrect verb and plural and replace the error with a new, improved version.

Dear Adelie,

Oh, my little fluffy sweetheart, how I long to be with you on this cold, cold day! Neither of the iron bars of my cell have kept me from dreaming about sweeping you away to our long-planned vacation in Antarctica. Through the vast blue skys, speeding swiftly as wild turkies, go my heart.

Either my jailors or my honey, who is the best of all possible honies, have taken over every thought in my brain. I never think about the fishes in the sea. Every single one of my waking moments are devoted to you, cuddliest of all the cuddly teddy bear.

But, Cow Pat, I and all the other prisoners, except for my cellmate, has waited impatiently for your visit. Two months has passed, and everyone (though not the cellmate, as I said) are impatient. I know you was busy, but the taxs are paid, your new downhill racing skies are waxed (I know you love to ski!), and still you is not here!

Here is two tickets for the policemans you befriended. They can accompany you on the train. (I know you hate to travel alone.) Speaking of alone, please bring the loots from our last job. I need escape money. Also bring two gold watchs, which are very handy for bribes.

Your Cutie Patootie,

Charlie

Figure 2-1:
Practice letter with subject and verb errors.

Answers to Subject and Verb Pairing Problems

1   **clinics**. For a regular plural, just add *s*.

2   **nuthouses**. Regular plural here: Add an *s*.

3   **thatches**. For a noun ending in *ch*, add *es*.

4   **sexes**. To a noun ending in *x*, add *es* to form a plural.

5   **graphs**. Did I fool you? The *h* at the end of the noun doesn't, all by itself, call for *es*. Only words ending in *sh* or *ch* require an added *es* in the plural form. For *graph*, a plain *s* will do.

6   **turkeys**. For nouns ending in *ay, ey,* and *oy*, add *s* to form a plural.

7   **women, lashes**. The plural of *woman* is irregular. The second noun ends in *sh*, so you must tack on *es* for a plural.

8   **sighs**. Regular plurals are fun; just add *s*.

9   **belfries**. The plural of a noun ending in consonant-*y* is created by dropping the *y* and adding *ies*.

10   **deer, squirrels, geese**. The first and third nouns form irregular plurals, but good old *squirrels* follows the rule in which you simply add *s* to the singular.

11   **is, wriggles**. You need two singular forms here: blue *is* and Nadine *wriggles*.

12   **has, suffers**. The verbs *has* and *suffers* are singular, as they should be, because the subject-verb pairs are *hair has* and *he suffers*.

13   **are**. The plural verb *are* matches the plural subject *we*.

14   **believe, give**. The pronoun *you* always takes a plural verb such as *believe* and *give*.

15   **Do, tell**. Both verbs are plural, matching the plural subjects *you and friends*. In the first pair, the subject is tucked between the two parts of the verb because the sentence is a question.

16   **Has**. You need a singular form here to pair with the singular subject *his story*.

17   **knows, is**. Both answers are singular and match the singular subjects *no one* and *John*.

18   **has**. Because *he* is singular, the verb *has* must also be singular.

19   **does**. The pronoun *everyone* is singular, so it matches the singular form *does*.

20   **was**. The singular verb *was* matches the singular subject *I*.

21   **were**. The subject is *guards; there* is never a subject. *Guards* is plural and takes the plural verb *were*.

22   **was**. Ignore the interrupters *(as well as . . . Alissa)* and zero in on the real subject *David*. Match the singular verb *was* to the singular subject.

23 **is**. The subject is *arrest,* not *charges* or *variety. Arrest* is singular, so you need the singular verb *is.*

24 **were**. Add one *movie director* to one *agent* and what do you get? A big fat check, that's what . . . and a plural subject that takes the plural verb *were.*

25 **include**. The subject is *offers,* which matches the plural verb *include.* Everything else is camouflage.

26 **waddle**. The subjects in this sentence appear at the end of the sentence. *David* and *Kristin* = plural, so pair them with the plural verb *waddle.*

27 **has**. Pay no attention to *series,* which is a distraction. The real subject is *producer,* which needs the singular verb *has.*

28 **is**. The little word *or* tells you to take the subjects one at a time, thus requiring the singular verb *is.*

29 **Is**. The subject is *hope,* which takes the singular verb *is.*

30 **broadcasts**. The subject is *Network.* Don't be distracted by the interrupter *but not its partner stations. Network* needs the singular verb *broadcasts.*

31 **are**. You can count *dancers,* so *are* is best.

32 **has**. Without a partner, *either* is always singular and rates a singular verb, such as *has.*

33 **is**. The word *every* may as well be Kryptonite, because it has the power to change *seat and balcony* to a singular concept requiring the singular verb *is.*

34 **does**. The subject is *no one,* which is singular, so it must be paired with *does,* a singular verb.

35 **have**. The pronoun *most* may be singular (if it's used with a measurable quantity) or plural (if it's used with a countable quantity). You can count *songs,* so the plural *have* is best.

36 **has, is**. The pronouns ending in *-one* are always singular, even though they seem to convey a plural idea at times. They need to be matched with singular verbs.

37 **is**. The closest subject is Lola, so the singular verb *is* wins the prize, the only prize likely to be associated with Lola's musical.

38 **have**. The pronoun *any* may be either singular or plural, depending upon the quantity to which it refers. Reviews may be counted (and you can be sure that Lola's investors will count them extremely carefully), so *any* takes the plural verb *have* in this sentence.

39 **Has**. This sentence can be decided by distance. The sentence has two subjects, *director* and *musicians.* The verb in this sentence has two parts, *has* and *agreed.* The subject *director* is closer to the part of the verb that changes (the *has* or the *have*); *agreed* is the same for both singular and plural subjects. The changeable part of the verb is the one that governs the singular/plural issue. Because that part of the verb is near the singular subject *director,* the singular *has* is correct.

40 **agrees**. The singular verb *agrees* matches the singular subject *everyone.*

41 **are**. The pronoun *most* can be either singular or plural. In this sentence, *members* can be counted (and it won't take too long, either, once the reviews are in), so the plural verb *are* is what you want.

42   has. The pronoun *neither* is always singular and needs to be paired with the singular verb *has.*

43   is. Did I catch you here? The expression *20 tattoos* suggests plural, but the subject is actually *one,* a singular.

44   are. You can count tattoos, so the pronoun *some* is a plural subject and needs to match the plural verb *are.*

45   has. The word *each* has the power to turn any subject to singular; *has* is a singular verb.

46   is. You can measure, but not count, *fame,* so a singular verb matches the singular pronoun *all.*

47   believe. *Accountants* are countable, so *all* is plural in this sentence and needs the plural verb *believe.*

48   Has. The pronoun *someone,* like all the pronouns ending in *-one,* is singular, and so is the verb *has.*

49   are, enters. In an *either/or* sentence, go with the closer subject, in this case, *producers.* Because *producers* is plural, it is paired with *are,* a plural verb. The singular verb *enters* matches the singular pronoun *nobody.* All pronouns ending with *-body* are singular.

50   is. The word *every* has the ability to make the subject singular, matching the singular verb *is.*

51   has. The pronoun *neither* is singular, so the singular verb *has* is needed here.

52   has. Pronouns ending in *-one* are always singular and thus always match with singular verbs. Here the subject is *someone,* so *has* wins.

53   are. The pronoun *both* is plural, as is the verb *are.*

54   Was. This sentence illustrates a common error. The pronoun *either* is singular and calls for the singular verb *was.* If I had a nickel for every time I heard someone pair *either* with a plural, I could retire to a luxury hotel and sip margaritas all day.

55   Is. A sentence with an *either/or* combo is easy; just match the verb to the closest subject. In this sentence, the singular *Lola* is closer to the verb than *brothers,* so you need a singular verb.

56   believe. The pronoun *most* shifts from singular to plural and back, depending upon context. If it's associated with something that you can count (such as *us*), it's plural. Tacked onto something that you can measure but not count (*fame,* perhaps), *most* becomes singular. Here *most* is plural and joins with the plural verb *believe.*

57   sparkle. *Some* is a pronoun that may be either singular or plural, like *most* in the preceding explanation. Here it's associated with *Oscars,* a countable item. Thus the plural verb *sparkle* is the one you want.

58   is. This sentence has another changeable pronoun; this time it's *all.* As explained in the preceding two answers, *all* is singular if it's attached to something that you can't count, such as *attention.* Go for the singular verb *is.*

59   attend. Any sentence with a *neither/nor* pair requires a ruler: The subject that's closer to the verb dominates. If the closer subject is singular, go for a singular verb. If the closer subject is plural, opt for a plural verb. In this sentence the plural *costars* is closer to the verb than the singular *Tom Cruise,* so a plural verb (that is, *attend*) is called for.

60 **is**. *Each* is a magic word that automatically creates a singular subject, no matter what it precedes. The logic is that *each* requires you to think of the subject as a series of singular units. Pair *each* with the singular verb *is*.

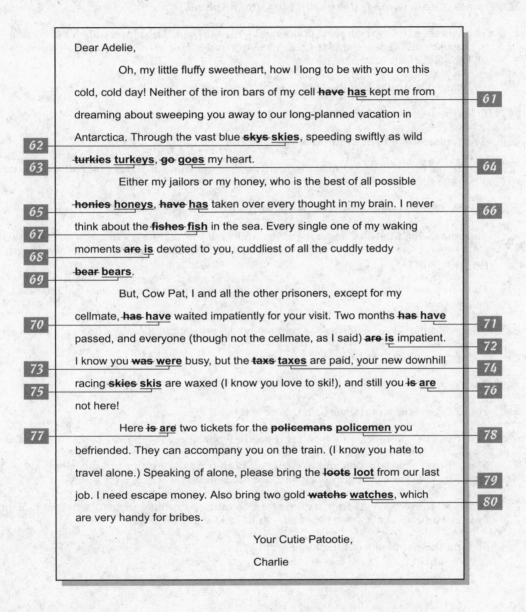

Dear Adelie,

Oh, my little fluffy sweetheart, how I long to be with you on this cold, cold day! Neither of the iron bars of my cell ~~have~~ **has** kept me from dreaming about sweeping you away to our long-planned vacation in Antarctica. Through the vast blue ~~skys~~ **skies**, speeding swiftly as wild ~~turkies~~ **turkeys**, ~~go~~ **goes** my heart.

Either my jailors or my honey, who is the best of all possible ~~honies~~ **honeys**, ~~have~~ **has** taken over every thought in my brain. I never think about the ~~fishes~~ **fish** in the sea. Every single one of my waking moments ~~are~~ **is** devoted to you, cuddliest of all the cuddly teddy ~~bear~~ **bears**.

But, Cow Pat, I and all the other prisoners, except for my cellmate, ~~has~~ **have** waited impatiently for your visit. Two months ~~has~~ **have** passed, and everyone (though not the cellmate, as I said) ~~are~~ **is** impatient. I know you ~~was~~ **were** busy, but the ~~taxs~~ **taxes** are paid, your new downhill racing ~~skies~~ **skis** are waxed (I know you love to ski!), and still you ~~is~~ **are** not here!

Here ~~is~~ **are** two tickets for the ~~policemans~~ **policemen** you befriended. They can accompany you on the train. (I know you hate to travel alone.) Speaking of alone, please bring the ~~loots~~ **loot** from our last job. I need escape money. Also bring two gold ~~watchs~~ **watches**, which are very handy for bribes.

Your Cutie Patootie,

Charlie

61 The subject of this sentence is *neither*, which, when it appears alone, is always singular, requiring the singular verb *has*.

62 To form the plural of a word ending in consonant-*y*, change the *y* to *i* and add *es*.

63 To form the plural of a word ending in vowel-*y*, just add *s*.

64   The singular subject of the verb *to go* is *heart,* which in this sentence is located after the verb, an unusual but legal spot. Singular subjects take singular verbs, and *goes* is singular.

65   *Honey* ends in vowel-*y,* so just add *s* to form the plural.

66   The sentence has two subjects connected with *either/or.* The closer subject is *my honey,* which is singular and takes a singular verb. The interrupter *best of all possible honeys* has no bearing on the subject/verb match.

67   *Fish* has an irregular plural — *fish.*

68   *Every* creates a singular subject, so you need the singular verb *is.*

69   *Bear,* unlike *fish* and *deer,* forms a regular plural. Just add *s.*

70   The *except for my cellmate* may distract you, but the true subject is *I and all the other prisoners,* a plural, which pairs with *have.*

71   *Two months* = plural, so use the plural verb *have.*

Time may sometimes be singular ("Five minutes is a long time") when you're referring to the total amount as one block of time. In question 71, David is counting the months separately, so plural is better.

72   *Everyone,* as well as all the pronouns with the word *one* tucked inside, is singular and takes the singular verb *is.*

73   The pronoun *you* can refer to one person or to a group, but it always takes a plural verb.

74   To form the plural of a noun ending in *x,* add *es.*

75   The noun *ski* is regular, so to form the plural, just add *s.*

76   *You* always takes a plural verb, in this case it's *are.*

77   *Here* can't be a subject, so look after the verb. Voila! *Tickets,* a plural, takes the plural verb *are.*

78   Many things separate men and women, but both form their plurals in the same way — by changing the *a* to *e.* Hence, *policemen,* not *policemans.*

79   *Loot* is whatever you get from a crime (not counting a criminal record), whether it be one diamond or a thousand Yankee tickets. *Loots* doesn't exist.

80   To form the plural of a noun ending in *ch,* add *es.*

Chapter 3

Who Is She, and What Is It? The Lowdown on Pronouns

Pronouns aren't for amateurs, at least when it comes to formal grammar. These tricky little words (most are quite short) take the place of nouns and frequently come in handy. Who can make a sentence without *I, me, ours, them, us, that,* and similar words? Unfortunately, pronouns can trip you up in a hundred ways. Never fear: In this chapter I show you how to distinguish singular from plural pronouns (and when to use each) and how to use possessive pronouns (the kind that won't let you go out on Saturday night). I also help you avoid vague pronouns and guide you through the maze of *its/it's, their/there/they're, whose/who's,* and *your/you're.*

Separating Singular and Plural Pronouns

Pronouns bump nouns from your sentences and make the words flow more smoothly. When choosing pronouns, you must follow two basic rules:

✔ Replace a singular noun with a singular pronoun.

✔ Replace a plural noun with a plural pronoun.

Pronouns have another characteristic — gender. Fortunately, the rules governing pronoun gender are nowhere near as complicated as the ones about who pays for what on the first date. Masculine pronouns *(he, him, himself)* take the place of masculine nouns, and feminine pronouns *(she, her, herself)* fill in for feminine nouns. Some pronouns are noncombatants in the gender wars *(it, itself, who, which, and that,* for example) and function in a neutral way.

Other rules also govern pronoun behavior, but I'll leave those for another time and place — specifically Chapters 2, 10, and 11, and, for those who want to perfect the most obsessive points of pronoun usage, Chapter 21.

Just for the record, here are the most common singular and plural pronouns:

✔ **Singular:** I, me, you, he, she, it, my, your, his, her, its, myself, yourself, himself, herself, itself, either, neither, everyone, anyone, someone, no one, everything, anything, something, nothing, everybody, anybody, somebody, nobody, each, and every

✔ **Plural:** we, us, you, they, them, our, ours, your, yours, their, theirs, ourselves, yourselves, themselves, both, and few

The *-self* pronouns — *myself, himself,* and so on — have very limited usage. They can add emphasis *(I myself will blow up the mud balloon)* or circle back to the person doing the action in the sentence *(She will clean herself later)*. If you're tempted to use a *-self* pronoun without the circling back action *(Rachel and myself hate mud balloons,* for example), resist the temptation.

Okay, get to work. Without peeking at the answers (and I *am* watching), decide which pronoun may replace the underlined noun. Consider the singular/plural and gender issues. Write your choice in the blank provided.

Q. I hope that Charlie Burke and <u>Dr. Eileen Burke</u> will attend tonight's symphony, even though Charlie is tone deaf and Eileen tends to sing along during the quieter moments. _____

A. **she**. Dr. Eileen has been known to hit the doughnut tray a little too often, but Eileen is still just one person. *She* is a singular, feminine pronoun.

1. Eileen wore a purple and red plaid hat last year, and <u>the hat</u> made quite an impression on the fashion press. _____

2. "Who is your designer, Eileen?" <u>the photographers</u> screamed. _____

3. <u>Charlie's hairpiece</u>, on the other hand, attracted almost no attention. _____

4. At one point during the evening Eileen muttered, "Charlie, you should have ordered a limousine for <u>Charlie and Eileen</u>. _____

5. Unlike his mother, Charlie likes to travel in luxury; <u>Mama</u> usually takes public transportation. _____

6. Charlie and Eileen told <u>Charlie and Eileen</u> that they would never set one foot in a subway. _____

7. Mama says that if you're in trouble, you can always ask the subway conductor and <u>the subway conductor</u> will help. _____

8. Eileen once tried the subway but fainted when the conductor said to her, "Miss, <u>Eileen</u> will need a ticket." _____

9. Until Eileen hit the floor, <u>the subway cars</u> had never before been touched by mink. _____

10. "Give <u>Eileen</u> a ticket, please," gasped Eileen when she awoke. _____

11. After Eileen's subway experience, <u>Eileen</u> opted for the bus. _____

12. The bus driver, Henry Todd, was very gracious to his passenger, as <u>Henry Todd</u> was to all passengers. _____

13. Because Eileen is a little slow, the driver of the bus parked <u>the bus</u> at the stop for a few extra minutes. _____

14. As Eileen mounted the bus steps, Eileen said, "Thank you, Driver, for waiting for <u>Eileen</u>. _____

15. "I am happy to wait for <u>Eileen</u>," replied the driver. "I have 12 more years until retirement." _____

Taking Possession of the Right Pronoun

When I was a kid I often heard the expression, "Possession is nine-tenths of the law." I never quite understood the legal meaning, but I do know that possessive pronouns (*my, mine, your, his, her, hers, its, our, ours, their, theirs,* and *whose*) are governed by just a few, easy laws:

  ✔ Use a possessive pronoun to show ownership.

  ✔ Match singular pronouns with singular owners.

  ✔ Match plural pronouns with plural owners.

  ✔ Take note of masculine (for males), feminine (for female), and neutral pronouns.

  ✔ *Never* insert an apostrophe into a possessive pronoun. (If a pronoun has an apostrophe, it's a contraction. See the next section for more information.)

Okay, here's a mini-test. Choose the correct possessive pronoun from the choices in parentheses and plop it into the blank.

Q. The little boy grabbed a grubby handkerchief and wiped _____ nose. *(his/her/its/he's)*

A. **his**. Because you're talking about a *little boy,* you need a masculine pronoun. Did I catch you with the last choice? *He's = he is.*

16. Jessica spent the morning polishing _____ new motorcycle, for which she had paid a rock-bottom price. *(her/hers/she's/her's)*

17. She found two scratches, so she took the cycle back to the store to get _____ fender repaired. *(it/its/her)*

18. When the store employees didn't satisfy her demand for a new fender, Jessica threatened to scratch something of _____. *(their/theirs/their's)*

19. Jessica talks a lot, but she has never taken revenge by damaging a single possession of _____. *(my/mine/mines/mine's)*

20. However, Neil and Rachel claim that Jessica once threw paint on something of _____. *(his/hers/her's/their/their's/theirs)*

21. Also, I heard a rumor that Neil had to bury _____ favorite wig, the one he styled himself, after Jessica got hold of it. *(his/her/he's)*

22. When Rachel's poodle dug up the wig, she had to use paint remover to clean _____ paw. *(it/its/their)*

23. Just to be safe, Neil will never let Jessica borrow another wig of _____ unless she takes out an insurance policy. *(his/his'/he's)*

24. Tomorrow, Neil is going to Matthews Department Store to buy a spare wig. The store is selling wigs at a 50 percent discount, and _____ wigs are Neil's favorites. *(its/their)*

25. Whenever Neil yells at Jessica, she screams, "Don't criticize _____ actions!" *(my/mine)*

26. Neil usually replies, in a voice that is just as loud, "I wouldn't dream of criticizing any action of _____." *(your/your's/yours/yours')*

27. When Neil speaks to _____ hairdresser, he will request a rush job. *(his/his'/he's)*

28. "Neil will never get his hands on any hairpiece of _____," declared Rachel and Jessica. *(our/ours/our'/ours'/our's)*

29. I think that Rachel took _____ hairpiece, and I told Neil so. *(his/his'/he's)*

30. Neil explained that he itches to get his hands on a wig of _____ someday. *(my/mine)*

31. "Over _____ dead body," I replied. *(my/mine)*

32. "I can't work on _____ dead body," answered Neil in a puzzled voice. *(your/yours/you're)*

33. As she dipped _____ fingers in paint remover, Jessica added, "You can't work on a live one either." *(her/hers/her's)*

34. Jessica and Neil seriously need to work on _____ people skills. *(his/her/their)*

35. I will buy a wig for Jessica, Neil, and me and then style _____ new hairpieces. *(our/ours/our's)*

It's All in the Details: Possessives versus Contractions

Think of this section as a map of a desert island with "scary monster's favorite cave," "poisoned water source," and "cannibal headquarters" clearly labeled. In other words, this section points out some dangers in the pronoun world and shows you how to steer clear of them. Specifically, I take you through the wonderful world of *its/it's, their/there/they're,* and *whose/who's.* Briefly, here's how to tell them apart:

- **Its/it's:** The first shows possession (the bird grasped a seed in *its* beak), and the second is a contraction meaning *it is.*

- **Their/there/they're:** The first shows possession (the birds grasped seeds in *their* beaks). The second is a location (don't go *there*). The third is a contraction meaning *they are.*

- **Whose/who's:** The first shows possession (the bird *whose* beak is longest). The second is a contraction meaning *who is.*

PRACTICE

Try the following questions. Choose the correct word from the choices in parentheses. Underline your selection.

Q. Marybelle sewed (their/there/they're) lips shut because the little brats refused to keep quiet.

A. **their**. The sentence expresses possession, so you want the first choice. The second *there* is location, and the third means *they are*. If you plug *they are* into the sentence, you're not making any sense.

36. George and Josh need watches because (their/there/they're) always late.

37. George found a watch that keeps atomic time, but (its/it's) too expensive.

38. Josh, playing with the atomic watch, broke (its/it's) band.

39. I notice that (your/you're) band is broken also.

40. "(Whose/Who's) watch is this?" Josh asked innocently.

41. "(Your/You're) sure that (its/it's) not Jessica's?" asked George.

42. "Put it over (their/there/they're) and pretend you never touched it," said George.

43. "I can't lie," whispered Josh. "(Their/There/They're) security cameras caught me."

44. (Its/It's) impossible for Josh to lie anyway because he is totally honest.

45. "(Your/You're) honor demands only the truth," sighed George.

46. (Whose/Who's) going to pay for the watch, you may wonder, Josh or George?

47. (Your/You're) wrong; Josh isn't willing to pay the full cost.

48. (Their/There/They're) funds are limited, so each will probably pay half the cost of a new watch band.

49. George, (whose/who's) ideas of right and wrong are somewhat fuzzy, asked Rachel whether she would contribute to (their/there/they're) "charity campaign for underprivileged watches."

50. Rachel replied, "(Your/You're) joking!"

51. "(Whose/Who's) going to help my watch?" she added.

52. "I don't think (its/it's) battery has ever been changed," continued Rachel.

53. (Its/It's) slowing down, according to Rachel, as the battery begins to die.

54. George told Rachel, "(Your/You're) battery is crucial and should be changed or recharged regularly."

55. "Who thinks about batteries?" commented Jessica. "(Their/There/They're) easy to overlook."

Avoiding Double Meanings

Unless you're a politician bent on hiding the fact that you've just increased taxes on everything but bubble gum, you're probably interested in communicating clearly. Double meanings, the darling of all sorts of elected officials, have no place in *your* speaking and writing, right? Self-interest dictates that you choose a pronoun that can't be misunderstood because accuracy and specificity in pronouns invariably lead to the correct interpretation of your meaning. One basic rule says it all:

> If any confusion arises about the meaning of a pronoun, dump it and opt for a noun instead.

In practice, this rule means that you shouldn't say things like "My aunt and her mother-in-law were happy about her success in the Scrabble tournament," because you don't know who had success, the aunt, the mother-in-law, or some other lady.

College entrance exams often hit you with a double-meaning sentence. Frequently the faulty pronoun is underlined. When asked to point out the error, keep your eye out for double-meaning pronouns.

Pronoun practice now begins. Hit these exercises with brainpower, rewriting if a pronoun may have more than one meaning. (When you rewrite, choose one of the possibilities, or, if you love to work, provide two new unmistakably clear sentences. If everything is hunky-dory, write "correct" in the blank.

Q. Stacy and Alice photographed her tattoos.

_____

A. **Stacy and Alice photographed Alice's tattoos.** Or, **Stacy and Alice photographed Stacy's tattoos.** Which answer is better? Neither. If you're saying something like this in real life, you know whose tattoos are under the lens. The reason the sentence needs a revision is that either meaning fits the original. To be clear, rewrite without the pronoun.

56. Chad and his sister are campaigning for an Oscar nomination, but only she is expected to get one.

_____

_____

57. Chad sent a donation to Mr. Hobson in hope of furthering his cause.

_____

58. If Chad wins an Oscar, he will place the statue on his desk, next to his Emmy, Tony, Obie, and Best-of-the-Bunch awards. It is his favorite honor.

_____

_____

59. Chad's sister has already won one Oscar for her portrayal of a kind but slightly cracked artist who can't seem to stay in one place without extensive support.

   _____

   _____

60. Rachel, who served as a model for Chad's sister, thought her interpretation of the role was the best.

   _____

   _____

61. In the film, the artist creates giant sculptures out of discarded hubcaps, although these are seldom appreciated by museum curators.

   _____

   _____

62. When filming was completed, Rachel was allowed to keep the leftover chair cushions and hubcaps, which she liked.

   _____

   _____

63. Rachel loves what she calls "found art objects," which she places around her apartment.

   _____

   _____

64. Chad's sister kept one for a souvenir.

   _____

65. Rachel, Chad, and Chad's sister went out for a cup of coffee, but he refused to drink his because the cafe was out of fresh cream.

   _____

   _____

66. Rachel remarked to Chad's sister that Chad could drink her iced tea if he was thirsty.

   _____

   _____

67. Chad called his brother and asked him to bring the cream from his refrigerator.

   _____

68. "Are you crazy?" asked Rachel as she gave Chad's sister her straw.

_____

69. Chad's sister took a straw and a packet of sugar, stirred her coffee, and then placed it on the table.

_____

_____

Calling All Overachievers: Extra Practice with Basic Pronouns

Sharpen your (that's _your,_ not _you're_) editing skills. Look for ten mistakes involving pronouns in the letter in Figure 3-1, written by an unfortunate merchant. After you find an error, correct it. Take note of singular/plural, gender, clarity, and confusion.

May 31, 2010

Dear Mr. Baker:

Its come to my attention that the watch you looked at yesterday in our Central Avenue store is broken. The band is disconnected from the watch, which is quite valuable. Their is no record of payment beyond a very small amount. The clerk, Mr. Sievers, told me that you paid her exactly 1 percent of the watch's price. When you and you're brother left the store, Mr. Sievers was still asking for additional funds. He's blood pressure still has not returned to normal levels.

Frankly I do not care whose to blame for the broken watchband or Mr. Sievers's medical problem. I simply want it fixed. The watch and it's band are not your property. The store needs their merchandise in good condition.

Sincerely,

E. Neil Johnson

Figure 3-1:
Error-filled sample letter.

Answers to Pronoun Problems

1. **it**. The hat is singular, and so is *it*.

2. **they**. More than one photographer means that you need the plural pronoun *they*.

3. **it**. The hairpiece is singular and has no gender, so *it* is the best choice.

4. **us**. Two nouns are underlined, so you're in plural territory. Because Eileen is talking about herself and Charlie, *us* fits here.

5. **she**. Mama is a singular feminine noun, so *she* is your best bet.

6. **themselves**. Two people make a plural, so *themselves,* a plural pronoun, is best.

7. **he or she**. You don't know whether the subway conductor is male or female, though you do know that you're talking about one and only one person. The best answer is *he or she,* covering all the bases.

8. **you**. Because the conductor is talking to Eileen, *you* is the best choice. *You,* by the way, functions as both a singular and a plural.

9. **they**. Cars is a plural noun, so *they* works best.

10. **me**. Because Eileen is talking about herself, *me* is your answer.

11. **she**. The singular, feminine (she always wears a skirt, never pants!) *Eileen* calls for a singular, feminine pronoun, in this case, *she*.

12. **he**. The singular, masculine (he never wears a skirt) *Henry Todd* calls for a singular, masculine pronoun, *he*.

13. **it**. The singular *bus* isn't masculine or feminine, so *it* fills the bill.

14. **me**. *Eileen* is talking about herself here (not a surprise, because she never talks about anything else!), so *me* is appropriate.

15. **you**. The driver is talking to Eileen, using the pronoun *you*.

16. **her**. You need a feminine singular pronoun, no apostrophe. Bingo: *her*.

17. **its**. I placed a trap here: her. The sentence does refer to a female, but the female doesn't have a fender; the *cycle* does. Thus you need the possessive pronoun *its*.

18. **theirs**. One of the choices — *their's* — doesn't exist in proper English. The first choice, *their*, should precede the thing that is possessed (*their* books, for example). The middle choice is just right.

19. **mine**. The last two choices don't exist in standard English. *My* does its job by preceding the possession (*my* blanket, for example). The second choice, *mine,* can stand alone.

20. **theirs**. You need a word to express plural possession, because you're talking about Neil and Rachel. Of the three plural choices (the last three), the first should precede the possession (*their* motorcycle, for example), and the second has an apostrophe, a giant no-no in possessive-pronoun world. Only the last choice works.

21 **his**. The hairpiece belongs to Neil, so *her,* a feminine pronoun, is out. The last choice is a contraction of *he is*.

22 **its**. The first choice isn't possessive, so you can rule *it* out easily. The second choice is plural, but the pronoun refers to *poodle,* a singular noun. Bingo: The last choice, a singular possessive, is correct.

23 **his**. No possessive pronoun ever contains an apostrophe, so the first choice is the only possibility. *He's,* by the way, means *he is*.

24 **its**. Did I catch you here? In everyday speech, people often refer to stores and businesses as "they," with the possessive form "their." However, a store or a business is properly referred to with a singular pronoun. The logic is easy to figure out. One store = singular. So Matthews Department Store is singular, and the possessive pronoun that refers to it is *its*.

25 **my**. The pronoun *mine* stands alone and doesn't precede what is owned. *My,* on the other hand, is a pronoun that can't stand being alone. A true party animal, it must precede what is being owned (in this sentence, *actions*).

26 **yours**. In contrast to sentence 25, this sentence needs a pronoun that stands alone. *Your* must be placed in front of whatever is being possessed — not a possibility in this sentence. All the choices with apostrophes are out because possessive pronouns don't have apostrophes. The only thing left is *yours,* which is the correct choice.

27 **his**. The contraction *he's* means *he is*. That choice doesn't make sense. The second choice is wrong because possessive pronouns don't have apostrophes.

28 **ours**. Okay, first dump all the apostrophe choices, because apostrophes and possessive pronouns don't mix. You're left with two choices — *our* and *ours*. The second is best because *our* needs to precede the thing that is possessed, and *ours* can stand alone.

29 **his**. The possessive pronoun *his*, like all possessive pronouns, has no apostrophe. The last choice, *he's*, means *he is* and isn't possessive at all.

30 **mine**. The pronoun *mine* works alone (it secretly wants to be a private detective, operating solo). In this sentence it has a slot for itself after the preposition *of*. Perfect!

31 **my**. The form that attaches to the front of a noun is *my*. In this sentence, *my* precedes and is linked to *dead body*.

32 **your**. The possessive pronoun *your* has no apostrophe. The second choice, *yours*, doesn't attach to a noun, so you have to rule it out in this sentence. The last choice, *you're*, is short for *you are*.

33 **her**. Right away you can dump the last choice, *her's*, because possessive pronouns are allergic to apostrophes. The pronoun *hers* works alone, but here the blank precedes the item possessed, *fingers*. *Her* is the possessive you want.

34 **their**. Because you're talking about both *Jessica* and *Neil*, go for *their*, the plural.

35 **our**. In this sentence the possessive pronoun has to include *me*, so *our* is the winner. *Ours* isn't appropriate because you need a pronoun to precede what is being possessed *(hairpieces)*. As always, apostrophes and possessive pronouns don't mix.

36 **they're**. The sentence tells you that *they are* always late, and the short form of *they are* is *they're*.

37   **it's**. The meaning needed here: *it is* too expensive. No possessive is called for.

38   **its**. The band belongs to the watch, so possession is indicated. The possessive pronoun *its* does the job.

39   **your**. The contraction *you're* is short for *you are,* clearly not right for this context.

40   **Whose**. The sentence doesn't say, "Who is watch is this?" so go for the possessive *whose*.

41   **You're, it's**. Two pronouns, neither possessive. The sentence really means "*You are* sure that *it is* not Jessica's?"

42   **there**. The meaning of the sentence calls for a location, so *there* is the one you want.

43   **Their**. The security cameras belong to them, so *their* is needed to show possession.

44   **It's**. The sentence should begin with "*It is* impossible" and *it's* = *it is*.

45   **Your**. A possessive is called for here, not a contraction (*You're* = *You are*).

46   **Who's**. The sentence should begin with *Who is,* and *who's* = *who is*.

47   **You're**. Here you want the contraction *you're* = *you are*.

48   **Their**. The funds belong to them, so *their* is needed to show possession.

49   **whose, their**. Both spots require a possessive, showing that the fuzzy ideas belong to George and that the campaign belongs to both George and his more honest brother Josh.

50   **You're**. The joking isn't a possession. The sentence calls for the contraction *you're* = *you are*.

51   **Who's**. You need *Who is* in this sentence, so go for the contraction.

52   **its**. The battery belongs to the watch, so the possessive pronoun *its* fits well here. The contraction *(it's,* for *it is),* doesn't belong here at all.

53   **It's**. In this sentence you want the contraction of *it is*.

54   **Your**. Here the possessive pronoun is called for, to show that the battery belongs to *you*.

55   **They're**. The contraction *They are* makes sense in this sentence, not the possessive *their* or the location word *there*.

56   **correct**. Chad is male and his sister is female, so *she* may refer only to one person, Chad's sister. No double meanings, so no corrections.

57   **Chad sent a donation to Mr. Hobson in hope of furthering Chad's cause. Or, Chad sent a present to Mr. Hobson in hope of furthering Mr. Hobson's cause.** The problem with the original is the *his*. Does *his* mean Chad's or Mr. Hobson's? The way the original reads, either answer is possible.

58   **If Chad wins an Oscar, he will place the statue on his desk, next to his Emmy, Tony, Obie, and Best-of-the-Bunch awards. The Oscar is his favorite honor.** Okay, maybe the Tony is his favorite honor, or maybe the Obie. The original is so unclear that almost anything may be plugged into the blank. Whichever one you choose, fine. Just don't let *It* stand for any one of five awards, which is what it does in the original.

59 **correct**. The two pronouns in this sentence, *her* and *who*, can only refer to Chad's sister. Everything is clear, and no changes are necessary.

60 **Rachel, who served as a model for Chad's sister, thought her own interpretation was the best.** Or, **Rachel, who served as a model for Chad's sister, thought the sister's interpretation was the best.** Either answer is okay, illustrating the problem with the original. You can't tell what *her* means — *Rachel's* or *Chad's sister's*.

61 **In the film, the artist creates giant sculptures out of discarded hubcaps, although the hubcaps are seldom appreciated by museum curators.** Or, **In the film the artist creates giant sculptures out of discarded hubcaps, although these sculptures are seldom appreciated by museum curators.** The problem with the original sentence is the pronoun *these*. (Did you know that *that*, *this*, *these*, and *those* may function as pronouns?) You have two groups of objects in the sentence: the sculptures and the hubcaps. *These* could refer to either. To eliminate the uncertainty, replace *these* with a more specific statement.

62 **Rachel was pleased to be allowed to keep the leftover chair cushions and hubcaps.** Or, **Rachel liked the leftover chair cushions, which she was allowed to keep. She also held onto the hubcaps.** Or, **Rachel liked the leftover hubcaps, which she was allowed to keep. She also kept the chair cushions.** If you've read all three suggested answers (and more variations are possible), you understand the problem with the original sentence. What does *which* mean? *Cushions? Hubcaps? Keeping leftovers?* That last possibility, by the way, can't be expressed by a pronoun, at least not according to the strictest grammar cops. Reword so that your reader knows what *which* means.

63 **correct**. Surprised? All the pronouns are clear, in the context of this story about Rachel. The *she* refers to *Rachel*, and the *which* refers to *objects*.

64 **Chad's sister kept one hubcap for a souvenir.** Or, **Chad's sister kept one sculpture for a souvenir.** Or, **Chad's sister kept one Rachel for a souvenir.** Just kidding about the last possible answer. (There's only one Rachel.) In the original sentence, *one* is too vague. Clarify by adding a specific souvenir.

65 **correct**. The sentence refers to two females (Rachel and Chad's sister) and one male. Because only one male is in the sentence, the masculine pronouns *he* and *his* are clear.

66 **Rachel remarked to Chad's sister, "Chad can drink my iced tea if he is thirsty."** Or, **Rachel remarked to Chad's sister, "Chad can drink your iced tea if he is thirsty."** In the original sentence, you can't tell whether *her* refers to Rachel or to Chad's sister.

67 **Chad called his brother and asked him to bring the cream from Chad's refrigerator.** If you want to make Chad a cheapo who is always mooching someone else's stuff, reword the sentence so that Chad is asking for his brother's cream, perhaps using a direct quotation, as in *Chad called his brother and asked, "Bring me some cream from your refrigerator."*

68 **"Are you crazy?" asked Rachel, giving her own straw to Chad's sister.** Or, **"Are you crazy?" asked Rached as she picked up Chad's sister's straw and gave it to her.** The original sentence doesn't make clear who owns the straw.

69 **Chad's sister took a straw and a packet of sugar, stirred her coffee, and then placed the coffee on the table.** The original sentence contains a pronoun (*it*) with several possible meanings (the straw, the sugar packet, or the coffee).

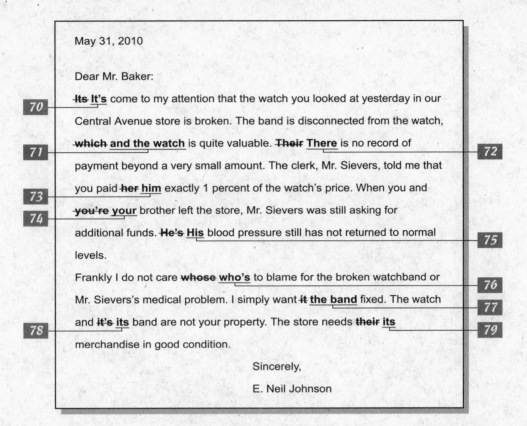

May 31, 2010

Dear Mr. Baker:

70 ~~Its~~ **It's** come to my attention that the watch you looked at yesterday in our Central Avenue store is broken. The band is disconnected from the watch,

71 ~~which~~ **and the watch** is quite valuable. 72 ~~Their~~ **There** is no record of payment beyond a very small amount. The clerk, Mr. Sievers, told me that

73 you paid ~~her~~ **him** exactly 1 percent of the watch's price. When you and

74 ~~you're~~ **your** brother left the store, Mr. Sievers was still asking for additional funds. 75 ~~He's~~ **His** blood pressure still has not returned to normal levels.

76 Frankly I do not care ~~whose~~ **who's** to blame for the broken watchband or

77 Mr. Sievers's medical problem. I simply want ~~it~~ **the band** fixed. The watch

78 and ~~it's~~ **its** band are not your property. The store needs 79 ~~their~~ **its** merchandise in good condition.

Sincerely,

E. Neil Johnson

70 In this sentence, *it's* is short for *it has*.

71 What's valuable — the watch or the band? Better to clarify by inserting the specific information.

72 *Their* is possessive, not called for in the sentence.

73 *Mr. Sievers* is male and needs a masculine pronoun *(him)*.

74 *You're* = *you are*, but the sentence needs the possessive pronoun *your*.

75 *He's* = *he is,* but the sentence calls for the possessive pronoun *his*.

76 *Who's* = *who is*. The sentence needs to read "I do not care who is to blame . . ."

77 What should be fixed, the band or the blood pressure? Clarify by changing *it* to *the band*.

78 Here the possessive *its* is needed.

79 A store is singular (one store), so *its* (singular) is what you want.

Chapter 4

Finishing What You Start: Writing Complete Sentences

In This Chapter
▶ Recognizing what makes a sentence complete
▶ Avoiding fragments and run-ons
▶ Combining sentences legally
▶ Placing endmarks properly

Have you heard the story about the child who says nothing for the first five years of his life and then begins to speak in perfect, complete sentences? Supposedly the kid grew up to be something important, like a Supreme Court Justice or a CEO. I question the story's accuracy, but I don't doubt that Supreme Court Justices, CEOs, and everyone else with a good job know how to write a complete sentence.

You need to know how to do so too, and in this chapter I give you a complete (pardon the pun) guide to sentence completeness, including how to punctuate and how to combine thoughts using proper grammar.

To write a proper, complete sentence, follow these rules:

✔ **Every sentence needs a subject/verb pair.** More than one pair is okay, but at least one is essential. Just to be clear about the grammar terms: a verb expresses *action* or *state of being;* a subject tells you *who* or *what* is acting or being.

✔ **A complete sentence contains a complete thought.** Don't leave the reader hanging with only half an idea. ("If it rains" = incomplete thought, but "If it rains, my paper dress will dissolve" = complete and truly bizarre thought.)

✔ **Two or more ideas in a sentence must be joined correctly.** You can't just jam everything together. If you do, you end up with a run-on or a "fused" sentence, which is a grammatical felony. Punctuation marks and what grammarians call *conjunctions* — joining words — glue ideas together legally.

✔ **Every sentence finishes up with an endmark.** Endmarks include periods, question marks, and exclamation points.

Just four little rules. Piece of cake, right? In theory, yes. But sometimes applying the rules gets a little complicated. In the following sections I take you through each rule, one at a time, so you can practice each step.

Seeking Out the Subject/Verb Pair

The subject/verb pair is the heart and soul of the sentence. To check your creation, zero in on the verb. At least one word must express action or a state of being. Next look for a word that expresses who or what is doing that action or is in that state of being; that's the subject. Now for one more, essential step: Check to see that the subject and verb match. They must go together and make sense ("Mike has been singing," "Lindsay suffered," and so forth). For practice on properly matching subjects and verbs, flip to Chapter 2.

Some words that look like verbs don't function as verbs. So you may wrongly identify a verb. Checking for a match between a subject and a verb eliminates these false verbs from consideration, because the pairs sound incomplete with false verbs. A couple of mismatches illustrate my point: "Lindsay watching," "Mike's message having been scrambled."

You try some. In the blank, write the subject (S)/verb (V) pair. If you find no true pair, write "incomplete." (By the way, Duke, who appears several times in the following sentences, is my grand-dog.)

Q. Mike, with a cholesterol count climbing higher and higher, gave in and fried some sausages. _____

A. **Mike (S)/gave (V), fried (V)**. Did I catch you with *climbing*? In the preceding sentence, *climbing* isn't a verb. One clue: *cholesterol count climbing* sounds incomplete. Just for comparison, *cholesterol count is climbing* makes a match. See the difference?

1. Duke, sighing repeatedly and frustrated by her inability to score more than ten points at the dog show. _____

2. Dogcatcher Charlie fed a chopped steak to Truffle, his favorite entry in the Dog of the Century contest. _____

3. Duke, my favorite entry, snarfed a bowl of liver treats and woofed for about an hour afterward. _____

4. Entered in the Toy breed category, Duke is sure to win the Most Likely to Fall Asleep Standing Up contest. _____

5. Having been tired out by a heavy schedule of eating, chewing, and pooping. _____

6. Duke sleeps profoundly. _____

7. Once, having eaten through the kibble bag and increased the size of her stomach by at least 50 percent. _____

8. One of the other dogs, biting the vet gently just to make a point about needles and her preference not to have them. _____

9. The vet is not upset by Duke's reaction. _____

10. Who would be surprised by a runoff between Truffle and Duke? _____

11. Not surprised by anything, especially with liver treats. _____

12. Truffle, sniffing the new dog toy on the couch. _____

13. Toto, the winner of last century's contest in running, jumping, and sleeping.
_____

14. Duke is guided by a strong handler around the judges' platform and television booth.
_____

15. Duke loves her time in the spotlight and the attention from the national media.
_____

16. Dogcatcher Charlie, covered in tanning cream and catching a few rays at the side of the arena. _____

17. Truffle and Duke sniffed the tanning cream while running around the arena.
_____

18. Swiftly across the arena sped the two dogs. _____

19. Stopping next to Dogcatcher Charlie at the arena wall, Truffle and Duke.
_____

20. They lapped a few gallons of tanning cream from his skin.
_____

Checking for Complete Thoughts

Some subject/verb pairs form a closed circle: The thought they express is complete. That's the quality you want, because otherwise your reader echoes the outlaw who, with his head in the noose, said: "Don't leave me hanging!"

Some expressions are incomplete when they're statements but complete when they're questions. To illustrate my point: "Who won?" makes sense, but "Who won" doesn't.

Try this one on for size. If you have a complete thought, write "complete." If the reader is left in suspense, write "incomplete." Remember, the number of words doesn't indicate completeness. The thought does.

O. Whenever the cow jumps over the moon. _____

A. **incomplete**. Aren't you wondering, "What happens *whenever the cow jumps over the moon*?" The thought is not complete.

21. The cow, who used to work for NASA until she got fed up with the bureaucracy.
_____

22. On long-term training flights, the milking machine malfunctioned. _____

23. Why didn't the astronauts assume responsibility for milking procedures? _____

24. For one thing, milking, which wasn't in the manual but should have been, thus avoiding the problem and increasing the comfort level of the cow assigned to the jump. _____

25. The cow protested. _____

26. Because she couldn't change NASA's manual. _____

27. Applying to NASA, her mother, when she was only a calf. _____

28. Not a bad decision, however. _____

29. Still, 20 years of moon-jumping is enough for any cow. _____

30. Unless they come up with a way to combine moon-jumping and milk-producing, the NASA administration will have to recruit other species. _____

31. Sheep, which were once rejected from moon duty. _____

32. Will NASA send a flock of sheep to the moon someday? _____

33. Not needing milking on a regular basis, though female sheep produce milk. _____

34. This species may be a better fit for life in a spacecraft. _____

35. However much the sheep practice, the training doesn't come as easy to them as it does to cows. _____

Going for Flow: Joining Sentences Correctly

Some sentences are short. Some are long. Joining them is good. Combined sentences make a narrative more interesting. Have I convinced you yet? The choppiness of the preceding sentences makes a good case for gluing sentences together. Just be sure to do so legally, or else you'll end up with a run-on sentence.

To join sentences correctly, you need one of the following:

✔ **A conjunction:** Don't worry about the grammatical terminology. But if you must know, a *conjunction* is a verbal rubber band that unites things. To connect two complete sentences more or less equally, use *and, or, but, nor,* and *for,* and put a comma before the conjunctions. To highlight one thought and make the other less important, use such conjunctions as *because, since, when, where, if, although, who, which,* and *that* — among others. These conjunctions are sometimes preceded by commas and sometimes not. For more information on comma use, check out Chapter 5.

✔ **A semicolon:** A *semicolon* (a little dot over a comma) pops up between two complete sentences and glues them together nicely. The two complete thoughts need to be related in some way.

Some words look like conjunctions, but aren't. Don't use *nevertheless, consequently, therefore, however,* or *then* to join complete thoughts. If you want to place one of these "false conjunctions" between two complete thoughts, add a semicolon and place a comma after the "false conjunction." For more information on commas, see Chapter 5.

Okay, put on your thinking cap and decide whether you have a legally combined, correct sentence or (gasp) an illegal, glued-together mess. In the blank after the sentence, write "correct" or "incorrect." Likewise, take a stab at changing the messes to legal, complete sentences. Notice the teacher trick? I provide space to revise every sentence, including the correct ones, so you can't judge the legal sentences by the length of the blanks.

0. Kathy broke out of jail, five years for illegal sentence-joining was just too much for her.

_____

_____

A. **incorrect. Kathy broke out of jail; five years for illegal sentence-joining was just too much for her.** The comma can't unite two complete thoughts. Change it to a semicolon and you're in business. An alternate correction: **Kathy broke out of jail because five years for illegal sentence-joining was just too much for her.** The *because* connects the two ideas correctly.

36. The grammarian-in-chief used to work for the Supreme Court, therefore his word was law.

_____

_____

37. His nickname, "Mr. Grammar," which had been given to him by the court clerks, was not a source of pride for him.

_____

_____

38. Nevertheless, he did not criticize those who used the term, as long as they did so politely.

_____

_____

39. He often wore a lab coat embroidered with parts of speech, for he was truly devoted to the field of grammar.

_____

_____

40. Kathy's escape wounded him deeply; he ordered the grammar cops to arrest her as soon as possible.

_____

_____

41. Kathy hid in a basket of dirty laundry, then she held her breath as the truck passed the border.

_____

_____

42. Kathy passed the border of sanity some time ago, although she is able to speak in complete sentences if she really tries.

_____

_____

43. She's attracted to sentence fragments, which appeal to something in her character.

_____

_____

44. "Finish what you start," her mother often exclaimed, "You don't know when you're going to face a grammar judge."

_____

_____

45. While she is free, Kathy intends to burn grammar textbooks for fuel.

_____

_____

46. Grammar books burn exceptionally well, nevertheless, some people prefer history texts for fuel.

_____

_____

47. History books create a satisfactory snap and crackle while they are burning, the flames are also a nice shade of orange.

_____

_____

48. Because she loves history, Kathy rejected _The Complete History of the Grammatical World,_ she burned _Participles and You_ instead.

_____

_____

49. _Participles and You,_ a bestseller for more than two years, sizzled, therefore it gave off a lot of heat.

_____

_____

50. Kathy found a few sentence fragments in the ash pile, but she disposed of them quickly.

_____

_____

Finishing with Flair: Choosing Endmarks

When you're speaking, the listener knows you've completed a sentence because the thought is complete and your tone says that the end has arrived. In writing, the tone part is taken care of by a period, question mark, or exclamation point. You must have one, and only one, of these marks at the end of a sentence, unless you're writing a comic book, in which characters are allowed to say things like "You want my what??!!?" Periods are for statements, question marks are for (surprise) questions, and exclamation points scream at the reader. Endmarks become complicated when they tangle with quotation marks. For tips on endmark/quotation mark interactions, check out Chapter 8.

Punch the time clock now and go to work on this section, which is filled with sentences desperately in need of an endmark. Write the appropriate endmark in the blank provided.

Q. Did Lola really ride to the anti-noise protest on her motorcycle _____

A. ? (question mark). You're clearly asking a question, so the question mark fits here.

51. No, she rode her motorcycle to the mathematicians' convention _____

52. You're not serious _____

53. Yes, Lola is a true fan of triangles _____

54. Does she bring her own triangles or expect to find what she needs at the convention _____

55. I'm not sure, but I think I heard her say that her math colleagues always bring triangles that are awesome _____

56. Do you think that she really means awful _____

57. I heard her scream that everyone loves triangles because they're the best shape in the universe _____

58. Are you going also _____

59. I'd rather have root canal surgery than attend a math convention _____

60. I heard Lola exclaim that equilaterals turn her on _____

61. Are you sure that Lola loves equilaterals _____

62. I always thought that she was fond of triangles _____

63. Who in the world wants an "I love math" tee shirt _____

64. I can't believe that Lola actually bought one _____

65. Will she give me her old "I love grammar" hat _____

Complete or Incomplete? That Is the Question

Time to get it together, as quite a few second-rate songwriters sang during the 1960s, one of my favorite decades that I almost remember. If you've plowed your way through this entire chapter (and if you have, my compliments), you've practiced each sentence skill separately. But to write well, you have to do everything at once — create subject/verb pairs, finish a thought, combine thoughts properly, and place the appropriate endmark.

Length and completeness aren't related. A very long sentence may be incomplete. Similarly, a very short sentence ("Grammar bores me," for example) may be complete. Make sure that the sentence follows the rules outlined in this chapter instead of counting words.

Take a test drive with the questions in this section. Decide whether the sentence is complete or incomplete and plop a label in the blank. If the sentence is incomplete, repair the damage. Notice that I've cleverly included a fix-it blank even for sentences that are already correct. In the military, that's called camouflage. In teaching, it's called a dirty trick.

Q. Though the spaghetti sticks to the ceiling above the pan on rainy days when even one more problem will send me over the edge.

_____

_____

A. **incomplete**. The statement has no complete thought. Possible correction: Omit "Though" and begin the sentence with "The."

66. Bill's holiday concert, occurring early in October, honors the centuries-old tradition of his people.

_____

_____

67. The holiday, which is called Hound Dog Day in honor of a wonderful dog breed.

_____

_____

68. Tradition calls for blue suede shoes.

_____

_____

69. Having brushed the shoes carefully with a suede brush, which can be bought in any shoe store.

_____

_____

70. The citizens lead their dogs to the town square, Heartbreak Hotel is located there.

_____

_____

71. "Look for the ghost of Elvis," the hotel clerk tells every guest, "Elvis has often been seen haunting these halls."

_____

_____

72. Elvis, ghost or not, apparently does not attend the Hound Dog Day festivities because no one has seen an aging singer in a white jumpsuit there.

_____

_____

73. Why should a ghost attend Bill's festival

_____

_____

74. How can you even ask?

_____

_____

75. The blue suede shoes are a nostalgic touch, consequently, the tourists always wear them.

_____

_____

Calling All Overachievers: Extra Practice with Complete Sentences

I can't let you go without pitching one more curveball at you. Read the letter in Figure 4-1, written by lovestruck Greg to his special squeeze, Alissa. Greg, who is better at romance than grammar, managed to write ten sentences about Alissa's charms, but only five are complete and correct. Can you find the five that don't make the grade?

Dear Alissa,

Your smile, with its capped teeth and strikingly attractive knotty pine denture. I can think of nothing I would rather do than contemplate the gap between your molars. Inspired by your eyebrows, I think of stars, constellations, and furry little bears. In the future, when I will have the time to write poetry about those brows. Your nose alone merits a poem, a sonnet should be dedicated to its nostrils. A wrestler would be proud to have a neck such as yours. Your shoulders slope invitingly, moreover, your hips swivel better than my office chair. Across those noble shoulders slides your hair, as thick as extra-strength glue. How can I forget your eyes I am yours forever, Alissa, unless I get distracted by a better offer.

Your friend,

Greg

Figure 4-1:
Sample letter with incomplete and run-on sentences.

Answers to Complete Sentence Problems

1. **incomplete**. Did you zero in on *sighing?* That's part of a verb (a present participle, if you absolutely have to know), but all by itself it isn't enough to fill the verb category. Likewise, if you try to pair *sighing* with a subject, the only candidate is *Duke. Duke is sighing* would be a match, but *Duke sighing* isn't. No subject/verb pair, no sentence.

2. **Dogcatcher (S)/fed (V)**. Start with a verb search. Any action or being verbs? Yes, *fed.* Now ask who or what *fed.* Bingo: *dogcatcher fed.* You have a good subject/verb match.

3. **Duke (S)/snarfed (V), woofed (V)**. Your verb search (always the best first step) yields two, *snarfed* and *woofed.* Who *snarfed* and *woofed? Duke.* There you go — an acceptable subject/ verb pair.

4. **Duke (S)/is (V)**. Were you tricked by *entered? Entered* may be a verb in some sentences, but in this one it isn't, because it has no subject. But *is* does have a subject, *Duke.*

5. **incomplete**. Something's missing here: *a subject* and *a verb!* What you have, in grammarspeak, is a participle, a part of a verb, but not enough to satisfy the subject/verb rule.

6. **Duke (S)/sleeps (V)**. Start with a verb search, and you immediately come up with *sleeps,* which, by the way, is an action verb, even though sleeping seems like the opposite of action. Who *sleeps? Duke,* bless her snoring little self.

7. **incomplete**. You have some action — *having eaten* — but no subject. Penalty box!

8. **incomplete**. The sentence has action *(biting),* but when you ask who's *biting,* you get no answer, because *one biting* is a mismatch.

9. **vet (S)/is (V)**. No action in this one, but *is* expresses being, so you're covered on the verb front. Who or what *is?* The *vet is.*

10. **Who (S)/would be (V)**. Are you surprised to see *who* as a subject? In a question, *who* often fills that role.

11. **incomplete**. A quick glance tells you that you have a verb form *(surprised),* but no subject.

12. **incomplete**. Another verb form *(sniffing)* is easy to find here, but when you ask who is doing the sniffing, you come up blank. *Truffle sniffing* doesn't match.

13. **incomplete**. In this one you have a subject, *Toto,* but no matching verb. True, the statement talks about *running, jumping,* and *sleeping,* but those aren't matches for *Toto.* (If you care, they're actually nouns functioning as objects of the preposition *in.*)

14. **Duke (S)/is guided (V)**. Start with a verb search. Any action or being verbs? Yes, *is guided.* Now ask who or what *is guided.* Bingo: *Duke is guided.* You have a good subject/verb match.

15. **Duke (S)/loves (V)**. A verb hunt gives you *loves,* and asking that universal question (who loves?) yields *Duke loves.* Bingo — a subject/verb pair and a legal sentence.

16. **incomplete**. Dogcatcher Charlie makes a fine subject, but in this one he's not matched with a verb. The two verb forms in the statement, *covered* and *catching,* describe Charlie. (They're participles, if you like these grammar terms.) Neither makes a good match. *Charlie covered* sounds like a match, but the meaning here is incorrect because Charlie isn't performing the action of covering. *Charlie catching* sounds like a mismatch because it is.

17 **Truffle (S), Duke (S)/sniffed (V).** First, find the verb. If you sniff around this sentence looking for an action word, you come up with *sniffed.* Now ask, *Who sniffed?* Bingo: *Truffle* and *Duke sniffed.* A good compound (double) subject for a good verb — you're all set with a complete sentence.

18 **dogs (S)/sped (V).** This one may have surprised you because the subjects follow the verb — an unusual, but perfectly fine position. If you follow the normal procedure (locating the verb and asking who did the action), you find *dogs,* even though they appear last in the sentence.

19 **incomplete.** This statement contains a verb form, *stopping,* but no subject matches it. Verdict: ten years in the grammar penitentiary for failure to complete the sentence.

20 **They (S)/lapped (V).** The action here is *lapped,* which unites nicely with *they.* Completeness rules!

21 **incomplete.** The reader is waiting to hear something about the *cow.* The way the sentence reads now, you have a description of *cow — who used to work for NASA until she got fed up with the bureaucracy —* but no action word to tell the reader what the cow is doing.

22 **complete.** The sentence tells you everything you need to know, so it's complete.

23 **complete.** The question makes sense as is, so the sentence is complete.

24 **incomplete.** The statement gives you an idea — *milking* — and some descriptions but never delivers with a complete thought about milking.

25 **complete.** Short, but you have everything you need to know about the *protesting cow.*

26 **incomplete.** The word *because* implies a cause-and-effect relationship, but the sentence doesn't supply all the needed information.

27 **incomplete.** What did the mama cow do when she was only a calf? The sentence doesn't actually say, so it's incomplete.

28 **incomplete.** Not enough information appears in this sentence, which, by the way, also lacks a subject/verb pair.

29 **complete.** All you need to know about moon-jumping (that it's enough for any cow) is in the sentence.

30 **complete.** This sentence contains enough information to reform NASA, should it indeed choose to enter the field of moon-jumping.

31 **incomplete.** The sentence begins to make a statement about *sheep* but then veers off into a description *(which were once rejected from moon duty).* No other thought is ever attached to *sheep,* so the sentence is incomplete.

32 **complete.** This question makes sense as is. You may wonder what NASA will do, but you won't wonder what's being asked here because the question — and the sentence — is complete.

33 **incomplete.** The first part of the sentence is a description, and the second is a qualifier, explaining a condition *(though female sheep produce milk).* Neither of these two parts is a complete thought, so the sentence is incomplete.

34 **complete.** You have everything you need to know here except why anyone would want to send sheep to the moon. Grammatically, this is a complete thought.

35 **complete**. The statement comparing sheep performance to cow performance is finished, and the cows win. You're not left hanging, wondering what the sentence is trying to say. Verdict: complete.

36 **incorrect**. Here you have two complete thoughts (everything before the comma equals one complete thought; everything after the comma = another complete thought). A comma isn't strong enough to hold them together. Try a semicolon or insert *and* after the comma.

37 **correct**. No problems here! The extra information about the nickname *(which had been given to him by the court clerks)* is a description, not a complete thought, so it can be tucked into the sentence next to the word it describes *(nickname)*. The *which* ties the idea to *nickname*.

38 **correct**. Surprised? The *nevertheless* in this sentence is not used as a joiner, so it's legal.

39 **correct**. Did I get you on this one? The word *for* has another, more common grammatical use in such expressions as *for the love of Pete, for you, for the last time,* and so on. However, *for* is a perfectly fine joiner of two complete thoughts when it means "because."

40 **correct**. The semicolon here joins two complete thoughts correctly.

41 **incorrect**. To connect these two ideas, look for a stronger connection word. *Then* can't do the job. Try *and then* or *but then*. Still another good solution is to replace the comma with a semicolon (; then).

42 **correct**. The words *although* and *if* join thoughts to another, more important, main idea about Kathy's sanity.

43 **correct**. The tacked-on description *(which appeal to something in her character)* is legal because the *which* refers to the preceding word *(fragments)*.

44 **incorrect**. Just because you're quoting, don't think you can ignore run-on rules. The quotation itself contains two complete thoughts and thus needs to be expressed in two complete sentences. Easiest fix: Place a period after *exclaimed*.

45 **correct**. No grammatical felonies here: Two ideas *(she is free* and *Kathy intends to burn grammar textbooks for fuel)* are linked by *while*.

46 **incorrect**. *Nevertheless* is a long word. It looks strong enough to join two complete thoughts, but in reality it isn't. Plop a semicolon before *nevertheless* and you're legal.

47 **incorrect**. One complete thought *(History books create a satisfactory snap and crackle while they are burning)* is glued to another *(the flames are also a nice shade of orange)* with nothing more than a comma. Penalty box! Use a semicolon or add a comma after *burning,* followed by the conjunction *and*.

48 **incorrect**. As in the preceding question, one complete thought *(Because she loves history, Kathy rejected* The Complete History of the Grammatical World*)* and another *(she burned* Participles and You *instead)* are attached by a comma. I don't think so! Use a semicolon or place a *but* after *World*.

49 **incorrect**. *Therefore* isn't a legal joiner. Substitute *so* or place a semicolon before *therefore*.

50 **correct**. The word *but* is short, but it does the job of joining two complete sentences without even working up a sweat.

51 **. (period)**. Because this sentence makes a statement, a *period* is the appropriate endmark.

52   ! (exclamation point). These words may also form a question, but an *exclamation point* is certainly appropriate, because the speaker may be expressing amazement that a biker chick likes math.

53   . (period). Another statement, another *period*.

54   ? (question mark). The *does* in this sentence signals a question, so you need a *question mark*.

55   . (period). The *period* is the endmark for this statement.

56   ? (question mark). Here the *question mark* signals a request for information.

57   . (period). This statement calls for a *period*.

58   ? (question mark). This sentence requests information, so place the *question mark* at the end.

59   ! (exclamation point). Okay, a period would do fine here, but an *exclamation point* adds extra emphasis. And shame on you for avoiding math. Some of my best friends are math teachers!

60   . (period). This statement needs a *period* as an endmark.

61   ? (question mark). The sentence requests information, so a question mark is the one you want.

62   . (period). I've chosen a period, but if you're bursting with emotion, opt for the exclamation point instead.

63   ? (question mark). I see this one as a true inquiry, but you can also interpret it as a scream of disbelief, in which case an exclamation point works well.

64   ! (exclamation point). I hear this one as a strong blast of surprise, suitable for an exclamation point.

65   ? (question mark). If you're asking for information, you need a question mark.

66   **complete**.

67   **incomplete**. The sentence is incomplete because it gives you a subject *(the holiday)* and a bunch of descriptions *(which is called Hound Dog Day in honor of a wonderful dog breed)* but doesn't pair any verb with *holiday*. Several corrections are possible. Here's one: The holiday, which is called Hound Dog Day in honor of a wonderful dog breed, requires each citizen to attend dog obedience school.

68   **complete**.

69   **incomplete**. This sentence has no subject. No one is doing the brushing or the buying. One possible correction: Having brushed the shoes carefully with a suede brush, which can be bought in any shoe store, Bill proudly displayed his feet.

70   **incomplete**. This sentence is a run-on, because a comma can't join two complete thoughts. Change it to a semicolon or reword the sentence. Here's a possible rewording: The citizens lead their dogs to the town square, where Heartbreak Hotel is located.

71   **incomplete**. Another run-on sentence. The two quoted sections are jammed into one sentence, but each is a complete thought. Change the comma after *guest* to a period.

72 **complete.**

73 **incomplete.** The sentence is incomplete because it has no endmark. Add a question mark.

74 **complete.**

75 **incomplete.** This sentence is a run-on. *Consequently* looks like a fine, strong word, but it's really a 98-pound weakling that doesn't get enough vitamins. In other words, it can't join two complete thoughts, which you have in this sentence. Add a semicolon after *touch,* and dump the comma.

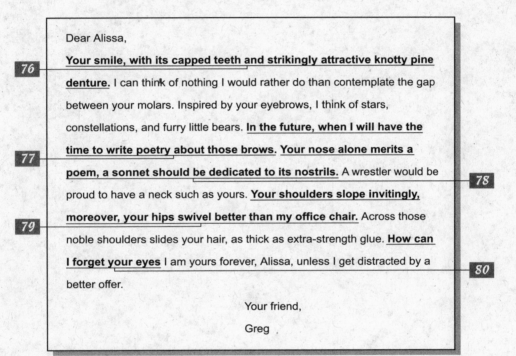

Dear Alissa,

76 **Your smile, with its capped teeth and strikingly attractive knotty pine denture.** I can think of nothing I would rather do than contemplate the gap between your molars. Inspired by your eyebrows, I think of stars, constellations, and furry little bears. **In the future, when I will have the** **77** **time to write poetry about those brows. Your nose alone merits a poem, a sonnet should be dedicated to its nostrils.** A wrestler would be **78** proud to have a neck such as yours. **Your shoulders slope invitingly, 79** **moreover, your hips swivel better than my office chair.** Across those noble shoulders slides your hair, as thick as extra-strength glue. **How can I forget your eyes** I am yours forever, Alissa, unless I get distracted by a **80** better offer.

Your friend,

Greg

76 Incomplete: no verb

77 Incomplete: *When* implies more information; no complete thought

78 Run-on

79 Run-on

80 Incomplete: no endmark

Part II
Mastering Mechanics

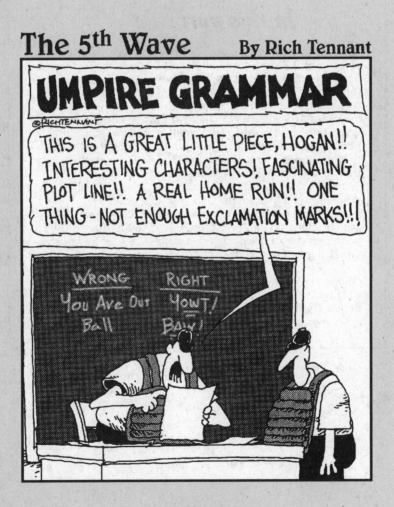

In this part . . .

In my hometown, it's possible to find stores where signs proclaim "merchant's sell Bagels." You have to give me a minute to shudder at the small but important mistakes (and I don't mean *mistake's*) in bagel signage. First of all, the apostrophe (the little hook at the end of the word *merchant*) is wrong, as are, in my informal count, 99.99 percent of the apostrophes I see in all sorts of official spots. Plus, despite the fact that *bagels* are extremely delicious, they don't deserve a capital letter. Sigh. Such are the daily trials of a grammarian in New York City.

Wherever you live, in this part, you can practice some aspects of what grammarians call *mechanics* — punctuation and capitalization. When you're done, you'll be the master of the dreaded comma (Chapter 5), apostrophe (Chapter 7), and the quotation mark (Chapter 8). Plus, you'll know how to place hyphens and dashes and semicolons, not to mention colons (Chapter 6). Tucked into Chapter 9 are the basics of capitalization. If all these details fry your brain, feel free to refresh yourself with a bagel or two.

Chapter 5

Exercising Comma Sense

- -

In This Chapter

▶ Punctuating lists correctly

▶ Signaling a direct address

▶ Placing commas in dates and addresses

▶ Using commas to insert introductory words and interrupters

▶ Deciding when descriptions need to be set off by commas

- -

The well-dressed writing of a hundred years ago boasted far more commas than today's fashionable sentences. The current trend toward what grammarians term *open style punctuation* calls for commas to be used sparingly. Dwindling though they may be, these little punctuation marks have their place — in lists, direct address, dates and addresses, introductory expressions, interrupters, and certain types of descriptions. In this chapter you can practice inserting and deleting commas until your writing is as proper as a maiden aunt and as stylish as a supermodel.

Making a List and Checking It Twice

When you're writing a free-standing list, line breaks signal when one item in a list ends and another begins. Commas do the same thing in sentences. Perhaps Professor MacGregor wants you to do the following:

- ✔ Go on the Internet.
- ✔ Locate the origin of the handheld meat patty.
- ✔ Write a paper on hamburger history.

Inserted into a sentence, the line breaks in the preceding list turn into commas:

> Professor MacGregor wants you to go on the Internet, locate the origin of the handheld meat patty, and write a paper on hamburger history.

Notice that the first item isn't preceded by a comma and that the last two items are separated by *and,* which has a comma in front of it. Although that last comma is optional, many style manuals, which are stricter than the bouncer at this year's most popular club, want you to insert a comma before the *and* or whatever word joins the last two items of the list.

If any item in a list has a comma *within* it, semicolons are used to separate the list items. Imagine that you're inserting this list into a sentence:

- Peter McKinney, the mayor
- Agnes Hutton
- Jeannie Battle, magic expert

In a sentence using only commas, the reader wouldn't know that Peter McKinney is the mayor and may instead think that Peter and the mayor are two separate people. Here's the properly punctuated sentence:

> Because he has only one extra ticket to the magic expo, Daniel will invite Peter McKinney, the mayor; Agnes Hutton; or Jeannie Battle, magic expert.

Get to work! Insert the list from each question into a sentence (I supply the beginning), and punctuate it properly.

Q. List of things to buy at the pharmacy:

industrial-strength toenail clippers

green shoe polish

earwax remover

Getting ready for his big date, Rob went to the pharmacy to purchase _____

_____

A. **Getting ready for his big date, Rob went to the pharmacy to purchase industrial-strength toenail clippers, green shoe polish, and earwax remover.** You have three items and two commas; no comma is needed before the first item on the list.

1. Supermarket shopping list:

pitted dates

chocolate-covered mushrooms

anchovies

pickles

Rob planned to serve a tasteful selection of _____

_____

2. Guests:

Helen Ogilbee, supermodel

Natasha Nakovee, swimsuit model

Blair Berry, automotive salesperson

Hannah Umbridge, former Miss Autoclave

Rob's guest list is heavily tilted toward women he would like to date, such as _____

_____

3. Activities:

bobbing for cabbages

pinning the tail on the landlord

playing double solitaire

After everyone arrives, Rob plans an evening of _____

_____

4. Goals:

get three phone numbers

arrange at least one future date

avoid police interference

Rob will consider his party a success if he can _____

_____

5. Results:

the police arrived at 10:00, 11:00, and 11:30 p.m.

no one gave out any phone numbers

everyone thought his name was Bob

Rob didn't meet his goals because _____

_____

You Talkin' to Me? Direct Address

If the name or title of the person to whom you're talking or writing is inserted into the sentence, you're in a direct-address situation. Direct-address expressions are set off from everything else by commas. In these examples, *Wilfred* is being addressed:

Wilfred, you can have the squash court at 10 a.m.

I expect you to remove all the seeds from the squash, Wilfred.

When you hit a zucchini, Wilfred, avoid using too much force.

The most common direct-address mistake is to send one comma to do a two-comma job. In the last of the three preceding examples, two commas must set off *Wilfred.*

Can you insert commas to highlight the direct-address name in these sentences?

Q. Listen Champ I think you need to get a new pair of boxing gloves.

A. **Listen, Champ, I think you need to get a new pair of boxing gloves.** In this example, you're talking to *Champ,* a title that's substituting for the actual name. Direct-address expressions don't have to be proper names, though they frequently are.

6. Ladies and Gentlemen I present the Fifth Annual Elbox Championships.

7. I know Mort that you are an undefeated Elbox competitor. Would you tell our audience about the sport?

8. Elboxing is about 5,000 years old Chester. It originated in ancient Egypt.

9. Really? Man I can't believe you knew that!

10. Yes, the sport grew out of the natural movement of the elbow when someone tried to interfere with a diner's portion by "elbowing" Chester.

11. Excuse me a moment. The reigning champion has decided to pay us a visit. Miss William could you tell us how you feel about the upcoming match?

12. Certainly Sir. I am confident that my new training routine will pay off.

13. What type of exercises did you do Placida? I may call you "Placida," right?

14. Sure! I arm-wrestled for eight hours a day Mort and then swam a mile or so for the aerobic benefit.

15. We wish her the best of luck, don't we folks?

Dating and Addressing

No, this section doesn't tell you what to wear when taking a comma to dinner and a movie. Nor does this section deal with what sort of speech you need to make when you first meet a comma. Instead, this section enables you to practice placing commas in dates (as in July 20, 2009) and addresses (as in Boise, Idaho).

The date rules are fairly simple:

✔ **For a date that includes (in order) the month, day, and year,** place a comma after the day. If this kind of date is in a sentence that continues beyond the year, place a comma after the year. ("I plan to blow up the rutabaga patch on August 4, 2006, unless I find a more enticing vegetable.")

✔ **For a date that includes (in order) the day, month, and year,** open-style punctuation, which drops commas faster than Superman drops Kryptonite, favors no commas anywhere — before, after, inside, over, or under. You get the idea; no commas. ("The last rutabaga will be harvested on 4 August 2006 and sold at auction.") Some very traditional English teachers (I'm one) always place a comma after the month and after the year, unless the year ends the sentence, in which case the endmark follows the year. ("The last cabbage will be picked on 30 September, 2008, and made into a doll.") If you're writing for a particular person (a professor or a boss), you should check his or her preference. As always, whatever style you choose should be consistent throughout.

✔ **For a date that includes (in order) only the month and day,** you don't need any commas. ("In honor of farmer Bill, I will send a contribution to Save the Rutabaga on September 12.")

✔ **For a date that includes (in order) the month and year,** no commas are required. ("Bill bought the farm in January 2006 and sold it five years later.")

Traditional punctuation places a comma between the month and the year and after the year within a sentence; however, open-style punctuation favors fewer commas, and that's what I'm advocating. Many style manuals drop both commas if the sentence continues. Which style should you follow? Your call, unless the Authority Figure for whom you're writing has a preference. No matter what you do, be consistent.

As far as addresses are concerned, the following rules apply:

- **If you're writing an address in block form (not in a sentence),** use a comma to separate only the city from the state.

- **If the address is inserted into a sentence,** use a comma to show where one line of the address ends and the next begins and between the city and state, which is standard practice. If the sentence continues after the address, insert a comma after the last bit of the address. ("I sent the rutabagas to Evelyn O'Hara, 1322 Wilson Street, Corville, Iowa 70202, but she never replied.") *Note:* No comma is placed between the state and the ZIP code.

PRACTICE

Punctuation party time! Place commas where you need them in these sentences.

Q. On December 12 2007 I received a letter from Evelyn O'Hara, who now resides at 722 Park Avenue New York City New York 10027 in the heart of Manhattan's Upper East Side.

A. **On December 12, 2007, I received a letter from Evelyn O'Hara, who now resides at 722 Park Avenue, New York City, New York 10027, in the heart of Manhattan's Upper East Side.** Commas separate the day from the year, the whole date from the rest of the sentence, and each part of the address (the house number and street, city, and state). A comma also follows the address. Notice that no comma ever comes between the state and the ZIP code. (They've been going steady for years and allow nothing to come between them. Ah, love.)

16. An article in *The New York Times* of 12 November 2006 reports that rutabagas have very few calories.

17. Evelyn is partial to the rutabagas sold by Clearview Nurseries 17 Fort Benn Parkway Kalama Florida 05789 although they are quite expensive and its rates are going up in September 2007.

18. Her last will and testament is dated April 8 1990 and specifies that rutabaga roses be placed on her grave.

19. Her attorney, Hubert Wilberforce, may be contacted at 78 Crescent Square London Connecticut 86689 for more information.

20. Instead of flowers, Evelyn wrote that friends and loved ones should contribute to the United Rutabaga Society 990 Pacific Street Northwest Agonis Oregon 98989.

Introducing (and Interrupting) with the Comma

Do you want to start your sentences off with a bang, or at least a small pop? Fine. Just don't forget to set off the introductory expression with a comma. Grammatically, *introductory expressions* are a mixed bag of verbals, prepositional phrases, adverbial clauses, and lots of other things you don't have to know the names of. In short, an introductory expression makes a comment on the rest of the sentence or adds a bit of extra information. It may include a verb form or just mention a place; it may even be as short as *yes, no,* or *well;* or it may be much longer. Check out the italicized portion of each of these sentences for examples of introductory expressions:

> *Snaking through the dark tunnel,* Brad Jones thought about the book deal he'd get for his memoirs.

> *To get out in one piece,* Brad planned a diversion.

> *While he was crossing the lighted area,* an order of takeout pizza would be delivered.

Interrupters vary in length. A direct-address element (see the "You Talkin' to Me? Direct Address" section earlier in this chapter) may be considered a type of interrupter and so may some of the introductory expressions in the preceding samples, even when you move the introducers to the middle of the sentence. The same principle that applies to direct-address elements applies to interrupters: They comment on or otherwise *interrupt* the main idea of the sentence and thus are set off by commas. In these sentences, the interrupters are italicized:

> Cindy Jones, *snaking through the dark tunnel,* didn't think about the book deal she'd get for her memoirs.

> There was no guarantee, *of course,* that Cindy would even be asked to write about herself.

Some short introductory expressions or interrupters don't require commas. For example, in the sentence "In the morning Brad drank 12 cups of coffee," *in the morning* isn't set off by a comma. If the expression doesn't have a verb in it and is tied strongly to the main idea of the sentence, you can sometimes get away without commas. This test may help: Say the sentence aloud (or in your head, if you're afraid of attracting the wrong sort of attention). If you hear a natural pause, plop in a comma. If everything runs together nicely, don't plop.

Up for some practice? Insert commas where needed and resist the temptation to insert them where they're not wanted in these sentences.

Q. Disgruntled after a long day delivering pizza Elsie was in no mood for fireworks.

A. **Disgruntled after a long day delivering pizza, Elsie was in no mood for fireworks.** The comma sets off the introductory expression, *Disgruntled after a long day delivering pizza.* Notice how all that applies to *Elsie?* She's the subject of the sentence.

21. In desperate need of a pizza fix Brad turned to his cellphone.

22. Cindy on the other hand checked the phone number in the pizza directory she had thoughtfully stashed in her purse.

23. Yes pizza was an excellent idea.

24. The toppings unfortunately proved to be a problem.

25. Restlessly Brad pondered pepperoni as the robbers searched for him.

26. Cindy wondered how Brad given his low-fat diet could consider pepperoni.

27. Frozen with indecision Brad decided to call the supermarket to request the cheapest brand.

28. Cindy of course wanted to redeem her coupons.

29. To ensure fast delivery was crucial.

30. Lighting a match and holding it near his trembling hand Brad realized that time was almost up.

31. Worrying about toppings had used up too many minutes.

32. Well the robbers would have a good story to tell.

33. With renewed determination Cindy speed-dialed the market and offered "a really big tip" for ten-minute service.

34. As the robbers chomped on pepperoni and argued about payment Brad slipped away.

35. Cindy let's just say was left to clean up the mess.

Setting Off Descriptions

Life would be much simpler for the comma-inserter if nobody ever described anything. No descriptions would mean no comma problems. However, solving your punctuation problems in that way leads to writing that resembles a pay-by-the-word text message — limited in scope, expensive, and not a good idea!

A better plan is to find out more about these basic principles behind punctuating descriptive expressions:

- ✔ **If the description *follows* the word being described, decide whether it's extra information or essential, identifying material.** If the description falls into the "nice to know but I didn't really need it" (extra) category, surround it with commas. If the description is in the "gotta have it" bin, omit the commas. For example, in the sentence, "The dictionary *on the table* is dusty," the description in italics is necessary because it tells *which* dictionary is dusty. However, in the sentence, "Charlie's dictionary, *which is on the table,* is dusty," the description in italics is set off by commas, because you already know *Charlie's dictionary* is the one being discussed. The part about the table is extra information.

- ✔ **For descriptions that precede the word described, place commas only when you have a list of two or more descriptions of the same type and importance.**

You can you tell when two or more descriptions are equally important; they can be written in different order without changing the meaning of the sentence. For example, in the sentence, "The *tan, dusty* dictionary has never been opened," the two descriptions — *tan* and *dusty* — can be reversed without changing the meaning, so you need a comma. However, in the sentence, "*Two dusty* dictionaries need some cleaning power now!" the two descriptions aren't the same type — one is a number, and one is a condition. You can't say, *Dusty two,* so you don't insert commas.

> ✔ **When descriptions containing verb forms introduce a sentence (see the preceding section on introductory elements), they always are set off by commas.** An example: Sighing into his handkerchief, Charlie looked for a dust cloth. The description, *sighing into his handkerchief,* has a verb form (sighing) and thus is set off by a comma from the rest of the sentence.

Got the idea? Now try your comma skills on the following sentence. If the italicized words need to be set off, add the commas. If not, go waterskiing. (Just kidding. Leave the sentence alone if no commas are needed.)

Q. The *ruffled striped* blouse belongs to my oldest sister *Mary*.

A. **The *ruffled, striped* blouse belongs to my oldest sister, *Mary*.** The first two descriptions precede the word being described (blouse) and may be interchanged without a problem, so a comma is needed between them. The second description (which, the strictest grammarians would tell you is really an equivalent term or *appositive*) follows the word described (my oldest sister). Because you can have only one *oldest sister*, the name is extra, not essential identifying information, and it's set off by commas.

36. Oscar's favorite food *which he cooks every Saturday night* is hot dogs.

37. The place *where he feels most comfortable during the cooking process* is his *huge brick* barbecue.

38. Oscar stores *his wheat* buns in a *large plastic* tub.

39. One of the horses *that live in Oscar's barn* often sniffs around the horseshoe.

40. Oscar rode *his three favorite* horses in an important race *honoring the Barbecue King and Queen*.

41. Oscar will never sell one of his horses *because he needs money*.

42. Oscar dedicated a song to the filly *that was born on his birthday*.

43. The jockeys became annoyed by Oscar's song *which he played constantly*.

44. The *deep horrible* secret is that Oscar can't carry a tune.

45. His guitar *a Gibson* is missing a *few important* strings also.

Calling All Overachievers: Extra Practice with Commas

Figure 5-1 shows an employee self-evaluation with some serious problems, a few of which concern commas. (The rest deal with the truly bad idea of being honest with your boss.) Forget about the content errors and concentrate on commas. See if you can find ten commas that appear where they shouldn't and ten spots that should have commas but don't. Circle the commas you're deleting and insert commas where they're needed.

Annual Self-Evaluation: Kristin DeMint

Well Ms. Ehrlich that time of year has arrived again. I, must think about

my strengths and weaknesses as an employee, of Toe-Ring

International. First and most important let me say that I love working for

Toe-Ring. When I applied for the job on September 15 2005 I never

dreamed how much fun I would have taking two, long lunches a day.

Sneaking out the back door, is not my idea of fun. Because no one ever

watches what I am doing at Toe-Ring I can leave by the front door

without worrying. Also Ms. Ehrlich, I confess that I do almost no work at

all. Transferred to the plant in Boise Idaho I immediately claimed a

privilege given only to the most experienced most skilled, employees and

started to take an extra week of vacation. I have only one more thing to

say. May I have a raise?

Figure 5-1:
Comma
problems
in an
employee
self-
evaluation.

Answers to Comma Problems

1. **Rob planned to serve a tasteful selection of pitted dates, chocolate-covered mushrooms, anchovies, and pickled radishes.** Each item on Rob's list, including the last one before the *and,* is separated from the next by a comma. No comma comes before the first item, *pitted dates.*

2. **Rob's guest list is heavily tilted toward women he would like to date, such as Helen Ogilbee, supermodel; Natasha Nakovee, swimsuit model; Blair Berry, automotive salesperson; and Hannah Umbridge, former Miss Autoclave.** Did you remember the semicolons? The commas within each item of Rob's dream-date list make it impossible to distinguish between one dream date and another with a simple comma. Semicolons do the trick.

3. **After everyone arrives, Rob plans an evening of bobbing for cabbages, pinning the tail on the landlord, and playing double solitaire.** Fun guy, huh? I can't imagine why he has so much trouble getting dates. I hope you didn't have any trouble separating these thrilling activities with commas.

4. **Rob will consider his party a success if he can get three phone numbers, arrange at least one future date, and avoid police interference.** Fortunately, Rob's standards of success are fairly low. So is the standard for a correctly punctuated list. All you have to do is plop a comma between each item.

5. **Rob didn't meet his goals because the police arrived at 10:00, 11:00, and 11:30 p.m.; no one gave out any phone numbers; and everyone thought his name was Bob.** Even with low standards, Rob is in trouble. You're in trouble too if you forgot to use a semicolon to distinguish one item from another. Why? The first item on the list has commas in it, so a plain comma isn't enough to separate the list items.

6. **Ladies and Gentlemen, I present the Fifth Annual Elbox Championships.** Even though *Ladies and Gentlemen* doesn't name the members of the audience, they're still being addressed, so a comma sets off the expression from the rest of the sentence.

7. **I know, Mort, that you are an undefeated Elbox competitor. Would you tell our audience about the sport?** Here you see the benefit of the direct-address comma. Without it, the reader thinks *I know Mort* is the beginning of the sentence and then lapses into confusion. *Mort* is cut away with two commas, and the reader understands that *I know that you are . . .* is the real meaning.

8. **Elboxing is about 5,000 years old, Chester. It originated in ancient Egypt.** You're talking to *Chester,* so his name needs to be set off with a comma.

9. **Really? Man, I can't believe you knew that!** Before you start yelling at me, I know that *Man* is sometimes simply an exclamation of feeling, not a true address. But it can be, and in this sentence, it is. Hence the comma slices it away from the rest of the sentence.

10. **Yes, the sport grew out of the natural movement of the elbow when someone tried to interfere with a diner's portion by "elbowing," Chester.** No one's hitting Chester's funny bone. Instead, *Chester* is being addressed directly, so you need the comma.

11. **Excuse me a moment. The reigning champion has decided to pay us a visit. Miss William, could you tell us how you feel about the upcoming match?** Here the person being addressed is *Miss William.*

12. **Certainly, Sir. I am confident that my new training routine will pay off.** The very polite *Miss William* from the previous exercise talks to *Sir* in this sentence, so that term is set off by a comma.

13 **What type of exercises did you do, Placida? I may call you "Placida," right?** *Placida* is being addressed, so the name requires a comma. Also, as reigning champ, she requires a bowl of jelly beans with the green ones removed. It's in her contract.

14 **Sure! I arm-wrestled for eight hours a day, Mort, and then swam a mile or so for the aerobic benefit.** The direct address term *Mort* is in the middle of the sentence, so two commas are needed to cut it away from the main idea.

15 **We wish her the best of luck, don't we, folks?** In this sentence, *folks* are being addressed, so the term must be set off by a comma.

16 **An article in *The New York Times* of 12 November 2006 reports that rutabagas have very few calories.** Or, **An article in *The New York Times* of 12 November, 2006, reports that rutabagas have very few calories.** Surprise! Two answers are possible. The more modern solution calls for no commas. The very traditional, "I learned English when quill pens were the rage" style calls for commas between the month and year and the year and the rest of the sentence.

17 **Evelyn is partial to the rutabagas sold by Clearview Nurseries, 17 Fort Benn Parkway, Kalama, Florida 05789, although they are quite expensive, and its rates are going up in September 2007.** Each line of the address is separated from the next by a comma. A comma also follows the address. The last date doesn't need a comma, but you may place one between the month and the year if you wish to follow the older, traditional style.

18 **Her last will and testament is dated April 8, 1990, and specifies that rutabaga roses be placed on her grave.** Traditional month-day-year style dates take commas between the day and the year and also after the year within a sentence.

19 **Her attorney, Hubert Wilberforce, may be contacted at 78 Crescent Square, London, Connecticut 86689, for more information.** The lines of Hubert's address are separated by commas, and the whole thing is followed by a comma. No comma ever appears between the state and the ZIP code.

20 **Instead of flowers, Evelyn wrote that friends and loved ones should contribute to the United Rutabaga Society, 990 Pacific Street Northwest, Agonis, Oregon 98989.** Did the *Northwest* throw you? I made it part of the street line, so it doesn't need to be set off by a comma from *Pacific Street*. If you interpreted the location as *Northwest Agonis,* no problem. In that case the comma follows *Street.* (Neither *Agonis* nor *Northwest Agonis* exists, so I don't care which you choose. In real life, of course, you have to use the proper address.)

21 **In desperate need of a pizza fix, Brad turned to his cellphone.** The introductory expression here merits a comma because it's fairly long. Length doesn't always determine whether you need a comma, but in general the longer the introduction, the more likely you'll need a comma.

22 **Cindy, on the other hand, checked the phone number in the pizza directory she had thoughtfully stashed in her purse.** The expression inside the commas makes a comment on the rest of the sentence, contrasting it with the actions of *Brad*. As an interrupter, it must be separated by commas from the rest of the sentence.

23 **Yes, pizza was an excellent idea.** *Yes* and *no,* when they show up at the beginning of a sentence, take commas if they comment on the main idea.

24 **The toppings, unfortunately, proved to be a problem.** The *unfortunately* is short and closely tied to the meaning of the sentence. However, setting the word off with commas emphasizes the emotional, judgmental tone. I've gone with the commas, as you see, but I can accept a case for omitting them.

25 **Restlessly Brad pondered the pepperoni question as the robbers searched for him.** The introductory word *restlessly* is short and clear. No comma is necessary.

26 **Cindy wondered how Brad, given his low-fat diet, could consider pepperoni.** The expression *given his low-fat diet* interrupts the flow of the sentence and calls for commas.

27 **Frozen with indecision, Brad decided to call the supermarket to request the cheapest brand.** Introductory expressions with verb forms always take commas.

28 **Cindy, of course, wanted to redeem her coupons.** The *of course* interrupts the flow of the sentence and comments on the main idea. Hence the commas.

29 **To ensure fast delivery was crucial.** Did I catch you here? This sentence doesn't have an introductory expression. *To ensure fast delivery* is the subject of the sentence, not an extra comment.

30 **Lighting a match and holding it near his trembling hand, Brad realized that time was almost up.** Introductory expressions containing verbs always take commas. This introductory expression has two verbs, *lighting* and *holding*.

31 **Worrying about toppings had used up too many minutes.** This sentence has no introductory expression, so no comma is needed. The verb form *(Worrying about toppings)* is the subject of the sentence, not an introduction to another idea.

32 **Well, the robbers would have a good story to tell.** Words such as *well, indeed, clearly,* and so forth take commas when they occur at the beginning of the sentence and aren't part of the main idea.

33 **With renewed determination, Cindy speed-dialed the market and offered "a really big tip" for ten-minute service.** I admit that this one's a judgment call. If you didn't place a comma after *determination,* I won't prosecute you for comma fraud. Neither will I scream if you, like me, inserted one. This sentence falls into a gray area. With a comma, the introductory expression stands out a little more. Your call.

34 **As the robbers chomped on pepperoni and argued about payment, Brad slipped away.** This introductory expression has a subject and a verb and clearly needs a comma.

35 **Cindy, let's just say, was left to clean up the mess.** This sentence is another that couldn't possibly make sense without the commas. *Cindy* isn't attached to the interrupter, *let's just say,* but absent the commas, the reader runs all those words together. Penalty box! You have to add the commas.

36 **Oscar's favorite food, *which he cooks every Saturday night,* is hot dogs.** After you find out that the food is *Oscar's favorite,* you have enough identification. The information about Oscar's datefree Saturday nights is extra and thus set off by commas. Descriptions beginning with *which* are usually extra.

37 **The place *where he feels most comfortable during the cooking process* is his *huge brick* barbecue.** The term *place* is quite general, so the description is an essential identifier. The two descriptions preceding *barbecue* aren't of the same type. One gives size and the other composition. You can't easily reverse them (a brick huge barbecue sounds funny), so don't insert a comma.

38 **Oscar stores *his wheat* buns in a *large plastic* tub.** The paired descriptions (*his* and *wheat, large* and *plastic*) aren't of the same type. *His* is a possessive, and you should never set off a possessive with a comma. (They get very annoyed. Don't ask!) *Large* indicates size and *plastic,* composition.

39 **One of the horses *that live in Oscar's barn* often sniffs around the tub.** Which horses are you talking about? Without the barn information, you don't know. Identifying information doesn't take commas. *Hint:* Descriptions beginning with *that* are nearly always essential identifiers and thus aren't set off by commas.

40 **Oscar rode *his three favorite* horses in an important race *honoring the Barbecue King and Queen*.** The three descriptions preceding *horses* aren't of the same type: One *(his)* is posses-sive, and another *(three)* is a number. Commas never set off possessives and numbers. The second descriptive element explains which race you're talking about. Without that information, the topic could be any important race. As an identifier, it isn't set off by a comma.

41 **Oscar will never sell one of his horses *because he needs money*.** Without a comma the itali-cized information is essential to the meaning of the sentence. The comma-free sentence means that Oscar may sell a horse because he hates the animal or wants to please the prospective buyer, but never for financial reasons. (Perhaps he bought into Microsoft early on or won the lottery.) With a comma, the italicized material is extra. The sentence then means that Oscar will never sell a horse, period. The reason — *he needs the money* — may mean that the horses are worth more in Oscar's stable than they would be anywhere else. The first interpretation makes more sense, so don't drop in a comma.

42 **Oscar dedicated a song to the filly *that was born on his birthday*.** Which filly? You don't know without the italicized identification. Thus you need no comma.

43 **The jockeys became annoyed by Oscar's song, *which he played constantly*.** Even without the italicized material, you know which song the jockeys hate. The italicized material gives you a little more info, but nothing essential.

44 **The *deep, horrible* secret is that Oscar can't carry a tune.** These two descriptions may be reversed without loss of meaning, so a comma is appropriate.

45 **His guitar, *a Gibson,* is missing a few important strings also.** The *his* tells you which guitar is being discussed, so the fact that it's *a Gibson* is extra and should be set off by commas.

Annual Self-Evaluation: Kristin DeMint

46
47 Well, Ms. Ehrlich, that time of year has arrived again. I must think about **48**

my strengths and weaknesses as an employee of Toe-Ring International. **49**

50 First and most important, let me say that I love working for Toe-Ring.

51 When I applied for the job on September 15, 2005, I never dreamed how **52**

53 much fun I would have taking two long lunches a day. Sneaking out the

back door is not my idea of fun. Because no one ever watches what I am
54

doing at Toe-Ring, I can leave by the front door without worrying. Also, Ms.
55 **56**

Ehrlich, I confess that I do almost no work at all. Transferred to the plant in

Boise, Idaho, I immediately claimed a privilege given only to the most
57 **58**

59 experienced, most skilled employees and started to take an extra week of **60**

vacation. I have only one more thing to say. May I have a raise?

46 Commas surround *Ms. Ehrlich* because she's being directly addressed in this sentence.

47 See the preceding answer.

48 The pronoun *I* is part of the main idea of the sentence, not an introductory expression. No comma should separate it from the rest of the sentence.

49 The phrase *of Toe-Ring International* is an essential identifier of the type of employee being discussed. No comma should separate it from the word it describes (employee).

50 A comma follows the introductory expression, *First and most important*.

51 In this date, a comma separates the day from the year.

52 A comma follows a year when a date is inserted into a sentence.

53 Two descriptions are attached to *lunches* — *two* and *long*. These descriptions aren't of the same type. *Two* is a number, and *long* is a different sort of quantity. Also, numbers are never separated from other descriptions by a comma. The verdict: Delete the comma after *two*.

54 In this sentence the expression *sneaking out the back door* isn't an introductory element. It's the subject of the sentence, and it shouldn't be separated from its verb *(is)* by a comma.

55 The introductory expression *Because no one ever watches what I am doing at Toe-Ring* should be separated from the rest of the sentence by a comma.

56 *Also* is an introduction to the sentence. Slice it off with a comma.

57 A comma separates the city from the state.

58 A comma follows *Idaho* for two reasons. If an address is embedded in a sentence, a comma generally follows the last bit of the address — in this case, the state. Also, *Idaho* is the last bit of an introductory element.

59 Two descriptions are attached to *employees: most experienced* and *most skilled*. Because these descriptions are more or less interchangeable, a comma separates them from each other.

60 No comma ever separates the last description from what it describes, so the comma before *employees* has to go.

Chapter 6

Made You Look! Punctuation Marks That Demand Attention

In This Chapter

▶ Placing hyphens where needed

▶ Using dashes for drama and interruptions

▶ Examining colons and semicolons

The punctuation marks I discuss in this chapter don't sit in the corner at parties murmuring, "Just forget about me." Instead, they scream, "I'm important! Pay attention, NOW," wherever they appear. Happily, placing these marks in the proper spots is a cinch.

Connectors and Dividers: Hyphens

Hyphens (-) are the shortest horizontal marks in the punctuation world. (Dashes are the long ones.) Sometimes, hyphens function as word breakers. When you arrive at the right-hand margin in the middle of a word, a hyphen enables you to finish the word on the next line. Just break the word at the end of a syllable (the dictionary guides you on this point), but don't leave only one or two letters all by themselves, and don't attempt to divide any one-syllable words, even a long one such as *through* (if you're working on a computer, though, you can count on your word processing program to take care of end-of-line hyphenation for you).

Hyphens also create *compounds* (two words linked to create one meaning) and sometimes to attach a prefix to a word. Prefixes (*pre-, post-, ante-, un-,* and so on) grab onto the front of other words, thereby changing the meaning. Most prefixes attach without hyphens, but a couple (*self-,* for example) tend to appear with hyphens.

As with other punctuation marks, the hyphen is subject to fashion. Many prefixed and hyphenated compounds of a hundred years ago have now become single words. What used to be *non-negotiable* is *nonnegotiable* these days. To make matters worse, the major style guides and publishing companies sometimes differ on the to-hyphenate-or-not question. The dictionary is a good guide for the everyday writer who's unsure about a particular case. If you can't find a dictionary, follow these guidelines:

✔ **You need a hyphen if your reader will become confused without one.** You may, for example, be going to *re-create* a work of art or *recreate* at your local amusement park. Without the hyphen, how can the reader tell?

✔ **If two vowels show up together, chances are you need a hyphen.** *Anti-insurance* and *re-examine,* for example, need hyphens.

> ✔ **If a prefix latches onto a capitalized word, a hyphen separates the two.** Consider *anti-Republican* and *post-Renaissance*.
>
> ✔ **If you're talking about part of a word (as I did earlier in this section when I listed the prefixes *pre-, post-,* and others), a hyphen signals that the word isn't complete.** The hyphen functions in this way when you want to link two prefixes to one root word, as in the expression *pre- and postwar anxiety.*

Hyphens also link two words that form one description of the same person or thing. You may make a *third-base error* (one bungled play) and allow a run to score. Or, if you're having a really bad day, you may make a *third base-error* (the third of three bad throws to any base, made obvious by the creation of compound *base-error*). The hyphen brings clarity, though it can't improve your baseball skills.

Enough talk. Time for some action. Use a caret (^) to tuck a hyphen wherever it's needed in this sentence. If you find a misplaced hyphen, cross it out with a vertical slash. If the sentence is okay, go bowling.

Q. The best known actress of the preSpielberg era has recently begun to respond to fans via email.

A. **best-known**, **pre-Spielberg**, **e-mail**. Both *best* and *known* describe *actress,* so the descriptions are hyphenated. The *pre-* is attached to a capitalized word; hence the hyphen. The current spelling of *e-mail* includes a hyphen. Ten years from now, however, you may be sending *email* . . . or teleporting, for all I know.

1. Jim, the second string quarterback, hates mice.

2. Among the antirodent forces was Megan, who doesn't like glue-traps.

3. Megan prefers a short preexecution period.

4. As a matter of fact, Megan is profoundly antiPestbegone, a new product that traps mice in a sticky web.

5. Debbie is too wrapped up in a selfimprovement program to worry about pests.

6. In Debbie's opinion, the supremely-annoying pest is Calvin, who insists on taking her skiing this weekend.

7. Calvin is into both tele- and miscommunication.

8. A two or a three way telephone call is Calvin's favorite way to arrange a ski-trip.

9. Tomorrow Megan, who is Latvian-American, will ask Calvin to take her skiing instead of Debbie.

10. Megan wants to show off her extremely-expensive ski equipment.

Just Dashing Through

The dash is the egotist of punctuation marks. It calls your attention faster than a fire drill in the middle of a test. Hence you need to use the dash sparingly, in these situations only:

- **To interrupt the flow of thought with another idea.** "I will not attend the ball — how could I when my glass slipper is cracked? — no matter how much you beg." Notice that the material inserted into the sentence between the two dashes doesn't begin with a capital letter, even though in another situation it can stand alone as a complete sentence.

- **To summarize or define a list.** "Lip gloss, bug repellent, stun gun — Megan had everything she needed for her big date." The dash divides the list from its definition, which is everything Megan thinks she needs on a date.

  If you're not feeling dramatic, use a colon to precede a list. A colon does the same job grammatically, with less flash than the dash.

- **To show incompleteness.** "You don't carry stun —" Megan was nearly speechless at the thought of a date without her trusty stun gun. The dash shows that the sentence is incomplete.

- **To create drama.** "May I introduce the best golfer in Antarctica — Sam Spearly." The dash is the equivalent of a drumroll in this sentence. In the sample sentence, "Sam Spearly" may be preceded by a comma, if you favor a quieter approach. (See Chapter 5 for more information on commas.)

When you plop a dash into a sentence, don't place a comma before or after it, unless you're showing incompleteness and the sentence requires a comma after the dash.

Dashes aren't appropriate in some situations. Keep these points in mind:

- Too many dashes are *really* annoying to the reader.
- Dashes can't be used to join complete sentences.
- You can't send a dash to do a hyphen's job.

Now dash through these questions, inserting dashes where appropriate. By the way, did you notice that I didn't say *where needed?* That's because dashes aren't required anywhere. Other punctuation marks (colons or parentheses, for example) may substitute for the dash, though they're usually less dramatic. Note that you may have to knock out another punctuation mark before inserting a dash.

Q. As usual Debbie brought too many snacks, chocolate antlers, cherry-coated sardines, and unsalted popcorn.

A. **As usual Debbie brought too many snacks — chocolate antlers, cherry-coated sardines, and unsalted popcorn.** The dash works better than the comma in this sentence, because the comma after *snacks* blends in with the list.

11. Jim plans to attend the truck race, I really don't know why, along with his personal trainer.

12. "I can scarcely believe that he has a trainer because . . ." sputtered Debbie.

13. He needs help with his fitness routine, four push-ups, a walk around the block, and a 20-minute nap.

14. His personal trainer worked with one of the best athletes on the planet, Karen Green.

15. Push-ups and walking, not exactly demanding exercises, are so easy that even an old lady can do them.

Sorting Out Semicolons

A semicolon (;) is the punctuation mark that people use to create winks in electronic messages. Not surprisingly, that isn't its main job. Instead, semicolons link two complete sentences and separate items in a list when at least one of those items contains a comma. (Chapter 5 tells you more about this function of the semicolon.) One important note: Don't join two sentences with a semicolon unless the ideas are closely related.

Get to work. Insert or delete semicolons as required in Fran's thoughts on a recent heat wave. If no semicolons need to be added or deleted, write "correct" in the blank after the sentence.

Q. Fran is allergic to hot weather, she plans to crank up her air conditioner to maximum cool. _____

A. **Fran is allergic to hot weather; she plans to crank up her air conditioner to maximum cool.** The original sentence sends a comma to do a semicolon's job. Not a good idea!

16. The reasons why I hate the summer are sweat; sweat; and sweat. _____

17. They say global warming is a myth; I bought two watermelons today. _____

18. Tomorrow I will plan trips to the North Pole; Ross, Alaska; and Antarctica. _____

19. I will turn on the weather report; but I am sure that it will be sunny and mild. _____

20. My saltshaker will run freely again; I may buy a winter coat. _____

21. Of course, winter coats are now on sale the fact that winter doesn't arrive for three more months is irrelevant. _____

22. Stores like to sell merchandise in advance shoppers prefer to buy season-appropriate goods. _____

23. Macy's has a sale on boots with fur linings; cashmere scarves; and leather gloves. _____

24. I should shop in Australia for clothes I need in the Northern Hemisphere; they sell summer clothes in July. _____

25. July is quite cool in Sydney, Australia; Canberra, Australia, and Wellington, New Zealand. _____

Placing Colons

A colon (:) often shows up — to grammarians' intense disapproval — in e-mails and the like to create smiley faces and other emoticons. Its real job is to introduce a long quotation or a list. Don't place a colon after a form of the verb *to be* or a preposition (*from, by, to,* and similar words). Also, in the absolute strictest English (and not even I am that picky), a colon may introduce a list or a quotation only when the words before the colon form a complete sentence. If you follow this rule, you can't insert a colon after *for example,* but you can use one after *take a look at this example.* Most business and technical handbooks allow colons after introductory phrases.

Time to "colon-ize" (or not) the sentences in this section. Add or remove colons (and, if necessary, subtract other punctuation). If everything's okay, write "correct" in the blank after the sentence.

0. The weather this year may be described with these words, horrible, freezing, humid, and windy. _____

A. **The weather this year may be described with these words: horrible, freezing, humid, and windy.** The list of weather descriptions doesn't include *words.* Placing a comma after *words* allows *words* to blend in with the list of descriptions. A colon marks the separation between the introduction and the list.

26. As I watched the thermometer rise, I told my friend what I felt: "There should be a national monument to the inventor of air-conditioning. If I had to live in the days when a bucket of ice and a fan were the only remedies for hot weather, I'd move to the North Pole." _____

27. Did I tell you that I bought books by: Marv Heatfree, Helen Icicle, and October Surprise? _____

28. When I return, I will say: "Great vacation." _____

29. The announcer will explain: that a strong cold front has wiped out the humidity. _____

30. I am astonished: a great, heat-free day! _____

Calling All Overachievers: Extra Practice with Hyphens, Dashes, Colons, and Semicolons

Fran recently received a travel brochure, and she's thinking about spending her vacation at La Bocaville Resort. Ignoring the wisdom of Fran's choice, read the following excerpt (see Figure 6-1) with an eye toward correct (actually, incorrect) punctuation. You need to find ten errors in hyphens, dashes, colons, and semicolons. Cross out the offending marks and substitute the correct punctuation. Enjoy your trip!

Figure 6-1:
Sample
brochure
excerpt
from a
less-than-
alluring
resort.

La Bocaville Resort welcomes — you to the best vacation of your life! When you arrive at the airport, you'll be greeted by: a stretch limo and a driver, a complimentary box of chocolates, and a bottle of mosquito repellent. No need to hike 10 miles to La Bocaville the limo will take you to the resort. After you've checked in to our lovingly-restored mansion, you can choose among many alternatives, including — volleyball played with a water filled balloon and a chat with our secretary treasurer, who is also our President of Having a Great Time! She's dedicated to your vacation; and she knows her job depends on your happiness with La Bocaville. You may also want to visit the BocaBite Restaurant: conveniently located inside the pool area. Be sure to take bug-spray along.

Answers to Punctuation Problems

1 **second-string**. You're not talking about *second quarterback* and *string quarterback*. These two words join forces to form one description of *quarterback* — one who isn't on the starting team but rather is on the second-string team.

2 **glue traps**. You don't normally need a hyphen between the prefix *anti* and the word it's glued onto. The word *glue* describes *traps* and doesn't form a compound.

3 **pre-execution**. Two vowels together, created by the attachment of a prefix, call for a hyphen.

4 **anti-Pestbegone**. The name of the product that Megan opposes is Pestbegone, which begins with a capital letter. When you clap a prefix onto a capitalized word, a hyphen needs to separate them.

5 **self-improvement**. The prefix *self-* likes to show up with a hyphen.

6 **supremely annoying**. These two words don't form one description. Instead, *supremely* describes *annoying*. How *annoying? Supremely annoying.* In general, descriptions ending in *-ly* aren't linked by a hyphen to other descriptions.

7 **correct**. The sentence links two prefixes to one word. The hyphen after the first prefix tells the reader to attach it to *communication*.

8 **two- or a three-way** and **ski trip**. Calvin likes a *two-way telephone call* or a *three-way telephone call*. The hyphen links the descriptions. *Ski* describes *trip* and doesn't form a compound.

9 **Latvian American** or **correct**. Here hyphens enter the realm of politics. If you hyphenate the term, you give equal importance to both, so Megan appreciates her Latvian and her American heritage equally. If you don't hyphenate, the second term dominates because it's described by the first. Without a hyphen, Megan sees herself as primarily American, though the Latvian side has some influence. Which form should you use? It depends on your point of view, but be consistent.

10 **extremely expensive**. The first word describes the second. How *expensive?* Like everything Megan buys, *extremely expensive!* They aren't linked as one description, so no hyphen should be inserted.

11 **Jim plans to attend the truck race — I really don't know why — along with his personal trainer.** The interrupting words *I really don't know why* are set off by dashes. But just so you know, parentheses can also do the job.

12 **"I can scarcely believe that he has a trainer because —" sputtered Debbie.** Or, **correct**. The *ellipses* (three dots) in the question do the job perfectly well, but the dash is more dramatic. Your call.

13 **He needs help with his fitness routine — four push-ups, a walk around the block, and a 20-minute nap.** The comma doesn't work after *routine* because otherwise the definition just blends in and creates a list of four things: *routine, push-ups, a walk,* and *a nap.* If you're allergic to dashes, a colon or parentheses may substitute here.

14 **His personal trainer worked with one of the best athletes on the planet — Karen Green.** Or, **correct**. Once again, if the comma is your preference, go for it.

15 **Push-ups and walking — not exactly demanding exercises — are so easy even an old lady can do them.** A dash sets off a comment on *push-ups and walking*.

16 **The reasons why I hate the summer are sweat, sweat, and sweat.** The items in this list are single words, not phrases containing commas. Semicolons therefore aren't needed to separate the items in the list. Commas do the job.

17 **They say global warming is a myth. I bought two watermelons today.** A semicolon can't join two unrelated ideas. These random thoughts — Fran always talks this way — shouldn't be linked by a semicolon. Apart from punctuation, throwing two unrelated ideas together isn't a good idea. The reader should have a logical thread to follow between one sentence and another.

18 **correct**. Surprised? This list contains one item (Ross, Alaska) that includes a comma. If the three places were separated only by commas, the reader would not be sure whether Ross and Alaska were two items or one. The semicolon tells the reader where one item ends and another begins.

19 **I will turn on the weather report, but I am sure that it will be sunny and mild.** The word *but* joins these two sentences, so you don't need a semicolon too. Change it to a comma. A comma precedes *and, but, or, nor,* and similar words when they connect two complete sentences.

20 **My saltshaker will run freely again. I may buy a winter coat.** The semicolon implies a relationship between the things it links. You can argue that the two halves of this sentence show what Fran wants out of the cold front, but if the relationship isn't immediately clear to the reader, add some words or make two separate sentences. Better yet, add one or more sentences that join the two ideas in a logical way.

21 **Of course, winter coats are now on sale; the fact that winter doesn't arrive for three more months is irrelevant.** These two complete thoughts both relate to the maddening habit of selling out-of-season merchandise. Because both statements are complete thoughts, a semicolon joins them legally.

22 **Stores like to sell merchandise in advance; shoppers prefer to buy season-appropriate goods.** Each of these two statements could stand alone as a complete sentence, and that's why they can't be mashed together without a legal connection. You need a semicolon to link them.

23 **Macy's has a sale on boots with fur linings, cashmere scarves, and leather gloves.** Take the semicolons out of this list. You need a semicolon to separate items in a list only if one of the items contains a comma — not the case here.

24 **correct**. In this sentence, two complete thoughts are correctly united by a semicolon.

25 **July is quite cool in Sydney, Australia; Canberra, Australia; and Wellington, New Zealand.** A comma separates the city and state in each of the items on this list, so a semicolon is needed to separate one item from another.

26 **correct**. This quotation from Fran is quite long and introduced by a complete sentence. Thus it may be introduced by a colon.

27 **Did I tell you that I bought books by Marv Heatfree, Helen Icicle, and October Surprise?** Don't place a colon after the preposition *by*; just dive into the list.

28 **When I return, I will say, "Great vacation."** The colon after *say* isn't a good idea, because the quotation is short and (I have to admit) run-of-the-mill. The colon is appropriate for long or extremely dramatic quotations only.

29 **The announcer will explain that a strong cold front has wiped out the humidity.** Drop the colon! It only interrupts the main idea, which shouldn't be interrupted, particularly in the case of cold fronts. (I'm writing this in mid-July, when everyone is sweating.) No punctuation is needed after *explain*.

30 **I am astonished — a great, heat-free day!** If you want the punctuation equivalent of a drumroll, go for a dash, not a colon.

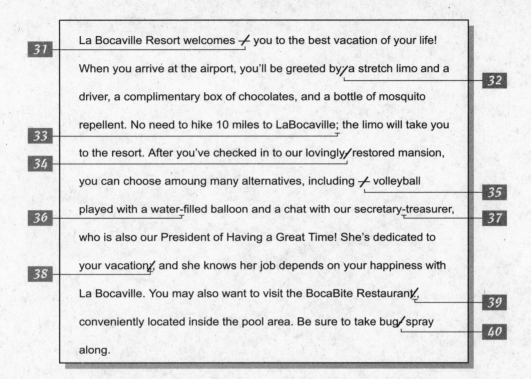

31 La Bocaville Resort welcomes ⫽ you to the best vacation of your life! When you arrive at the airport, you'll be greeted by⫽a stretch limo and a driver, a complimentary box of chocolates, and a bottle of mosquito repellent. No need to hike 10 miles to LaBocaville; the limo will take you to the resort. After you've checked in to our lovingly⫽restored mansion, you can choose amoung many alternatives, including ⫽ volleyball played with a water-filled balloon and a chat with our secretary-treasurer, who is also our President of Having a Great Time! She's dedicated to your vacation⫽ and she knows her job depends on your happiness with La Bocaville. You may also want to visit the BocaBite Restaurant⫽, conveniently located inside the pool area. Be sure to take bug⫽spray along.

31 No punctuation needed here. Why? The sentence has no interrupting thought that should be set off by a dash.

32 No punctuation needed here, because a colon should never follow a preposition (*by,* in this sentence).

33 Two complete sentences can't be placed next to each other without a joining word or appropriate punctuation. Insert a semicolon or make two separate sentences.

34 These two descriptions should not be linked because they don't form a single description of *mansion.* Instead, *restored* describes *mansion* and *lovingly* describes *restored.* In general, words ending in -*ly* aren't linked by hyphens to other descriptions.

35 The dash is out of place here because *including* introduces the list. Drop the dash. (I'd also leave La Bocaville Resort on the first available jet, but maybe that's just me.)

36 The hyphen is needed to join *water* and *filled* because they create one description of the balloon and a very messy volleyball game.

37 The term *secretary-treasurer* is always hyphenated.

38 The two complete sentences are already joined by *and.* The semicolon is overkill. Drop the *and,* or drop the semicolon.

39 The colon after *Restaurant* implies that a list or a quotation follows, but the next few words don't fit into those categories. A comma is better here.

40 *Bug* describes *spray.* No hyphen is needed, because you don't have a compound word.

Chapter 7

One Small Mark, a Whole New Meaning: Apostrophes

In This Chapter
▶ Shortening words and numbers with apostrophes
▶ Showing possession

An apostrophe is a little hook (') that snags many writers at some point. With a little practice, you can confidently plop apostrophes into the proper spots in your writing.

The most common apostrophe mistake is to place one where it's not appropriate. Don't use an apostrophe in either of these circumstances:

- **To create a plural:** You have *one arrow* and *two arrows,* not *two arrow's.* The no-apostrophe-for-plural rule holds true for names. I am one person named *Woods,* and members of my family are the *Woodses,* not the *Woods'.*

- **With a possessive pronoun:** Don't use an apostrophe in a possessive pronoun (*my, your, his, hers, its, ours, theirs, whose,* and so on).

Traditionally, an apostrophe was used to create a particular (and unusual) type of plural — the plural of symbols and numerals. It was also used to create the plural of a word referred to as a word. (Confused? Keep reading for an example.) In old books you may find a sentence like *Henry sprinkled 20's and therefore's throughout his story.* Don't panic. Grammar goes through changes. What was once correct is now passé. Just recognize an outdated custom and move on with your life.

Hook into the exercises in this chapter so that no apostrophe snags you ever again.

Putting Words on a Diet: Contractions

Apostrophes shorten words by replacing one or more letters. The shortened word, or *contraction* (not to be confused with the thing pregnant women scream through), adds an informal, conversational tone to your writing.

The most frequently used contractions, paired with their long forms, include those in Table 7-1.

Table 7-1		Frequently Used Contractions			
Long Form	**Contraction**	**Long Form**	**Contraction**	**Long Form**	**Contraction**
Are not	Aren't	I will	I'll	We are	We're
Cannot	Can't	I would	I'd	We have	We've
Could have	Could've	It is	It's	We will	We'll
Could not	Couldn't	She has	She's	Were not	Weren't
Do not	Don't	She is	She's	Will not	Won't
He has	He's	She will	She'll	Would have	Would've
He is	He's	Should have	Should've	Would not	Wouldn't
He will	He'll	Should not	Shouldn't	You are	You're
He would	He'd	They are	They're	You have	You've
I am	I'm	They have	They've	You will	You'll
I had	I'd	They will	They'll	You would	You'd

College entrance tests won't ask you to insert an apostrophe into a word, but they may want to know whether you can spot a misplaced mark or an improperly expanded contraction. An apostrophe shortens a word, and a common mistake is to re-expand a contraction into something it was never meant to be. The contraction *should've,* for example, is short for *should have,* not *should of.* The expressions *should of, could of,* and *would of* don't exist in standard English. If you see one of these turkeys on the SAT or the ACT, you know you've found a mistake.

Contractions aren't just for words. You also can slice numbers out of your writing with apostrophes, especially in informal circumstances. This punctuation mark enables you to graduate in '07, marry in '15, and check the maternity coverage in your health insurance policy by early '18.

Feel like flexing your apostrophe muscles? Look at the underlined words in these sentences and change them into contractions. Place your answers in the blanks.

Q. Adam said that <u>he would</u> go to the store to buy nuts. _____

A. **he'd**. This apostrophe is a real bargain. With it, you save four letters.

1. "Peanuts <u>are not</u> the best choice because many people are allergic to them," commented Pam. _____

2. "<u>I am</u> sure that <u>you will</u> choose a better appetizer," she added. _____ _____

3. The store <u>will not</u> take responsibility for your purchase. _____

4. <u>Do not</u> underestimate the power of a good appetizer. _____

5. Your guests will think that <u>you are</u> cheap if you <u>do not</u> provide at least one bowl of nuts. _____ _____

6. "Adam <u>would have</u> bought caviar, but I <u>would not</u> pass the walnut counter without buying something," commented Pam. _____ _____

7. "You <u>cannot</u> neglect the dessert course either," countered Adam. _____

8. Adam usually recommends a fancy dessert such as a maple walnut ice cream sundae, but <u>he is</u> watching his weight. _____

9. "If they created a better diet ice cream," he often says, "<u>I would</u> eat a ton of it." _____

10. "Yes, and then <u>you would</u> weigh a ton yourself," snaps Pam. _____

11 <u>She is </u>a bit testy when faced with diet food. _____

12. Of course, Adam <u>could have</u> been a little more diplomatic when he mentioned Pam's "newly tight" sweater. _____

13. Adam is planning to serve a special dessert wine, Chateau Adam <u>1999</u>, to his guests. _____

14. He always serves that beverage at reunions of the class of <u>2006</u>. _____

15. <u>We are</u> planning to attend, but <u>we will</u> bring our own refreshments! _____ _____

16. No one from the class of <u>1912</u> can attend; <u>they are</u> all too busy golfing. _____ _____

17. For this, our tenth reunion, <u>we are</u> preparing a guessing game. _____

18. Adam wants to know <u>who is</u> in charge of creating the questions. _____

19. <u>He is</u> in charge because he knows the most gossip. _____

20. <u>We will</u> have to check the questions before the party. _____

21. <u>He would</u> like nothing better than to shock us all with prying questions. _____

22. At our last reunion, Adam <u>should have</u> been more careful. _____

23. Three people cried because they <u>could not</u> remember the latest gossip item. _____

24. Adam <u>is not</u> qualified to work for the new gossip magazine. _____

25. I <u>cannot</u> tell a lie; I hope that Adam <u>does not</u> get the job. _____ _____

Taking Possession

The *pen of my aunt* that you learn in foreign-language class becomes *my aunt's pen* in standard English, with the help of an apostrophe. To show possession with apostrophes, keep these rules in mind:

- ✔ **Singular owner:** Attach an apostrophe and the letter *s* (in that order) to a singular person, place, or thing to express possession (*Henry's* tooth, *Rome's* dentists, the *drill's* annoying whine).

- ✔ **Plural owner:** Attach an apostrophe to a regular plural (one that ends in *s*) to express possession (the *boys'* restroom, the *cities'* mayors, the *billboards'* message).

- ✔ **Irregular plural owner:** Add an apostrophe and the letter *s* (in that order) to an irregular plural (one that doesn't end in *s*) to express possession (the *children's* toys, the *data's* significance).

- ✔ **Joint ownership:** If two or more people own something jointly, add an apostrophe and an *s* (in that order) to the last name (*Abe and Mary's* sofa; *George, Jeb, and Barbara's* memories).

> ✔ **Separate ownership:** If two or more people own things separately, everyone gets an apostrophe and an *s* (*Abe's and Mary's* pajamas; *George's, Jeb's, and Barbara's* shoes).
>
> ✔ **Hyphenated owner:** If the word you're working with is hyphenated, just attach the apostrophe and *s* to the end (*mother-in-law's* office). For plurals ending in *s*, attach the apostrophe only (*three secretary-treasurers'* accounts).
>
> ✔ **Time and money:** Okay, Father Time and Mr. Dollar Bill don't own anything. Nevertheless, time and money may be possessive in expressions such as *next week's test, two hours' homework, a day's pay,* and so forth. Follow the rules for singular and plural owners, as explained at the beginning of this bulleted list.

Easy stuff, right? See whether you can apply your knowledge. Turn the underlined word (or words) into the possessive form. Write your answers in the blanks provided.

0. The style of this <u>year</u> muscle car is <u>Jill</u> favorite.

A. **year's, Jill's**. Two singular *owners. Jill* is the traditional owner — a person, but the time expression also takes an apostrophe.

26. <u>Carol</u> classic car is entered in <u>tonight</u> show. _____

27. She invested three <u>months</u> work in restoring the finish. _____

28. Carol will get by with a little help from her friends; <u>Jess and Marty</u> tires, which they purchased a few years ago with their first allowance, will be installed on her car.

_____

29. The <u>boys</u> allowance, by the way, is far too generous, despite their <u>sister-in-law</u> objections.

_____

30. <u>Jill</u> weekly paycheck is actually smaller than the <u>brothers</u> daily income.

_____

31. Annoying as they are, the brothers donate <u>a day</u> pay from time to time to underfunded causes such as the <u>Women</u> Committee to Protect the Environment.

_____

32. Carol couldn't care less about the environment; the <u>car</u> gas mileage is ridiculously low.

_____

33. She cares about the car, however. She borrowed <u>Jess and Marty</u> toothbrushes to clean the dashboard. _____

34. Now she needs her <u>helpers</u> maximum support as the final judging nears. _____

35. She knows that the <u>judge</u> decision will be final, but just in case she has volunteered <u>two thousand dollars</u> worth of free gasoline to his favorite charity.

_____

36. <u>Carol</u> success is unlikely, because the <u>court</u> judgments can't be influenced by anything but the law. _____

37. Last week, for example, the judge ruled in favor of a developer, despite the <u>mother-in-law</u> plea for a different verdict. _____

38. <u>Ten hours</u> begging did no good at all. _____

39. Tomorrow the judge will rule on the <u>car show</u> effect on the native <u>animals</u> habitat.

_____

40. The <u>geese</u> ecosystem is particularly sensitive to automotive exhaust.
_____

41. The <u>fish</u> ecosystem is easily damaged as well. _____

42. In September, someone poured two <u>weeks</u> worth of used french-fry oil into a lake.
_____

43. All the marine <u>animals</u> oxygen was trapped in the oil. _____

44. Ten <u>months</u> cleaning was needed to restore the water to purity. _____

45. The restaurant that dumped the oil accepted responsibility for the <u>cook</u> actions.
_____

Calling All Overachievers: Extra Practice with Apostrophes

Marty's to-do list, shown in Figure 7-1, needs some serious editing. Check the apostrophe situation. You need to find nine spots to insert and six spots to delete an apostrophe.

Things to Do This Week

A. Call Johns doctor and arrange for a release of annual medical report.

B. Check on last springs blood pressure numbers to see whether they

    need to be changed.

C. Ask John about his rodent problem's.

D. Find out why networks cant broadcast Tuesdays speech live, as John

    needs prime-time publicity.

E. Ask whether his' fondness for long speeches' is a problem.

F. Send big present to network president and remind him that you are

    both Yale 06.

G. Order bouquet's for secretary and National Secretaries Week card.

H. Rewrite speech on cat litter' to reflect sister-in-laws ideas.

I. Tell opposing managers assistant that "you guys wouldnt stand a

    chance" in the old day's.

Figure 7-1:
Mock to-do
list, full of
apostrophe
mistakes.

Answers to Apostrophe Problems

1 **aren't**. The contraction drops the letter *o* and substitutes an apostrophe.

2 **I'm, you'll**. In the first contraction, the apostrophe replaces the letter *a*. In the second, it replaces two letters, *w* and *i*.

3 **won't**. This contraction is irregular because you can't make an apostrophe-letter swap. Illogical though it may seem, *won't* is the contraction of *will not*.

4 **Don't**. Drop the space between the two words, eliminate the *o*, and insert an apostrophe to create *don't*.

5 **you're, don't**. The first contraction sounds exactly like the possessive pronoun *your*. Don't confuse the two.

6 **would've, wouldn't**. Take care with the first contraction; many people mistakenly re-expand the contraction *would've* to *would of* (instead of the correct expansion, *would have*). The second contraction, *wouldn't,* substitutes an apostrophe for the letter *o*.

7 **can't**. Did you know that *cannot* is written as one word? The contraction also is one word, with an apostrophe knocking out an *n* and an *o*.

8 **he's**. The same contraction works for *he is* (as in this sentence) and *he has*.

9 **I'd**. You're dropping the letters *woul*.

10 **you'd**. The same contraction works for *you would* (as in this sentence) and *you had*.

11 **She's**. The apostrophe replaces the letter *i*.

12 **could've**. Be careful in re-expanding this contraction. A common mistake is to write *could of,* an expression that's a total no-no.

13 **'99**. A date may be shortened, especially if you're out with Adam. Just be sure that the context of the sentence doesn't lead the reader to imagine a different century (2099, perhaps). This one is fairly clear, given that we're nowhere near 2099, and 1899 is probably not the intended meaning.

14 **'06**. Not much chance of the reader misunderstanding which numbers are missing here (unless he or she is really old)!

15 **we're, we'll**. The apostrophes replace the letter *a* and *wi*.

16 **'12, they're**. In the first part of this sentence, the apostrophe replaces two numerals. It's okay to drop numerals as long as the reader is likely to understand what's been left out. In the second part of this sentence, the apostrophe replaces the letter *a*.

17 **we're**. The apostrophe replaces the letter *a* in this contraction of *we are*.

18 **who's**. The apostrophe replaces the letter *i* in this one.

19 **He's**. Only one letter is replaced here (*i*), but in this hurried world, every letter counts.

20 **We'll**. This one is a bargain. Drop two letters (*wi*) and plop in an apostrophe instead.

21   **He'd**. The apostrophe is a real space saver in this contraction; it replaces *woul*.

22   **should've**. If you take out the *ha,* you can insert an apostrophe and create a contraction.

23   **couldn't**. I'm not sure why anyone cares about gossip, but I'm sure that the contraction has an apostrophe in place of the letter *o*.

24   **isn't**. Drop the *o* and replace it with an apostrophe.

25   **can't, doesn't**. Two for the price of one here: In the first blank, you substitute an apostrophe for the letters *no*. In the second, just the *o* drops out in favor of the apostrophe.

26   **Carol's, tonight's**. Carol owns the car, so you just need to attach an apostrophe and an *s* to a singular form to create a singular possessive. The second answer illustrates a time/money possessive expression.

27   **three months'**. The value of time and money can be expressed with a possessive form. Because you're talking about *months,* a plural, the apostrophe goes after the *s*.

28   **Jess and Marty's**. The sentence tells you that the boys own the tires together, so only one apostrophe is needed. It's placed after the last owner's name. The possessive pronoun *her,* like all possessive pronouns, has no apostrophe.

29   **boys', sister-in-law's**. The plural possessive just tacks an apostrophe onto the *s,* in regular, *end-in-s* plurals. Hyphenated forms are easy too; just attach the apostrophe and an *s* to the end.

30   **Jill's, brothers'**. The first form is singular, so you add an apostrophe and an *s*. The second form is a regular plural, so you just add the apostrophe.

31   **a day's, Women's**. The first form falls into the time/money category, and because *day* is singular, you add an apostrophe and an *s*. The second is an irregular plural (not ending in *s*), so you tack on an apostrophe and an *s*.

32   **car's**. A singular possessive form calls for an apostrophe and an *s*.

33   **Jess's and Marty's**. Okay, the brothers are close, but they draw the line at shared toothbrushes. Each owns a separate brush, so each name needs an apostrophe.

> **TIP**   If a word ends in *s* (*Jess,* for example), adding an apostrophe and another *s* creates a spit factor: People tend to spray saliva all over when saying the word. To avoid this unsanitary problem, some writers add just the apostrophe (*Jess'*), even though technically they've neglected the extra *s*. Grammarians generally allow this practice, perhaps because they too dislike being spit upon. In all but the strictest situations, either form is correct.

34   **helpers'**. To create a plural possessive of a word ending in *s,* just attach an apostrophe.

35   **judge's, two thousand dollars'**. The first answer is a simple, singular possessive, so an apostrophe and an *s* do the trick. The second is a time/money possessive, and two thousand dollars is plural, so just an apostrophe is needed.

36   **Carol's, court's**. Two singular words, so only an apostrophe and the letter *s* are needed to make each possessive.

37   **mother-in-law's**. The apostrophe and the letter *s* follow the last word of the hyphenated term.

38   **Ten hours'**. The apostrophe creates an expression meaning *ten hours of begging*. Because *hours* is plural, only an apostrophe is added.

39 **car show's, animals'.** The first is a singular possessive, and the second is plural.

40 **geese's.** The word *geese* is irregular. In an irregular plural, an apostrophe and the letter *s* are added.

41 **fish's.** The word *fish* is irregular (and unusual); the singular and plural form are the same. To create a possessive, add an apostrophe and the letter *s*.

42 **weeks'.** To create a plural possessive, add an apostrophe after the letter *s*.

43 **animals'.** This regular plural ends with the letter *s*. To show possession, add an apostrophe.

44 **months'.** This regular plural needs only an apostrophe after the *s* to become possessive.

45 **cook's.** When one cook becomes possessive, he hogs all the desserts. Oops. That's life, not grammar. Just add an apostrophe and the letter *s*.

Things to Do This Week

46   A. Call John's doctor and arrange for a release of annual medical report.

47   B. Check on last spring's blood pressure numbers to see whether they

         need to be changed.

         C. Ask John about his rodent problem/s.   48

49   D. Find out why networks can't broadcast Tuesday's speech live, as John   50

         needs prime-time publicity.

51   E. Ask whether his/ fondness for long speeches/ is a problem.   52

         F. Send big present to network president and remind him that you are

         both Yale '06.

53

54   G. Order bouquet/s for secretary and National Secretaries' Week card.   55

56   H. Rewrite speech on cat litter/ to reflect sister-in-law's ideas.   57

58   I.   Tell opposing manager's assistant that "you guys wouldn't stand a   59

60   chance" in the old day/s.

---

46 The doctor belongs to John (in a manner of speaking), so the apostrophe is needed to show possession.

47 This time expression needs an apostrophe and an *s*.

48 A simple plural (not possessive, not a numeral, and so on) takes no apostrophe.

49 In this contraction, the apostrophe replaces the letters *n* and *o*.

50 Time expressions sometimes use apostrophes, as in *Tuesday's*.

51 Possessive pronouns don't have apostrophes.

52 A plural takes no apostrophe.

53 Missing numerals (in this case, *20*) are replaced by an apostrophe.

54 A simple plural doesn't take an apostrophe.

55 This plural possessive form — the secretaries own the week, symbolically — adds an apostrophe after the *s*.

56 In this sentence *litter* isn't possessive and doesn't need an apostrophe.

57 A hyphenated singular form takes an apostrophe and an *s* to become possessive.

58 A singular possessive is created by adding an apostrophe and an *s*.

59 In this contraction, the missing letter *o* is replaced by an apostrophe.

60 *Days* is just plural, not possessive, so it doesn't take an apostrophe.

Chapter 8

"Let Me Speak!" Quotation Marks

*W*hen I first started teaching, I used to curve and wiggle two fingers of each hand whenever I was quoting someone else's words. I assumed the students knew that my fingers represented the two little lines that precede and follow a direct quotation (" "). Big mistake. It was June before I discovered that they had interpreted my wiggles as a strange form of wave. Sadly, this error was only one of many they made with quotation marks.

Quotation marks may puzzle you, too, because they're subject to so many rules, most of which come from custom and tradition rather than logic. But if you're willing to put in a little effort, you can crack the code and ace this important punctuation mark.

Quotation marks have a few important jobs:

✔ **Directly quoted material:** Quotation marks surround words drawn from another person's speech or writing. In fiction, quotation marks indicate dialogue: "I would love to receive a single rose," sighed Sandy. Quotation marks don't belong in a sentence that summarizes speech, such as *He said that he had caught a cold.*

✔ **Titles:** Quotation marks surround the titles of certain types of literary or other artworks: Emily's first poem, "Ode on a Grecian Olive," was printed in the school magazine.

✔ **Distancing:** Quotation marks sometimes are used to indicate slang or to tell the reader that the writer doesn't agree with the words inside the quotation marks: I don't always appreciate Emily's "art."

In this chapter, you get to practice direct quotations and titles (lucky you!) along with a few other delights, including the interaction between quotation marks and other punctuation and quotations embedded inside other quotations. Let the games begin.

Lending Written Words a Voice: Punctuating Direct Quotations

The basic rule governing quotation marks is simple. Place quotation marks around words drawn directly from someone else's speech or writing to distinguish their ideas and expression from your own. Or, if you're writing the Great American Novel, place quotation marks around dialogue. The tricky part is the interaction between quotation marks and other punctuation, such as commas, periods, and the like:

- **If the quotation has a speaker tag (*he murmured, she screamed,* and so forth), the speaker tag needs to be separated from the quotation by a comma.**

  - If the speaker tag is *before* the quotation, the comma comes *before* the opening quotation mark: Sharon sighed, "I hate hay fever season."

  - If the speaker tag is *after* the quotation, the comma goes *inside* the closing quotation mark: "What a large snout you have," whispered Richard lovingly.

  - If the speaker tag appears *in the middle* of a quotation, a comma is placed before the first closing quotation mark and immediately after the tag: "Here's the handkerchief," said Richard, "that I borrowed last week."

  Just because you're quoting, don't think you have a license to create a run-on sentence. (See Chapter 4 for practice with run-ons.) If you have two complete sentences, quoted or not, they should be written as separate sentences or linked correctly with a semicolon or a joining word such as *and*.

- **If the quotation ends the sentence, the period goes *inside* the closing quotation mark.** Richard added, "I would like to kiss the tip of your humungous ear."

- **If the *quotation* is a question or an exclamation, the question mark or the exclamation mark goes *inside* the closing quotation mark.** "Why did you slap me?" asked Richard. "I was complimenting you!"

  Note: Question and exclamation marks serve as sentence-ending punctuation, so you don't need to add a period after the quotation marks.

- **If the quotation is *neither* question nor exclamation, but the *sentence* in which the quotation appears is, the question mark or exclamation point goes *outside* the closing quotation mark.** I can't believe that Richard said he's "a world class lover"! Do you think Sharon will ever get over his "sweet nothings"?

  If the quotation is tucked into the sentence without a speaker tag, as in the previous two sample sentences, no comma separates the quotation from the rest of the sentence. Nor does the quotation begin with a capital letter. Quotations with speaker tags, on the other hand, always begin with a capital letter, regardless of where the speaker tag falls. In an interrupted quotation (speaker tag in the middle), the first word of the first half of the quotation is capitalized, but the first word of the second half is not, unless it's a proper name.

- **Semicolons and colons always go outside the quotation marks.** Mary explained that the book was "too long"; I told her to read it anyway.

Enough with the explanation. Put the pedal to the metal in each of the following sentences. Your job is to identify the direct quotation, and fill in the proper punctuation, in the proper order, in the proper places. Here and there I add extra information in parentheses at the end of the sentence.

Q. The annual company softball game is tomorrow declared Becky.

A. **"The annual company softball game is tomorrow," declared Becky.** Don't count yourself right unless you placed the comma *inside* the closing quotation mark.

1. I plan to pitch added Becky, who once tried out for the Olympics.

2. Andy interrupted As usual I will play third base

3. No one knew how to answer Andy, who in the past has been called overly sensitive.

4. Gus said No one wanted Andy at third base; the entire Snyder family has terribly slow reaction time (The first part of the sentence — *No one wanted Andy at third base* — is a quotation, but the second part is not.)

5. Who wants to win asked the boss in a commanding, take-no-prisoners tone.

6. Did she mean it when she said that we were not hard-boiled enough to play decently

7. Sarah remarked I dare anyone to call Andy soft (The statement Sarah is making is an exclamation.)

8. The opposing team, everyone knows, is first in the league and last in our company's heart (The whole statement about the opposing team is an exclamation.)

9. The odds favor our opponents sighed Becky but I will not give up

10. The league handbook states that all decisions regarding player placement are subject to the umpire's approval

11. The umpire has been known to label us out-of-shape players who think they belong in the Olympics (The label is a direct quotation.)

12. Do you think there will be a rain delay inquired Harry, the team's trainer.

13. Harry also asked Has anyone checked Becky's shoes to make sure that she hasn't sharpened her spikes again

14. Surely the umpire doesn't think that Becky would violate the rule that states, Fair play is essential (Imagine that the writer of this sentence is exclaiming.)

15. Becky has been known to cork her bat commented Harry.

16. The corking muttered Becky has never been proved

17. Oh yes it has countered Sarah I drilled a couple of holes and found plenty of cork

18. Sarah has not often been called a team player

19. If we could just find a player of Babe Ruth's caliber (This whole sentence is an exclamation.)

20. Just then Becky hit her trademark frozen rope to left field.

Embedding One Quotation inside Another

You had to ask. Sigh. Embedded quotations don't turn up very frequently, but when they do, you must pay close attention. Here's the deal: The embedded quotation is enclosed in single quotation marks (' '), and the surrounding quotation is placed in the usual double quotation marks (" "). So far, so good. The problem comes when this sort of situation requires other punctuation, and it pretty much always does. Follow these guidelines:

✔ **If the embedded quotation is at the end of the larger quotation,** the two closing quotation marks are next to each other, with the single mark first. Any commas or periods you need go inside both closing marks. "I hate the term 'frozen rope,'" said Sharon. Question marks and exclamation points follow the rule of logic: If the internal quotation is a question or an exclamation, place the **?** or the **!** inside the single closing mark. If the internal quotation isn't a question or an exclamation but the larger quotation is, place the **?** or the **!** outside the single closing mark but inside the double closing mark (simply put, in between them).

✔ **If the embedded quotation is at the beginning or in the middle of the larger quotation,** any commas surrounding it follow the rules described in the previous section. In other words, commas that precede the embedded quotation go in front of the opening double quotation mark. Commas that follow the embedded quotation go inside the closing single quotation mark. Sharon exclaimed, "'A frozen rope' is what she hit!" and "When Sharon started talking about 'a frozen rope,' I cheered," said Harry, who is supposed to be neutral.

The rules in this chapter follow American-style English. In Britain, single and double quotation marks are called *inverted commas,* and they're reversed. If you're in London (lucky you! I love London!), you may want to write a single quotation mark wherever I've placed a double, and a double wherever I've plopped a single.

Can you place the quotation marks and other punctuation in the right places in these sentences? Write the appropriate punctuation marks in the appropriate spots. Some helpful information is in parentheses at the end of the sentence.

O. I think that I shall never see a summer's romance more lovely and more temperate intoned Richard, who believes that quoting Shakespeare is the best way to impress women. (The embedded quotation is *more lovely and more temperate.*)

A. **"I think that I shall never see a summer's romance 'more lovely and more temperate,'" intoned Richard, who believes that quoting Shakespeare is the best way to impress women.** Notice that the comma after *temperate* goes inside both closing quotation marks, the single and the double.

21. Jane Austen would have a lot to say to Richard about his more lovely nonsense commented Sharon. (The embedded quotation is *more lovely.*)

22. Sharon went on to say that her favorite quotation concerns a truth universally acknowledged (The embedded quotation is *a truth universally acknowledged.*)

23. Did Richard really ask about Shakespeare's sonatas asked Clair. (The embedded quotation is *Shakespeare's sonatas.*)

24. Betsy replied, No, he asked about Shakespeare's bonnets (The embedded quotation is *Shakespeare's bonnets.*)

25. I can't believe he talked about beauteous bonnets sighed Sharon. (The embedded quotation is *beauteous bonnets.* Just to make this one harder, make the larger quotation an exclamation.)

26. Betsy has no patience for what she terms Richard's posturing explained Clair. (The embedded quotation is *Richard's posturing.*)

27. Clair went on to ask Don't you think that Richard is what I call an educated guy who means well (The embedded quotation is *an educated guy who means well.*)

28. No, he claims he's just trying to make girls think he's a player commented Sharon. (The embedded quotation is *a player.*)

29. I can't believe that anyone would call him a player exclaimed Betsy.

30. I'm going to give him A Summer's Pay said Sharon, who had a copy of the poem in her bag. (The embedded quotation here is actually a poem title, *A Summer's Pay.* Poem titles, as I explain in the next section, belong in quotation marks. Treat the title like any other embedded quotation.)

Punctuating Titles

Punctuating titles is easy, especially if you're a sports fan. Imagine a basketball player, one who tops seven feet. Next to him place a jockey; most jockeys hover around five feet. Got the picture? Good. When you're deciding how to punctuate a title, figure out whether you're dealing with Yao Ming (NBA player) or Mike Smith (Derby rider), using theses rules:

- **Titles that are italicized or underlined:** The basketball player represents full-length works — novels, magazines, television series, plays, epic poems, films, and the like. The titles of those works are italicized or underlined.

- **Titles that are placed in quotation marks:** The jockey, on the other hand, represents smaller works or parts of a whole — a poem, a short story, a single episode of a television show, a song, an article — you get the idea. The titles of these little guys aren't italicized or underlined; they're placed in quotation marks.

Okay, I admit that my sports comparison falls apart in one case: Pamphlets, which can be short, fall into the underlined-title category because regardless of length, they're still considered full-length works.

These rules apply to titles that are tucked into sentences. Centered titles, all alone at the top of a page, don't get any special treatment: no italics, no underlining, and no quotation marks. The centering and placement are enough to call attention to the title, so nothing else is called for, unless the centered title refers to some other literary work. In that case the embedded title is punctuated as described in the previous bulleted list.

When a title in quotation marks is part of a sentence, it sometimes tangles with other punctuation marks. The rules in American English (British English is different) call for any commas or periods *after* the title to be placed *inside* the quotation marks. So if the title is the last thing in the sentence, the period of the sentence comes before the closing quotation mark. Question marks and exclamation points, on the other hand, don't go inside the quotation marks unless they are actually part of the title. For example, suppose you write a poem and call it "Why Is the Sky Blue Again?" because you can't stop wondering why the sky isn't green. The question mark must always appear inside the closing quotation mark because it's part of the title.

If a title that ends with a question mark is the last thing in a sentence, the question mark ends the sentence. Don't place both a period and a question mark at the end of the same sentence.

All set for a practice lap around the track? Check out the title in this series of sentences. Place quotation marks around the title if necessary, adding endmarks when necessary; otherwise, underline the title. Here and there you find parentheses at the end of a sentence, in which I add some information to help you.

Q. Have you read Sarah's latest poem, Sonnet for the Tax Assessor (The sentence is a question, but the title isn't.)

A. **Have you read Sarah's latest poem, "Sonnet for the Tax Assessor"?** The title of a poem takes quotation marks. Question marks never go inside the quotation marks unless the title itself is a question.

31. Sarah's poem will be published in a collection entitled Tax Day Blues

32. Mary's fifth best-seller, Publish Your Poetry Now, inspired Sarah.

33. Some of us wish that Sarah had read the recent newspaper article, Forget About Writing Poetry.

34. Julie, an accomplished violinist, has turned Sarah's poem into a song, although she changed the name to Sonata Taxiana.

35. She's including it on her next CD, Songs of April.

36. I may listen to it if I can bring myself to turn off my favorite television show, Big Brother and Sister

37. During a recent episode entitled Sister Knows Everything the main character broke into her brother's blog.

38. In the blog was a draft of Who Will Be My First Love?, a play that, trust me, will never be produced.

39. Tonight Mary and Sarah are drafting an article entitled A Resolution to Revolutionize Poetry

40. They plan to publish their article in The New York Times.

Calling All Overachievers: Extra Practice with Quotation Marks

Tommy Brainfree's classic composition is reproduced in Figure 8-1. Identify ten spots where a set of quotation marks needs to be inserted. Place the quotation marks correctly in relation to other punctuation in the sentence. Also, underline titles where appropriate.

What I Did during Summer Vacation

by Tommy Brainfree

This summer I went to Camp Waterbug, which was the setting for a famous poem by William Long entitled Winnebago My Winnebago. At Camp Waterbug I learned to paddle a canoe without tipping it over more than twice a trip. My counselor even wrote an article about me in the camp newsletter, Waterbug Bites. The article was called How to Tip a Canoe. The counselor said, Brainfree is well named. I was not upset because I believed him (eventually) when he explained that the comment was an editing error.

Are you sure? I asked him when I first read it.

You know, he responded quickly, that I have a lot of respect for you. I nodded in agreement, but that night I placed a bunch of frogs under his sheets, just in case he thought about writing How to Fool a Camper. One of the frogs had a little label on his leg that read JUST KIDDING TOO.

At the last campfire gathering I sang a song from the musical Fiddler on the Roof. The song was called If I Were a Rich Man. I changed the first line to If I were a counselor. I won't quote the rest of the song because I'm still serving the detention my counselor gave me, even though I'm back home now.

Figure 8-1:
Sample
school
report sans
quotation
marks.

Answers to Quotation Problems

1   **"I plan to pitch," added Becky, who once tried out for the Olympics.** The directly quoted words, *I plan to pitch,* are enclosed in quotation marks. The comma that sets off the speaker tag *added Becky* goes inside the closing quotation mark.

2   **Andy interrupted, "As usual I will play third base."** The speaker tag comes first in this sentence, so the comma is placed before the opening quotation mark. The period that ends the sentence goes inside the closing quotation mark.

3   **No one knew how to answer Andy, who in the past has been called "overly sensitive."** The quotation is short, but it still deserves double quotation marks. Single quotation marks, in American usage, are reserved for embedded quotations. British custom is different, perhaps because they eat all those cucumber sandwiches. The period at the end of the sentence is placed, as periods always are in American usage, inside the closing quotation mark. Notice that this quotation doesn't have a speaker tag, so it isn't preceded by a comma, and it doesn't start with a capital letter.

4   **Gus said, "No one wanted Andy at third base"; the entire Snyder family has terribly slow reaction time.** The speaker tag is followed by a comma. A semicolon always goes outside the closing quotation mark, unless you're quoting a long passage that has a semicolon somewhere inside. A period ends the sentence.

5   **"Who wants to win?" asked the boss in a commanding, take-no-prisoners tone.** Because the quoted words are a question, the question mark goes inside the closing quotation mark. Okay, everybody knows that boss's questions aren't real questions — they're more like threats. Grammatically speaking, however, they fall into the question category and thus take a question mark.

6   **Did she mean it when she said that we were "not hard-boiled enough to play decently"?** The quoted words aren't a question, but the entire sentence is. The question mark belongs outside the closing quotation mark. By the way, if both the sentence and the quotation are questions, the question mark belongs inside the closing quotation mark.

7   **Sarah remarked, "I dare anyone to call Andy soft!"** A comma separates the speaker tag *(Sarah remarked)* from the quotation and precedes the opening quotation mark. Because the quoted words are an exclamation, the exclamation point belongs inside the closing quotation mark.

8   **The opposing team, everyone knows, is "first in the league and last in our company's heart"!** The hint in parentheses gives rationale for the answer. Because the whole statement is an exclamation, the exclamation point belongs outside the closing quotation mark.

9   **"The odds favor our opponents," sighed Becky, "but I will not give up."** Here's an interrupted quotation, with the speaker tag in the middle. Unlike the rude comments that seem to occur every five minutes when I'm trying to make a point about grammar, this sort of interruption is perfectly proper. Just be sure that the two parts of the quotation are punctuated correctly. In this question, the quoted material makes up one sentence, so the second half begins with a lowercase letter.

If each part of the quotation can stand alone as a complete sentence (see Chapter 4 for more detail), don't run the two together as one sentence. Instead, put a period after the speaker tag and make the second half of the quotation into a separate sentence enclosed in quotation marks. Or, place a period after the first half of the quotation and capitalize the first word of the rest of the quotation. Here's an example, adapted from question 9: "The odds favor our opponents," sighed Becky. "I will not give up."

10 **The league handbook states that "all decisions regarding player placement are subject to the umpire's approval."** Here's a nice little quotation tucked into the sentence. Because it's tucked in without a speaker tag, it takes no comma or capital letter. The period at the end of the sentence goes inside the closing quotation mark.

11 **The umpire has been known to label us "out-of-shape players who think they belong in the Olympics."** Ah yes, the joy of amateur sport! This quotation is plopped into the sentence without a speaker tag, so the first word takes no capital and isn't preceded by a comma. It ends with a period, which is slipped inside the closing quotation mark.

12 **"Do you think there will be a rain delay?" inquired Harry, the team's trainer.** Harry's words are a question, so the question mark goes inside the closing quotation mark.

13 **Harry also asked, "Has anyone checked Becky's shoes to make sure that she hasn't sharpened her spikes again?"** This speaker tag *Harry also asked* begins the sentence. It's set off by a comma, which precedes the opening quotation mark. The quoted words form a question (actually, they're a last-ditch effort to avoid a trip to the emergency room), so the question mark belongs inside the quotation marks.

14 **Surely the umpire doesn't think that Becky would violate the rule that states, "Fair play is essential"!** Okay, the parentheses tell you that the writer is exclaiming. The whole sentence is an exclamation, and the quoted words are fairly mild, so the exclamation point belongs to the sentence, not to the quotation. Place it outside the closing quotation mark.

15 **"Becky has been known to cork her bat," commented Harry.** A straightforward statement with a speaker tag *commented Harry* calls for a comma inside the closing quotation mark. The quotation is a complete sentence. In quoted material, the period that normally ends the sentence is replaced by a comma, because the sentence continues on — in this case, with *commented Harry*. Periods don't belong in the middle of a sentence unless they're part of an abbreviation.

16 **"The corking," muttered Becky, "has never been proved."** A speaker tag breaks into this quotation and is set off by commas. The one after *corking* goes inside, because when you're ending a quotation or part of a quotation, the comma or period always goes inside. Ditto at the end of the sentence; the period needs to be inserted inside the closing quotation mark. (Think of these punctuation marks as couch potatoes who never go outside.)

17 **"Oh yes it has," countered Sarah. "I drilled a couple of holes and found plenty of cork."** Did I catch you here? The quoted words form two complete sentences. You can't join two complete sentences with a comma, even if the sentences are quotations. The comma is too weak to do the job. The first quotation ends with a comma tucked inside the quotation marks, and the first sentence ends with *Sarah*. The second sentence should be surrounded by quotation marks, and the last period goes inside.

18 **Sarah has not often been called "a team player."** Okay, dokey. No speaker tag (no one is identified as the one who called), so no comma or capital letter marks the quotation. The sarcasm of *team player* is indicated by the quotation marks.

19 **"If we could just find a player of Babe Ruth's caliber!"** Because the sentence is an exclamation, the exclamation mark takes its rightful place inside the closing quotation mark.

20 **Just then Becky hit her trademark "frozen rope" to left field.** These quotation marks tell the reader that *frozen rope* is slang, okay for informal speech or writing only.

21 **"Jane Austen would have a lot to say to Richard about his 'more lovely' nonsense," commented Sharon.** When one quotation is planted inside another, the embedded words are enclosed by single quotation marks. I'm talking about America here; in Britain, this practice is sometimes reversed.

22 **Sharon went on to say that her "favorite quotation concerns 'a truth universally acknowl-edged.'"** You may want to sort out all these squiggles with a magnifying glass! The embedded quotation gets single marks, and the embedder (sounds like someone you *don't* want to meet at a party) gets double quotation marks. When the two occur at the same spot — in this case at the end of the sentence — the period plops down inside both closing marks.

23 **"Did Richard really ask about 'Shakespeare's sonatas'?" asked Clair.** At first glance this sen-tence looks like a good example of why grammarians are unpopular. It appears far too compli-cated to punctuate correctly. The secret is that in this sentence, the punctuation actually makes sense. Just take it one step at a time. The embedded quotation takes single quotation marks. Because the embedded quotation is not a question, the question mark follows the closing single quotation mark. The larger quotation, on the other hand, is a question, so the question mark goes inside the closing double quotation mark. See, I told you it was easy!

24 **Betsy replied, "No, he asked about 'Shakespeare's bonnets.'"** Another fun sentence. The embedded quotation and the larger quotation are both statements, so the period goes inside both closing marks.

25 **"I can't believe he talked about 'beauteous bonnets'!" sighed Sharon.** Are you having a good time yet? The embedded quotation isn't an exclamation, so the exclamation point stays outside the single quotation marks. The larger quotation is an exclamation, so the exclamation point goes inside the closing double quotation mark.

26 **"Betsy has no patience for what she terms 'Richard's posturing,'" explained Clair.** When both quotations end at the same spot, any periods or commas go inside both closing marks.

27 **Clair went on to ask, "Don't you think that Richard is what I call 'an educated guy who means well'?"** This is a complicated one. The embedded quotation isn't a question, so its closing quotation mark precedes the question mark. The larger quotation is a question, so its closing quotation mark goes after the question mark.

28 **"No, he claims he's trying to make girls think he's 'a player,'" commented Sharon.** Once again, both the embedded and the larger quotation end at the same place. The comma goes inside both closing quotation marks.

29 **"I can't believe that anyone would call him 'a player'!" exclaimed Betsy.** The larger quotation is an exclamation, so the exclamation point belongs inside the closing double quotation mark. The embedded quotation is just a statement, so its closing quotation mark precedes the excla-mation point.

30 **"I'm going to give him 'A Summer's Pay,'" said Sharon, who had a copy of the poem in her bag.** Embedded titles are the same as embedded quotations, so the comma goes inside both closing quotation marks.

31 **Tax Day Blues.** If it's a collection, it's a full-length work. Full-length works are underlined or ital-icized, not placed in quotation marks.

32 **Publish Your Poetry Now.** The book title is underlined.

33 **"Forget About Writing Poetry."** The period following a quotation or a title in quotation marks goes inside the closing quotation mark.

34 **"Sonata Taxiana."** The period always goes inside a closing quotation mark, at least in America. In Britain the period is generally outside, playing cricket. Just kidding about the cricket.

35 **Songs of April.** A CD is a full-length work, so the title is underlined or italicized.

36 <u>**Big Brother and Sister**</u>. The title of the whole series is underlined. (You can italicize it instead.) The title of an individual episode goes in quotation marks.

37 **"Sister Knows Everything,"** I don't have a blog, but if I did, I wouldn't want anyone breaking in! The episode title belongs in quotation marks. The series title gets underlined. (Italics may sub for underlining, if you wish.) The introductory expression calls for a comma, which should be placed inside the quotation marks.

38 <u>**Who Will Be My First Love?**</u> This one is complicated. A question mark is part of the title, which is underlined because a play is a full-length work. The comma in the sentence follows the title. (See Chapter 5 for more information on commas.)

39 **"A Resolution to Revolutionize Poetry."** A *resolution* isn't a book-length work, so quotation marks do the trick. The period ending the sentence goes inside the closing mark.

40 <u>**The New York Times**</u>. The newspaper name is underlined or italicized, in contrast to an article title, which belongs in quotation marks.

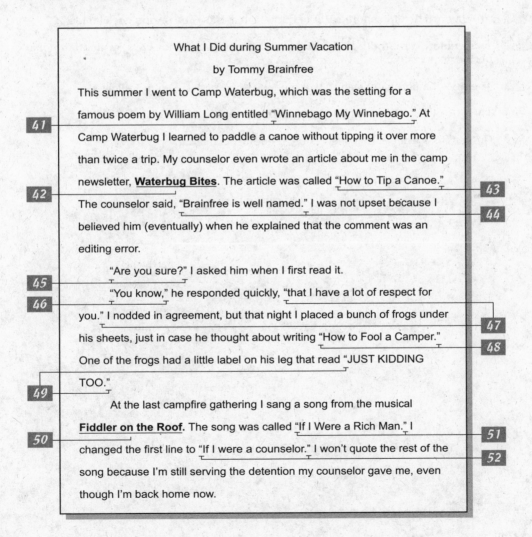

What I Did during Summer Vacation

by Tommy Brainfree

This summer I went to Camp Waterbug, which was the setting for a famous poem by William Long entitled "Winnebago My Winnebago." At **41** Camp Waterbug I learned to paddle a canoe without tipping it over more than twice a trip. My counselor even wrote an article about me in the camp newsletter, **Waterbug Bites**. The article was called "How to Tip a Canoe." **43**
42 The counselor said, "Brainfree is well named." I was not upset because I **44** believed him (eventually) when he explained that the comment was an editing error.

"Are you sure?" I asked him when I first read it.
45
"You know," he responded quickly, "that I have a lot of respect for **46** you." I nodded in agreement, but that night I placed a bunch of frogs under **47** his sheets, just in case he thought about writing "How to Fool a Camper." **48** One of the frogs had a little label on his leg that read "JUST KIDDING TOO."
49 At the last campfire gathering I sang a song from the musical **Fiddler on the Roof**. The song was called "If I Were a Rich Man." I **51** **50** changed the first line to "If I were a counselor." I won't quote the rest of the **52** song because I'm still serving the detention my counselor gave me, even though I'm back home now.

41 Poem titles belong in quotation marks. The title of a collection of poems, on the other hand, needs to be underlined.

42 The newsletter title is underlined.

43 An article title belongs in quotation marks. The period at the end of the sentence belongs inside the closing quotation mark.

44 Directly quoted speech belongs in quotation marks, with the period inside the closing mark.

45 The quoted words are a question, so the question mark goes inside the quotation marks.

46 The interrupted quotation, with an inserted speaker tag, needs two sets of marks. The comma at the end of the first part of the quotation goes inside the closing mark.

47 As in the preceding explanation, the period at the end of the sentence goes inside the closing mark.

48 Another article title, another set of quotation marks. The period goes inside.

49 This quotation reproduces the exact written words and thus calls for quotation marks. The period goes inside.

50 The title of a play, a full-length work, needs to be underlined or italicized.

51 The title of a song needs to be in quotation marks.

52 Quoted lines from a song need to be in quotation marks.

Chapter 9
Hitting the Big Time: Capital Letters

• •

In This Chapter

▶ Choosing capitals for job and personal titles

▶ Capitalizing geographical names

▶ Identifying school and business terms that should be capitalized

▶ Selecting capital letters for literary and media titles

▶ Placing capital letters in abbreviations

• •

Poetry is something I love, but even I have to admit that poets get away with murder. Specifically, they murder the rules for capital letters whenever they want to. A poet can write "i sent sally to sue," and no one blinks. Unfortunately, the rest of us have to conform to capitalization customs.

Most people know the basics: Capital letters are needed for proper names, the personal pronoun *I*, and the first letter of a sentence. Trouble may arrive with the finer points of capital letters — in quotations (which I cover in Chapter 8), titles (both people and publications), abbreviations, and school or business terms. Never fear. In this chapter you get to practice all those topics.

Even for nonpoets, the rules for capital letters may vary. The major style setters in the land of grammar (yes, grammar has style, and no, grammarians aren't immune to trends) sometimes disagree about what should be capitalized and what shouldn't. In this workbook I follow the most common capitalization styles. If you're writing for a specific publication or a particular teacher, you may want to check which twenty-pound book of rules (also known as a style manual) you should follow. The most common are those manuals published by the Modern Language Association (academic writing in the humanities), the American Psychological Association (science and social science writing), and the University of Chicago (general interest and academic publishing).

Bowing to Convention and Etiquette: People's Names and Titles

Unless you're a poet or an eccentric rock star who wants to buck the trend, you capitalize your name — first, last, and initials. Titles — job or personal — are a different story. The general rules are as follows:

✔ A title preceding and attached to a name is capitalized (*Mr. Smith, Professor Wiley, Lord Cummings,* and so forth). Small, unimportant words in titles (*a, the, of,* and the like) are always lowercased.

✔ Titles written after or without a name are generally not capitalized (*George Wiley, professor of psychology* or *Danielle Smith, director of paper distribution,* for instance).

✔ If the title names a post of the highest national or international importance (*President, Vice President, Secretary General,* and the like), it may be capitalized even when used alone, though some style manuals go for lowercase regardless of rank.

Now that you get the idea, test yourself. In the following sentences, add capital letters where needed. Lowercase any extra capitals. (Just cross out the offending letter and substitute the correct form.) *Note:* In this section, correct only personal names and people's titles — you can assume that everything else is correct.

0. The reverend archie smith, Chief Executive of the Homeless Council, has invited senator Bickford to next month's fundraiser.

A. **Reverend**, **Archie**, **Smith**, **chief**, **executive**, **Senator**. Personal names are always capitalized, so *Archie Smith* needs capitals. *Reverend* and *Senator* precede the names (*Archie Smith* and *Bickford*) and act as part of the person's name, not just a description of their jobs. Thus they should be capitalized. The title *chief executive* follows the name and isn't capitalized.

1. Yesterday mayor Victoria Johnson ordered all public servants in her town to conserve sticky tape.

2. Herman harris, chief city engineer, has promised to hold the line on tape spending.

3. However, the Municipal Dogcatcher, Agnes e. Bark, insists on taping "Lost Dog — Reward!" signs to every tree.

4. The signs placed by dogcatcher Bark seldom fall far from the tree.

5. The taping done by ms. Bark is so extensive that hardly any paper detaches.

6. Few Dogcatchers care as much as agnes about rounding up lost dogs.

7. The recent champion of the town dog show, BooBoo, was caught last week.

8. Surely Ms. Johnson is wrong when she insists that tape be rationed by Civil Servants.

9. Johnson, who also serves as director of marketing for a well-known thumbtack company, has an interest in substituting tacks for tape.

10. Until the issue is resolved, Agnes, herself the chief executive of Sticking, Inc., will continue to tape to her heart's content.

11. Sticking, Inc. has appointed a Vice President to oversee a merger with a thumbtack producer.

12. Vice president Finger of Thumbtack, Inc. is tired of jokes about his name.

13. When he was appointed Chief Financial Officer, George Finger asked the previous holder of the position for advice.

14. Alicia Bucks, who is now the President of a major thumbtack conglomerate, had little sympathy for Finger.

15. With a name like Bucks, she explained, everyone thinks you should work as a Bank President.

16. Finger next asked reverend Holy how he dealt with his unusual name.

17. However, Holy, who has been a Bishop for twelve years, was puzzled by the question.

18. "I feel fortunate compared to my brother, who was General Manager of the New Jersey Devils hockey team," Bishop Holy remarked.

19. Reginald Holy joined the Devils twenty years ago as a Player Development Director.

20. Holy hopes to be appointed President of the National Hockey League someday.

Entering the Worlds of Business and Academia

Whether you bring home a paycheck or a report card, you should take care to capitalize properly. Surprisingly, the worlds of business and education have a lot in common:

- **The place where it all happens:** Capitalize the name of the company or school (*Superlative Widgets International* or *University of Rock and Roll*, for example). General words that may refer to a number of businesses or academic institutions (*university, conglomerate*, and so forth) are written in lowercase.

- **Working units:** Business activities (*management, advertising*, or *marketing*, perhaps) and general academic tasks, years, and subjects (such as *research, sophomore*, and *history*) aren't capitalized. The name of a specific department (*Research and Development Division, Department of Cultural Anthropology*) may be capitalized. Project names (*the Zero Task Force*) and course names (*Psychological Interpretations of Belly-Button Rings*) are capitalized. In these capitalized terms, articles and prepositions (*a, the, for*, and so forth) are generally lowercased.

Course titles and the names of businesses or institutions are capitalized according to the "headline style" rules of titles, which I describe in "Capitalizing Titles of Literary and Media Works" later in this chapter. Briefly, capitalize the first word, all nouns and verbs, and any important words in the title. Short, relational words such as *of, for, by*, and *from* aren't capitalized, nor are articles such as *a, an*, and *the*.

- **Products:** General terms for items produced or sold (*widgets, guarantees, consultation fee*, and the like) aren't capitalized. Neither are academic degrees or awards (*master's, endowed chair, fellowship, doctorate*, and so forth). If a specific brand is named, however, roll out the big letters (*Christopher Columbus Award for Round-Trip Travel, Universal Widget Groove Simulator*, and so on).

Some companies take a tip from poets and change the usual capitalization customs. Sigh. As a grammarian, I'm not happy, but people (and companies) have the right to ruin their own names. So if you know that a company prefers a particular format (*eBay* or *Banjos 'n Strings*, for example), bow your head and accept fate.

Now that you have the basics, try these questions. I thoughtfully include both business and school references so that everyone feels at home. If a word needs a capital letter, cross out the offending letter and insert the capital. If a word has an unnecessary capital letter, cross out the offender and insert a lowercase letter.

Q. The eldest daughter of Matt Brady, founder of belly buttons are we, is a senior at the university of southeast hogwash, where she is majoring in navel repair.

A. **Belly Buttons Are We, University of Southeast Hogwash**. The name of the company is capitalized, as is the name of the school. The year of study *(senior)* isn't capitalized, nor is the major.

21. After extensive research, the united nose ring company has determined that most college freshmen prefer silver rings.

22. The spokesperson for the Company commented that "silver rocks their world."

23. "I wore a gold ring to the curriculum critique committee last semester," explained Fred P. Stileless, who is the student representative to all university committees.

24. "The gold ring definitely turned off some juniors I was interested in romantically," explained Fred, who hasn't had a date, he says, since he was a high school senior.

25. The spokesperson surveyed competing products, including a silver-gold combination manufactured by in style or else, inc., a division of klepto industrials.

26. The silver that the Jewelers use is imported from "four or five big countries."

27. The company claims that the silver attracts attention and costs less, though the department of product development has issued a statement denying "any attractive power" for the metal.

28. Stileless says that he doesn't care about scientific studies because, though he originally majored in chemistry, "introduction to fashion, a course I took in freshman year, opened my eyes to art and beauty."

29. Stileless expects to receive a bachelor's degree with a concentration in fashion imperatives.

30. Import-export Companies will have to switch from gold to silver.

Capitalizing Titles of Literary and Media Works

If you write an ode to homework or a scientific study on the biological effects of too many final exams, how do you capitalize the title? The answer depends on the style you're following:

- **Literary, creative, and general-interest works are capitalized in "headline style."** Headline style specifies capital letters for the first and last word of the title and subtitle, in addition to all nouns, verbs, and descriptive words, and any other words that require emphasis. Articles *(a, an, the)* and prepositions *(among, by, for,* and the like) are usually in lowercase. All the headings in this book are in headline style.

- **The titles of scientific works employ "sentence style,"** which calls for capital letters only for the first word of the title and subtitle and for proper nouns. Everything else is lowercased. (The title of a scientific paper in sentence style: "Cloning fruit flies: Hazards of fly bites.")

Ready to get to work? The following titles are written without any capital letters at all. Cross out the offending letters and insert capitals above them where needed. The style you should follow (headline or sentence) is specified in parentheses at the end of each title. By the way, titles of short works are enclosed in quotation marks. Titles of full-length works are italicized. (See Chapter 8 for more information on the punctuation of titles.)

Q. "the wonders of homework completed: an ode" *(headline)*

A. **"The Wonders of Homework Completed: An Ode"** The first word of the title and subtitle (*The, An*) are always capitalized. So are the nouns (*Wonders, Homework*) and descriptive words (*Completed*). The preposition (*of*) is left in lowercase.

31. moby duck: a tale of obsessive bird watching *(headline)*

32. "an analysis of the duckensis mobyous: the consequences of habitat shrinkage on population" *(sentence)*

33. "call me izzy smell: my life as a duck hunter" *(headline)*

34. the duck and i: essays on the relationship between human beings and feathered species *(sentence)*

35. duck and cover: a cookbook *(headline)*

36. "the duck stops here: political wisdom from the environmental movement" *(sentence)*

37. duck upped: how the duck triumphed over the hunter *(headline)*

38. "moby platypus doesn't live here anymore" *(headline)*

39. "population estimates of the platypus: an inexact science" *(sentence)*

40. for the love of a duck: a sentimental memoir *(headline)*

Placing Geographical Capitals

Where am I? I'm in a city (lowercase), popularly known as New York (capitalized), or, as my husband likes to say, on a small island (lowercase) off the coast of New Jersey (capitalized). The island, by the way, is Manhattan (capitalized).

Get the idea? Place names are in lowercase when they're generic, one-term-fits-all (*river, canyon, town, street,* and so forth). Place names are capitalized when they're the specific, proper names (*Manhattan, North Dakota, Tibet, Amazon River,* and such).

One more point about places: the compass points are in lowercase when they refer to directions (*head south for ten miles,* for example) and capitalized when they refer to areas of the country (*the Northeast, the South, the Midwest,* and so on).

Place names that have become so much a part of the common vocabulary that they no longer refer to actual locations aren't capitalized (*french fries, russian roulette, egyptian cotton,* and so on).

Now that you're oh-so-savvy about places and capital letters, peer at the underlined words in the following sentences and decide whether a capital letter is appropriate. If so, draw three lines under the letter needing to be capitalized. If not, leave the word alone.

Q. Megan often revs up her motorcycle and speeds <u>south</u>, arriving at the shores of the <u>mississippi river</u> around sunset.

A. **correct**, **Mississippi River**. The first underlined word is a direction, not an area, so lower-case is appropriate for *south*. The second underlined term is a proper, specific name, so capital letters are needed.

41. Rowing across the <u>hudson river</u> is difficult for Andy, who hates <u>oceans</u>, <u>lakes</u>, and all bodies of water.

42. Andy, who was born in <u>schenectady, new york</u>, pretends to be a <u>ukranian</u> prince.

43. His latest bride, Abby, hails from an <u>island</u> near Andy's castle, which is just <u>north</u> of the <u>strait of gibraltar</u>.

44. Megan gave a wedding present to the happy couple: two round-trip tickets to a beautiful natural <u>canyon</u> in the <u>southwest</u>.

45. The last time Megan visited <u>new mexico</u>, she was arrested by a constable visiting from <u>europe</u>.

46. "The fact that I am not from this <u>continent</u> is no reason to deny my arresting privileges," said Constable Creary. "The <u>north american</u> justice system was modeled after the one in my <u>country</u>."

47. "Do you expect me to honor a <u>trans-atlantic</u> arrest?" queried the judge.

48. The <u>european</u> cop, who was actually from <u>belgium</u>, was so discouraged that he grabbed a <u>turkish</u> towel and sent out for a <u>spanish omelet</u>.

49. Megan did no jail time in <u>santa fe</u>, but she was imprisoned briefly in a small <u>village</u> <u>north</u> of <u>omaha</u>.

50. Her offense was wading in a <u>stream</u> and trampling on six gardens in the <u>west</u>.

AM or p.m.? Capitalizing Abbreviations

Abbreviations save you time, but they also present you with a couple of annoying problems, namely whether to capitalize or lowercase and whether a period is needed. The world of abbreviations, I must confess, is prime real estate for turf wars. Some publications and institutions proudly announce that "*we* don't capitalize a.m." whereas others declare exactly the opposite, choosing "AM" instead. (Both are correct, but don't mix the forms.) So if you're writing for an organization with a chip on its collective shoulder, you're wise to ask in advance for a list of the publication's or school's preferences. In this section I give you the one-size-fits-most abbreviated forms. These are the general guidelines:

✔ **Acronyms** — forms created by the first letter of each word (NATO, UNICEF, OPEC, and so forth) — take capitals but not periods.

✔ **Initials and titles** are capitalized and take periods (George W. Bush and Msgr. Sullivan, for example). The three most common titles — Mr., Mrs., and Ms.— are always capitalized and usually written with periods, though the current trend is to skip the period because the long forms of these words are never used, with the exception of "Mister," and even that is rare.

✔ **Latin abbreviations** aren't usually capitalized but do end with a period. Latinate abbreviations include e.g. (for example), ibid. (in the same place), and etc. (and so forth). The abbreviations for morning and afternoon may be written with capital letters and no periods (AM and PM) or without capitals but with periods (a.m. and p.m.). Your choice, but be consistent.

✔ **State abbreviations** used to be written with an initial capital letter, lowercase letters as needed, and a concluding period (*Ind.* and *Ala.* for *Indiana* and *Alabama,* for example). However, people now use the two-letter, no-period, capitalized forms created by the post office (*IN* and *AL*).

✔ **A capitalized long form** normally has a capitalized abbreviation, and vice versa (lowercase long forms pair with lowercase abbreviations).

✔ **When an abbreviation comes at the end of a sentence,** the period for the abbreviation does double duty as an endmark. Don't place two periods in a row!

Okay, try your hand at abbreviating. Check out the full word, which I place in lowercase letters, even when capital letters are called for. See whether you can insert the proper abbreviation or acronym for the following words, taking care to capitalize where necessary and filling in the blanks with your answers.

Q. figure _____

A. **fig.**

51. illustration _____

52. before common era _____

53. mister Burns _____

54. united states president _____

55. national hockey league _____

56. reverend Smith _____

57. new york _____

58. Adams boulevard _____

59. irregular _____

60. incorporated _____

Calling All Overachievers: Extra Practice with Capital Letters

Use the information in this chapter to help you find ten capitalization mistakes in Figure 9-1, which is an excerpt from possibly the worst book report ever written.

Moby, the Life Of a Duck: A Book Report

If you are ever given a book about Ducks, take my advice and burn it. When i had to read *Moby Duck*, the Teacher promised me that it was good. She said that "Excitement was on every page." I don't think so! The story is set in the northwest, where a duckling with special powers is born. Moby actually goes to school and earns a Doctorate in bird Science! After a really boring account of Moby's Freshman year, the book turns to his career as a Flight Instructor. I was very happy to see him fly away at the end of the book.

Figure 9-1:
Sample
book report
of a lousy
read.

Answers to Capitalization Problems

1. **Mayor**. Titles and proper names take capitals; common nouns, such as *servants* and *tape,* don't.

2. **Harris**. Names take capitals, but titles written after the name usually don't.

3. **municipal dogcatcher, E.** The title in this sentence isn't attached to the name; in fact, it's separated from the name by a comma. It should be in lowercase. Initials take capitals and periods.

4. **Dogcatcher**. Now the title is attached to the name, and thus it's capitalized.

5. **Ms**. The title *Ms.* is always capitalized, but the period is optional. After you choose a style, however, be consistent. Write either *Mr., Mrs.,* and *Ms.* or *Mr, Mrs,* and *Ms* but not some from each set.

6. **dogcatchers, Agnes**. The common noun *dogcatchers* doesn't need a capital letter, but the proper name *Agnes* does.

7. **correct**. The name of the champion must be capitalized. About that name — people are allowed to spell their own names (and the names of their pets) as they wish. The capital letter inside the name is a style; you may not like it, but the namer's preference should be honored.

8. **civil servants**. Once again, the title and name are in caps, but the common job classification isn't.

9. **correct**. This title isn't attached to a name, so it takes lowercase.

10. **correct**. Names are in caps, but the title isn't, except when it precedes the name.

11. **vice president**. A title that isn't attached to a name shouldn't be capitalized.

12. **President**. In this sentence the title precedes the name and thus should be capitalized.

13. **chief financial officer**. This title isn't attached to a name. Go for lowercase.

14. **president**. Don't capitalize the title of president written without a name unless you're talking about a major world leader such as the President of the United States. (Even then, some style manuals call for lowercase.)

15. **bank president**. This title isn't connected to a name; therefore, it should be lowercased.

16. **Reverend**. The title precedes the name and becomes part of the name, in a sense. A capital letter is appropriate.

17. **bishop**. In this sentence *bishop* doesn't precede a name; lowercase is the way to go.

18. **general manager**. I love the Devils (my son's favorite team), but even so, lowercase is best for this title, which isn't connected to a name.

19. **player development director**. Another title that's all by itself. Opt for lowercase.

20. **president**. To be president is a big deal, but not a big letter.

21. **United Nose Ring Company**. Although college freshmen think they're really important (and, of course, they are), they rate only lowercase. The name of the company is specific and should be in uppercase.

22 **company**. A common noun such as *company* isn't capitalized.

23 **Curriculum Critique Committee**. The name of the committee and the person (*Stileless*) should be written in caps, but the other terms (*student representative, university,* and the like) aren't cap-worthy.

24 **correct**. Years in school and school levels aren't capitalized.

25 **In Style or Else, Inc., Klepto Industrials**. The names of companies are capitalized according to the preference of the company itself. Most companies follow "headline style," which is explained in the section "Capitalizing Titles of Literary and Media Works" in this chapter.

26 **jewelers**. Don't capitalize common nouns.

27 **Department of Product Development**. The name of a department should be capitalized, but the preposition (*of*) is lowercased.

28 **Introduction to Fashion**. Course titles get caps, but subject names and school years don't.

29 **correct**. School degrees (bachelor's, master's, doctorate) are lowercased, though their abbreviations aren't (B.A., M.S., and so on). School subjects aren't capitalized.

30 **companies**. This term isn't the name of a specific company, just a common noun. Lowercase is what you want.

31 ***Moby Duck: A Tale of Obsessive Bird Watching*** In headline style, the first word of the title (*Moby*) and subtitle (*A*) are in caps. Nouns (*Duck, Tale,* and *Watching*) and descriptive words (*Obsessive, Bird*) are also uppercased. The preposition *of* merits only lowercase.

32 **"An analysis of the *Duckensis mobyous*: The consequences of habitat shrinkage on population"** In sentence style capitalization, the first words of the title and subtitle are in caps, but everything else is in lowercase, with the exception of proper names. In this title, following preferred scientific style, the names of the genus and species are in italics, with only the genus name in caps.

33 **"Call Me Izzy Smell: My Life As a Duck Hunter"** Per headline style, the article (*a*) is in lowercase. Did I catch you on "As"? It's short, but it's not an article or a preposition, so it rates a capital letter.

34 ***The duck and I: Essays on the relationship between human beings and feathered species*** Sentence style titles take caps for the first word of the title and subtitle. The personal pronoun *I* is always capitalized.

35 ***Duck and Cover: A Cookbook*** Headline style calls for capitals for the first word of the title and subtitle and all other nouns. The joining word *and* is lowercased in headline style, unless it begins a title or subtitle.

36 **"The duck stops here: Political wisdom from the environmental movement"** Sentence style gives you two capitals in this title — the first word of the title and subtitle.

37 ***Duck Upped: How the Duck Triumphed over the Hunter*** Because this title is in headline style, everything is in caps except articles (*the*) and prepositions (*over*).

38 **"Moby Platypus Doesn't Live Here Anymore"** Headline style gives capital letters for all the words here, as this title contains no articles or prepositions.

39 **"Population estimates of the platypus: An inexact science"** Sentence style calls for capital letters at the beginning of the title and subtitle. The term *platypus* isn't the name of a genus (a scientific category), so it's written in lowercase.

40 ***For the Love of a Duck: A Sentimental Memoir*** Headline style mandates lowercase for articles (*the, a*) and prepositions (*of*). The first words of the title and subtitle, even if they're articles or prepositions, merit capital letters.

41 **Hudson River, correct, correct**. The proper name (*Hudson River*) is in caps, but the common terms (*oceans, lakes*) are lowercased.

42 **Schenectady, New York, Ukranian**. All proper names, all caps here.

43 **correct, correct, Strait of Gibraltar**. The names are all in caps, with a lowercase *of* for the *Strait of Gibraltar*. When capitalizing place names that contain several words, follow the "headline style" of capitalization described in detail in the section entitled "Capitalizing Titles of Literary and Media Works" in this chapter. The direction *north* is lowercased.

44 **correct, Southwest**. The common noun isn't capitalized, but the area of the country is.

45 **New Mexico, Europe**. All proper names, all caps.

46 **correct, North American, correct**. Two common nouns (*continent, country*) are lowercased, but the description *North American* is derived from a proper name (North America) and thus needs capital letters.

47 **trans-Atlantic**. This question is a tricky one. The prefix *trans-* isn't a proper name, so it's written in lowercase. The name of the ocean, on the other hand, needs a capital letter.

48 **European, Belgium, correct, correct**. Another tricky question. The first two are capitalized because they're proper, specific terms. The last two terms (*turkish, spanish*) are capitalized when they refer to the countries, but not when they refer to common, everyday objects. A *turkish towel* isn't really talking about the country of *Turkey* but rather about a household object. Ditto for the omelet.

49 **Santa Fe, correct, correct, Omaha**. Two names, both in caps. One common term (*village*) and one direction (*north*), no caps.

50 **correct, West**. The *stream* is a common term and doesn't deserve uppercase. The area of the country is capitalized.

51 **illus.**

52 **BCE** (The Latin expression *Anno Domini* — abbreviated "AD" — means "in the year of our Lord" and is used with dates that aren't "BC," or "before Christ." To make this term more universal, historians often substitute "CE" or *Common Era* for AD and "BCE" or *Before the Common Era* for BC.)

43 **Mr. Burns**

44 **U.S. Pres.**

45 **NHL** (an acronym)

46 **Rev. Smith**

47 **NY** (postal abbreviation) or **N.Y.** (traditional form)

48 **Adams Blvd.**

49 **irreg.**

50 **Inc.**

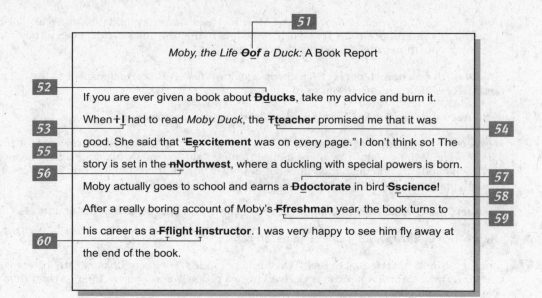

Moby, the Life ~~O~~of a Duck: A Book Report

51

52 If you are ever given a book about ~~D~~ducks, take my advice and burn it. When ~~i~~I had to read *Moby Duck*, the ~~T~~teacher promised me that it was **53** good. She said that "~~E~~excitement was on every page." I don't think so! The **54** **55** story is set in the ~~n~~Northwest, where a duckling with special powers is born. **56** Moby actually goes to school and earns a ~~D~~doctorate in bird ~~S~~science! **57** After a really boring account of Moby's ~~F~~freshman year, the book turns to **58** his career as a ~~F~~flight ~~I~~instructor. I was very happy to see him fly away at **59** the end of the book. **60**

51 In a headline-style title, prepositions aren't capitalized.

52 An ordinary term for animals, in this case *ducks,* is lowercased.

53 The personal pronoun *I* is always capitalized.

54 The name of the teacher isn't given, just the term *teacher,* which should be lowercased.

55 When a quotation is written without a speaker tag, the first word isn't capitalized.

56 Areas of the country are capitalized.

57 Academic degrees take lowercase.

58 School subjects are written in lowercase.

59 School years are in lowercase too.

60 Job titles, when they aren't attached to the beginning of a name, are in lowercase.

Part III
The Pickier Points of Correct Verb and Pronoun Use

The 5th Wave   By Rich Tennant

In this part . . .

When was the last time you chatted with a grammar teacher? Never? I'm not surprised. When people find out that someone cares about proper English, they tend to discover that silence is indeed golden. The urge to clam up rather than to risk an error is nearly overpowering. However, most grammar teachers aren't out to nail anyone for confusing verb tenses. Furthermore, most of the issues that people obsess about are actually extremely simple. Take *who* and *whom*, for example. Deciding which one is appropriate is not rocket science; it's just pronoun case, which you can practice in Chapter 10. Chapters 11 and 12 help you master tricky (okay, picky) points of pronoun and verb usage. If you've ever stumbled over *everyone brought their/his/her lunch* or *she said she has/had a cold*, these chapters rescue you. Finally, Chapter 13 explains how to deal with verb moods (not irritable or ecstatic but indicative, imperative, and subjunctive).

Chapter 10

The Case of It (And Other Pronouns)

Most kids I know can switch from *He and I are going to do our homework now* (reserved for adult audiences) to *Him and me are playing video games* (with peers) faster than an eye can blink. The second sentence, of course, is nonstandard English, but if you need a way to indicate that the world of rules and proprieties has been left behind, messing up pronoun case is a good bet. Just to be clear what I'm talking about: Pronouns are the words that stand in for the name of a person, place, or thing. Popular pronouns include *I, me,* and *my* (very big with swelled-head types), *you* and *yours* (for the less selfish), *he, she, it, they, them,* and a bunch of others (good, all-purpose choices).

Case is one of the qualities that all pronouns have. Subject and object pronouns form two of the three major cases, or families, of pronouns. The third is possessive. (Possessive pronouns want to know where you are every single minute. Oops, that's my mother, not possessive case.) In this chapter I deal mainly with subject and object pronouns. You can find the basics of possessive-pronoun usage, along with the lowdown on another quality of pronouns — number — in Chapter 3, and the really advanced (okay, obsessive) pronoun topics, such as double meanings, in Chapter 11. Here I discuss only one weird possessive situation — when a pronoun precedes a noun that was formed from a verb.

Meeting the Subject at Hand and the Object of My Affection

Subjects and objects have opposite jobs in a sentence. Briefly, the subject is the doer of the action or whatever is in the state of being talked about in the sentence. In the first paragraph of this chapter, *he* and *I* are better than *him* and *me* because the sentence needs a subject for its verb, *are going,* and *he* and *I* are subject pronouns. Objects receive; instead of acting, they are acted upon. If you scold *him* and *me,* those two pronouns resentfully receive the scolding and thus act as objects. Verbs have objects, and so do some other grammatical elements, such as prepositions. (I deal with prepositions later in this chapter.) Here are the contents of the subject- and object-pronoun baskets:

▶ **Subject pronouns** include *I, you, he, she, it, we, they, who,* and *whoever.*

▶ **Object pronouns** are *me, you, him, her, it, us, them, whom,* and *whomever.*

Some pronouns, such as *you* and *it*, appear on both lists. They do double duty as both subject and object pronouns. Don't worry about them; they're right for all occasions. Other one-case-fits-almost-all pronouns are *either, most, other, which,* and *that.*

Another type of pronoun is a reflexive, or *-self* pronoun (*myself, himself, ourselves,* and so forth). Use these pronouns only when the action in the sentence doubles back on the subject. ("I told myself that the grammar test would be easy." "They washed themselves 50 times during the deodorant shortage.") You may also insert the *-self* pronouns for emphasis. ("She herself baked the cake.") Don't place a *-self* pronoun in any other type of sentence.

In the following sentences, choose the correct pronoun from the parentheses. Take care not to send a subject pronoun to do an object pronoun's job, and vice versa. Violators will be prosecuted. Try your hand at an example before moving on.

Q. Matt took the precious parchment and gave (she/her) a cheap imitation instead.

A. **her**. In this sentence, Matt is the one taking and giving. The pronoun *her* is on the receiving end because Matt gave the imitation to *her*. *Her* is an object pronoun.

1. Matt, Peyton, and (I/me/myself) have a date with destiny.

2. The parchment, which (he/him) discovered in the back pocket of a pair of jeans made in 1972, is covered with strange symbols.

3. I wanted to call Codebusters because (they/them) solved the riddle of the Subway Tapestry last year.

4. I can't decide whether (they/them) should contact Matt first or wait until Matt realizes that he needs (they/them).

5. The president of Codebusters knows that Peyton is better at figuring out obscure symbols than (he/him).

6. Peyton won't tell (I/me) a thing about the parchment, but (she/her) did nod quietly when I mentioned Martians.

7. Peyton's friends — Lucy and (she/her) — are obsessed with Martians and tend to see Little Green Men everywhere.

8. If the Martians and (she/her) have a message for the world, (they/them) will make sure it gets out with maximum publicity.

9. Elizabeth and (I/me/myself) will glue (we/us/ourselves) to the all-news channel just in case Peyton decides to talk.

10. Sure enough, Peyton just contacted the relevant authorities, Dan Moore and (he/him), to arrange an interview.

11. Elizabeth favors sending NASA and (we/us/ourselves) the parchment.

12. I pointed out that NASA knows a lot more than (she/her) about space, but nothing about ancient parchments.

13. Matt checked the Internet, but it had little to offer (he/him), though Codebusters did.

14. (I/me/I myself) think that the parchment is a fake.

15. No one is more dishonest than Matt and (she/her).

16. Yesterday, Elizabeth told Matt and (I/me) that Peyton's room is filled with parchment scraps.

17. Elizabeth is as suspicious as (we/us) when it comes to Peyton's activities.

18. Peyton and (I/me/myself) were enrolled in several art classes last year.

19. The art class, which gave (we/us) instruction in sculpture, printmaking, and parchment design, was fascinating.

20. This semester Peyton and Elizabeth left art school and enrolled in the Classics Academy, where (they/them) are taking a class in symbolic language.

To "Who" or To "Whom"? That Is the Question

The dreaded pronouns, *who* and *whom,* deserve some, but not all, of the fear that people apply to them. Like all other subject/object pronoun decisions, you simply have to figure out how the pronoun functions in the sentence. If you need a subject (someone doing the action or someone in the state of being described in the sentence), *who* is your guy. If you need an object (a receiver of the action), go with *whom.* Why are *who* and *whom* such a pain? Probably because they tend to occur in complicated sentences. But if you untangle the sentence and figure out (pardon the expression) *who* is doing what to *whom,* you'll be fine.

Take a ride on the *who/whom* train and select the proper pronoun from the parentheses in the following sentences.

Q. (Who/Whom) can decode the message? Codebusters!

A. **Who.** The verb *can decode* needs a subject, someone to do that action. *Who* is for subjects, and *whom* is for objects.

21. Does Peyton know (who/whom) should get the information once she's finished decoding?

22. Matt will discuss the parchment with (whoever/whomever) the buyer sends.

23. (Who/Whom) is his buyer?

24. His buyer is (whoever/whomever) believes Matt's sales pitch.

25. Also, Matt will sell the parchment to (whoever/whomever) is willing to pay.

26. I don't think NASA is interested, despite Matt's claim that an expert from NASA, (who/whom) isn't saying much, was seen checking "Mars" and "Alien Life Forms" on the Internet.

27. Do you know (who/whom) the expert consulted?

28. No one seems to know (who/whom) Matt saw.

29. Peyton remains capable of conspiring with NASA, Codebusters, and (whoever/whomever) else is able to sell a fraudulent document.

30. Matt, (who/whom) I do not trust, has the most sincere face you can imagine.

31. Peyton, (who/whom) Matt once scolded for cutting class, has a reputation for sincerity.

32. I once heard Peyton explain that those (who/whom) have an honest face can get away with anything.

33. "If you are one of those people (who/whom) can fake sincerity," she said, "you can accomplish anything."

34. Peyton states this theory to (whoever/whomever) is willing to listen.

35. I think that (whoever/whomever) trusts Peyton is in big trouble.

Linking Up with Pronouns in "To Be" Sentences

Most verbs express action, but mingling with this on-the-go group are forms of the verb "to be" (*am, is, are, was, were, has been, will be,* and the like). These verbs are like giant equal signs linking two equivalents, and for that reason, they're sometimes called *linking verbs.* "Jeremy is the president" is the same as "Jeremy = president." If you've studied algebra, or even if you haven't, you know that these statements mean the same even when reversed ("The president is Jeremy.") This incredibly boring explanation leads to an important pronoun fact: A subject pronoun serves as the subject of a linking verb, and to preserve reversibility, subject pronouns also *follow* linking verbs, in the same spot where you normally expect an object. Therefore, the answer to *Who's there?* is "It is *she*" instead of "It is *her*" because you can reverse the first ("She is it") and not the second ("Her is it").

When you select pronouns for a linking-verb sentence, be aware that sometimes the verb changes, so to sound right, a reversible sentence may need a verb adjustment from singular to plural or vice versa. "It is they" is reversible, at least in theory, because *they* is a subject pronoun, even though "they is" doesn't pass a sound check until you change the verb to *are.*

Can you select the appropriate pronoun from the parentheses? Give it a whirl in the following example and practice exercises. Just to make life more interesting, I'm sprinkling action verbs into the mix — for more information on pronouns with action verbs, see the earlier section, "Meeting the Subject at Hand and the Object of My Affection."

Q. Angelina knows that the true culprit is (he/him) and not Brad.

A. **he.** Who is *he?* Only the gossip columnist knows for sure. The grammarian, on the other hand, is positive that a subject pronoun is the one you want after the linking verb *is.* Reverse that portion of the sentence to check yourself: *Him* is the *culprit?* I don't think so. *He* is the *culprit?* Bingo.

36. The FBI recently announced that the criminals responsible for the theft of a 1972-era parchment are (they/them).

37. Matt and Peyton met with three FBI agents and promised (they/them) that the parchment would be returned to the rightful owner.

38. The "rightful owner," according to Peyton, is (she/her), because Peyton herself purchased the jeans in which the document was located.

39. "I can't read the code," added Peyton, "but I know a good pair of jeans when I see one, and besides, the lawful purchaser of both the jeans and the parchment is (I/me)."

40. Matt isn't so sure; it is (he/him) who will have to go to jail if the FBI decides not to buy Peyton's story that "the seller said the document was included in the price."

41. Agent Tim told (they/them) that the document is vital to national security.

42. As Tim was explaining his theory of the code, his cell phone rang and drew (he/him) away from the crowd.

43. Tim is an expert in undercover work and claims that with just a bit of makeup and a good wig he can be "(whoever/whomever)."

44. This month he posed as a code breaker in order to entice Peyton to tell (he/him) more about the parchment.

45. "Who was on the phone?" I asked Agent Tim. "It was (he/him)," Tim replied, "the master criminal who created the fake parchment and sold it to Peyton."

You Talkin' to Me, or I? Pronouns as Objects of Prepositions

Prepositions, not to be confused with *propositions* (such as *Are you busy tonight?*) are words that express relationships. (Come to think of it, *propositions* concern relationships too.) Common prepositions include *by, for, from, in, on, of, about, after,* and *before.* Prepositions always have objects, and sometimes those objects are pronouns. Check out the italicized objects of prepositions in these examples:

> Give that umbrella to *me* or I'll break it over your *head.*

> The embroidery on the *umbrella* was done by *me* alone.

Got the idea? In the first sample sentence, *me* and *head* are objects of the prepositions *to* and *over.* In the second, *umbrella* and *me* are objects of *on* and *by.* Luckily, you don't have to worry about *umbrella* and *head.* They're nouns, and they don't change no matter where they appear in the sentence. But the pronoun does change (sigh), depending upon its job in the sentence. And if its job is to be an object of a preposition, it must be an object pronoun. You can't give an umbrella to *I,* nor was the embroidery done by *I* alone. Not in this grammatical universe, anyway.

Take a stab at the following sentences, selecting the correct pronoun from the pair in parentheses. In an attempt to fry your brain, I cleverly (she said modestly) scatter a few subjects in the exercise.

Q. I won't accept any packages from (he/him) because last week he sent a quart of pickled cabbage to (I/me), and my mailbox was sticky for days.

A. **him, me.** The preposition *from* needs an object, so your first answer has to be *him. To* is also a preposition and should be followed by the object pronoun *me.*

46. Jessica sang songs to Mom and (she/her) whenever the moon was full.

47. Her latest CD is entitled *Of Mom, (I/Me), and the Moon.*

48. I'm going to buy the CD, although a lot of issues remain between Jessica and (I/me).

49. For example, when she broke up with her boyfriend, she stated that she was prettier than (he/him).

50. However, she has been "looks-challenged" ever since her mother's dog Spike ran after (she/her) and took a large bite out of her nose.

51. Aggressive though he may be, you can't put much past (he/him), and for that reason Spike is a great watchdog.

52. Spike likes to walk behind (we/us) when we approach the house; he growls at (whoever/ whomever) comes too close.

53. "At (who/whom) is this dog snarling?" I once asked Jessica.

54. "He thinks the letter carrier wants to rob us, so he tries to keep an eye on (he/him)," she replied as she pieced together a ripped catalogue.

55. "You have to run around (they/them)," added Jessica, speaking of her mother and Spike.

56. Carefully separating the letters addressed to "Spike" from the letters meant for Jessica, the letter carrier gave the shredded mail to Jessica and (he/him).

57. Spike's penpals generally include a dog biscuit when writing to (he/him).

58. Spike and Jessica both enjoy getting mail, but Spike loves letters even more than (she/her).

59. Spike's letters sometimes contain meaty bones from (whoever/whomever) really wants to catch his attention.

60. Jessica is as fond of meaty bones as (he/him), but she hardly ever receives any.

Matching Possessive Pronouns to "-ing" Nouns

I cheated a bit with the title of this section. When I say -ing noun, I mean a noun made from the -ing form of a verb (swimming, smiling, puttering, and similar words). I'm not talking about nouns that just happen to contain those three letters, such as king, wingding, and pudding, among others. Nor am I talking about -ing verb forms used as verbs or as descriptions of other nouns. For those of you who enjoy grammar terms, the -ing-noun-made-from-a-verb-form is actually a gerund.

Here's the deal with pronouns and -ing nouns. You should put a possessive form in front of these nouns. Why? Because that form keeps the focus in the right place. Take a look at this sentence:

Carrie hates (me/my) auditioning for the new reality show, Nut Search.

Putting on your thinking cap, you can see that Carrie doesn't hate me. Instead, Carrie hates the whole reality-show effort. (My auditioning threatens her sense of privacy and pretty much guarantees that she won't get a slot on the show.) Back to grammar:

my is the best choice because it shifts the reader's attention to *auditioning,* where it belongs, because *auditioning* is what Carrie hates.

In the situation described in the preceding paragraph, the possessive form of a *noun* should also be your choice for the spot in front of an *-ing* noun. In the sample sentence there, the correct form is *Carrie hates Rick's auditioning . . . ,* not *Carrie hates Rick auditioning . . . .* The same reasoning applies; Carrie doesn't hate Rick. She just doesn't want him on television.

Try your hand at the following example and practice exercises. Circle the pronouns you love and ignore the ones you hate. To keep you alert, I've inserted a few sentences that don't call for possessive pronouns. Keep your eyes open!

Q. Although I'm not a literary critic, I think that (he/him/his) writing a novel about talking ocelots is a bad idea.

A. **his** The bad idea here is the *writing,* not *he* or *him.* The possessive pronoun shifts the attention to the task, which is the point of the sentence.

61. St. John Lincoln of the *Times* needs help with (he/him/his) editing and must hire additional editors.

62. Lincoln said that he loved everything the employment agency did last week except (they/them/their) sending him too many pronoun-obsessed writers.

63. When Lori went for an interview, she saw (he/him/his) reading a review of *The Pronoun Diet,* a new grammar text.

64. "I object to (she/her) insisting on one pronoun per paragraph," he muttered.

65. When I applied, Lincoln took (I/me/my) editing seriously.

66. However, he hated (I/me/my) pronouncing his first name incorrectly.

67. Apparently his relatives insist on something that sounds like "Sinjun," but (they/them/their) demanding special pronunciation has backfired.

68. The editor-in-chief calls him "Sin" for short; speaking at a recent awards dinner, (she/her) got a big laugh when she announced the nickname.

69. Do you think that St. John will appreciate (I/me/my) calling him "Johnny"?

70. I think that he will appoint (I/me/my) king of the newsroom.

Calling All Overachievers: Extra Practice with Pronoun Case

This advertisement for a garage sale (see Figure 10-1) has quite a few problems (including the fact that Anne stapled it to the police chief's favorite rose bush). In this advertisement I underlined 20 pronouns. Ten are correct, and ten aren't. Can you find the ten pronoun-case errors and correct them?

Garage Sale for You

On Monday, May 5, <u>my</u> brother cleaned out the garage and gave <u>our</u> neighbors and <u>I</u> a great opportunity. The merchandise, which, just between <u>you</u> and <u>I</u> is mostly junk, will go on sale tomorrow.

<u>Him</u> taking the initiative to earn a few bucks will put money in everyone's pocket as well! The gently used videotapes — a few surprises here for <u>whomever</u> looks really carefully at the subtitles — are priced to sell! Buy some for your friends and watch with <u>them</u> and <u>their</u> pets. <u>I</u> recommend *For Who the Dog Barks*. Other great items include a used refrigerator, given to Mom by <u>me</u> and my brother Doug and recently repaired by <u>our</u> dad and <u>I</u>. Only a little freon leaks now.

Come early to 5858 Wisteria Parkway and bring a wallet stuffed with bills, for it is <u>me</u> <u>who</u> will have to cart away unsold merchandise. I promise a free balloon to <u>whomever</u> buys the most, and <u>he</u> or <u>her</u> may blow it up and pop it right on the spot! As my mom says, "Give <u>she</u> a chance, and everyone will be happy."

Figure 10-1:
A pronoun-challenged garage-sale ad.

Answers to Pronoun Case Problems

1 **I.** The pronoun *I* is an actor, one of the subjects of the verb *have (I have). Me* is for objects. *Myself* is only for emphasis *(I myself)* or for actions that bounce back on the subject *(I told myself not to stand under a tree during a thunderstorm!).*

2 **he.** Who discovered? *He discovered. He* is a subject pronoun.

3 **they.** Someone has to do the *solving* referred to in the sentence. Therefore you need a subject pronoun, *they.*

4 **they, them.** This sentence illustrates the difference between subject and object pronouns. In the first parentheses, *they* is what you want because *they should contact Matt.* The pronoun *they* does the action. In the second half of the sentence, *he needs them,* and *them* receives the action from the verb *needs.*

5 **he.** Did I catch you here? If the sentence contains a comparison and some words are implied, supply the missing words before choosing a pronoun. In sentence 5, *Peyton is better . . . than he is.* After you throw in the verb *is,* you immediately see that you need a subject pronoun — *he.*

6 **me, she.** In the first part of the sentence, the pronoun receives the action *(Peyton won't tell whom? Me.)* In the second, you need someone to do the nodding, the subject pronoun *she.*

7 **she.** The tough part about this sentence is that the pronoun choice is camouflaged by other words *(Peyton's friends* and *Lucy).* If you isolate the pronoun, however, you see that it is *she* who is *obsessed* with Martians. You need the subject pronoun. To add a technical grammatical explanation — stop reading now before you die of boredom! — the subject is *Peyton's friends,* and *Lucy and she* forms an appositive to the subject. An appositive is always in the same case as the word it matches.

8 **she, they.** Two parentheses, two subjects. The verbs *have* and *will make* need subjects; *she* and *they* fill the bill.

9 **I, ourselves.** In the first part of the sentence, you need a subject for *will glue.* You can rule out *me* because *me* is an object pronoun. The pronoun *myself* works only for emphasis, in which case the sentence would read *Elizabeth and I myself.* In the second parentheses, you're looking for an object for the verb *will glue.* The pronoun *we* drops out right away because it's for subjects only. The next choice, *us,* is tempting, but because the actor and the receiver are the same, *ourselves* is better.

10 **him.** Like sentence 7, this one has lots of camouflage. Cover everything between *contacted* and the pronoun choice. What's left? *Peyton just contacted he/him.* Can you hear the correct answer? *Peyton contacted he?* I don't think so! You need the object pronoun *him.* If you really want a grammatical explanation, and surely you have better things to do with your time, *authorities* is the object of the verb *contacted,* and *Dan Moore and him* forms an appositive. An appositive is always in the same case as its equivalent.

11 **us.** Elizabeth is doing the action, and the pronoun's on the receiving end. You can't plug in *we* because *we* is for subjects, and receivers are objects. *Ourselves* doesn't fit because the *-self* pronouns are only for emphasis *(we ourselves will go . . .)* or for situations in which the actor and receiver are the same *(I told myself . . .).*

12 **she.** A word is missing in this sentence: *does.* If you insert the missing word after the pronoun, you'll hear it: *NASA knows a lot more than she does . . . .* The pronoun *she* is the subject of the implied verb *does.*

13 **him**. The verb *offer,* even in the infinitive form *(to offer)* takes the object pronoun *him.*

14 **I** or **I myself**. The first choice is an ordinary subject pronoun; the second is emphatic. Do you want to scream this phrase or just say it? Your call.

15 **she**. A word is missing. After you supply it, you see what's needed: *No one is more dishonest than Matt and she* are. That last little verb tells you that you need a subject pronoun.

16 **me**. The object pronoun *me* receives the action from the verb *told.* You can probably "hear" the correct answer if you use your thumb to cover the words *Matt and.* By isolating the pronoun, you can quickly determine that *Elizabeth told I* is a nonstarter. *Elizabeth told me* sounds — and is — correct.

17 **we**. In many comparisons, a word is missing. This sentence is easy if you insert the implied word, *are. Elizabeth is as suspicious as us are?* Nope. Try again: *Elizabeth is as suspicious as we are.* Bingo. The grammatical explanation is also simple: The implied verb *are* needs a subject pronoun.

18 **I**. Here you need a subject pronoun for the verb *were enrolled.* The *-self* pronoun isn't appropriate because *-self* pronouns are only for emphasis or for actions that double back upon the subject, as in *I told myself not to make a grammar mistake.*

19 **us**. The object pronoun *us* receives the action of the verb *gave* in this sentence.

20 **they**. The verb *are taking* needs a subject, and *they* fills the bill.

21 **who**. Focus on the part of the sentence containing the *who/whom* issue: *who/whom should get the information.* The verb *should get* needs a subject, so *who* is the proper choice.

22 **whomever**. The buyer is sending someone, so the pronoun you plug in receives the action of *sending.* Receivers are always object pronouns, so *whomever* wins the prize.

23 **Who**. The verb *is* needs a subject, and *who* is a subject pronoun — a match made in heaven.

24 **whoever**. The verb *believes* needs a subject. *Whoever* is a subject pronoun.

25 **whoever**. This one is tricky. When you hear the word *to* (a preposition), you may want to jump for the object pronoun, because *prepositions* are completed by object pronouns such as *whomever.* (Check out sentence 17, where *whomever* is the object of the preposition *with.*) But in this sentence, the verb *is* needs a subject, and *whoever* fills that role. For those who dig grammar (if you quake at the word, don't read this part), the object of the preposition *to* is the whole clause, *whoever is willing to pay.*

26 **who**. Somebody *isn't saying,* so you need a subject pronoun. *Who* fills the bill.

27 **whom**. This sentence is easier to figure out if you isolate the part of the sentence containing the who/whom choice: *who/whom the expert consulted.* Now rearrange those words into the normal subject-verb order: *the expert consulted whom. Whom* is the object of the verb *consulted.*

28 **whom**. As in the previous sentence, isolating and rearranging are helpful: *who/whom Matt saw, Matt saw whom.* The pronoun *whom* serves as the object of the verb *saw.*

29 **whoever**. The verb *is* needs a subject, so *whoever* has to do the job.

30 **whom**. Concentrate on the part of the sentence between the commas. Rearrange the words into the normal subject-verb order: *I do not trust who/whom.* Now do you see that it has to be *whom?* The pronoun *I* is the subject, and *whom* is acted upon, not an actor.

31 **whom**. The verb *scolded* needs an object, and the object pronoun *whom* does the job.

32 **who**. The verb *have* just has to have a subject (verbs are picky that way), so here you need *who*.

33 **who**. The verb *can fake* matches with the subject pronoun *who* in this sentence.

34 **whoever**. Did I fool you here? The preposition *to* needs an object, so at first glance *whomever* looks like a winner. However, the verb *is willing* requires a subject, and that subject is *whoever*. So what about the preposition? No sweat: The object of the preposition is the whole statement (a clause, in grammatical terms) *whoever is willing to listen.*

35 **whoever**. The verb *trusts* can't flap around without a subject, so you have to plug in *whoever*.

36 **they**. Okay, I know it doesn't sound right, but you can reverse "the criminals are they" to get "they are the criminals." To put it another way: *they* is a subject pronoun and belongs after the linking verb *are.*

37 **them**. *To promise* isn't a linking verb; it expresses action. After an action verb you need an object pronoun, and *them* fits the description.

38 **she**. The *rightful owner* is *she,* and *she* is the *rightful owner.* See how neatly that reverses?

39 **I**. The subject pronoun *I* belongs after the linking verb *is.*

40 **he**. *It* is *he* and *he* is *it* . . . in more ways than one! If Peyton points the FBI at Matt, he is certainly *it,* as far as felony charges go. Speaking grammatically, I must point out that *he* is a subject pronoun and should appear after the linking verb *is.*

41 **them**. Telling is an action, so you need an object pronoun here, and *them* is an object pronoun.

42 **him**. *Drew* is an action word that should be followed by an object pronoun such as *him.*

43 **whoever**. The verb *can be* is a linking verb, and *whoever* is a subject pronoun.

44 **him**. Peyton sings, rats, blabs, confesses, and *tells,* which is the action verb in this sentence and which should be followed by an object pronoun.

45 **he**. The linking verb *was* is completed by the subject pronoun *he.*

46 **her**. The preposition *to* needs an object, and here it has two: *Mom* and *her.*

47 **Me**. The preposition *Of* has three objects, including *Me.*

48 **me**. The preposition *between* calls for two objects. In this sentence, *Jessica* is one and *me* is the other. Don't fall into the *between-and-I* trap; *between* calls for objects, not subjects.

49 **he**. I did warn you that I'm throwing in a subject here and there! The verb *was* is missing at the end of this sentence. When you throw it in, you hear that *she was prettier than he was.* The missing word clarifies everything because you would never say that *she was prettier than him was.* (Everyone knows that he once won an "Ugly as a Wart" contest!)

50 **her**. The preposition *after* needs an object, and *her* takes that role.

51 **him**. Did you know that *past* may sometimes be a preposition? The object pronoun *him* works well here.

52 **us**, **whoever**. This is a hard one; if you got it right, you deserve an ice cream sundae. The pronoun *us* is best as an object of the preposition *behind.* But the preposition *at* is NOT completed by the pronoun *whomever.* Instead, *whoever* functions as the subject of the verb *comes.* The whole thing — *whoever comes too close* — is the object of the preposition *at.*

53 **whom**. Change the question to a statement and you'll get this one right away: *This dog is snarling at whom.* The preposition *at* is completed by the object *whom*.

54 **him**. The preposition *on* needs an object, and *him* got the job.

55 **them**. *Around* is a preposition in this sentence, so it takes the object *them*.

56 **him**. The preposition *to* needs an object, so opt for *him*.

57 **him**. You can't write *to he*, because *he* is a subject pronoun, and the preposition *to* can't bear to be without an object pronoun.

58 **she**. This sentence makes a comparison, and comparisons often contain implied verbs. The missing word is *does*, as in *Spike loves letters even more than she does*. Once you include the missing word, the answer is clear. You need *she* as a subject of the verb *does*.

59 **whoever**. The preposition *from* needs an object, but in this tricky sentence, the entire expression *whoever really wants to catch his attention* is the object, not just the first word. The pronoun *whoever* functions as the subject of the verb *wants*.

60 **he**. This implied comparison omits the verb *is*. Add the missing verb and the answer leaps off the page: *Jessica is as fond of meaty bones as he is*. You need the subject pronoun *he* to match with the verb *is*.

61 **his**. *Lincoln* doesn't need help with a person; he needs help with a task (editing). Whose editing is it? *His*.

62 **their**. Lincoln didn't hate the people at the agency (except that guy with bad breath who called him "Abe"). He didn't love *their sending* pronoun-lovers. The possessive pronoun shifts the focus to the action, where it should be.

63 **him**. I snuck this one in to see if you were awake. *Lori* saw *him*. What was he doing? *Reading*, but the *reading* is a description tacked onto the main idea, which is that she saw *him*. A possessive isn't called for in this sentence.

64 **her**. The objection isn't to a person *(she)* but to an action *(insisting)*.

65 **my**. The point in this sentence is Lincoln's reaction to the *editing*. The possessive pronoun *my* keeps the reader's attention on *editing*, not on *me*.

66 **my**. He didn't hate *me*, he hated the way I said his name, which no one can ever pronounce anyway. *My* ensures that the reader thinks about *pronouncing*.

67 **their**. *They* haven't backfired; the say-it-my-way-or-take-the-highway attitude is the problem. The possessive keeps you focused on *demanding*.

68 **she**. The expression inside the commas *(speaking at a recent awards dinner)* is just a description. Take it out for a moment and see what's left: *she got a big laugh*. The pronoun *she* is the one you want.

69 **my**. He does appreciate *me*, especially at bonus time. But in this sentence, I'm inquiring about the *calling*. This *-ing* noun should be preceded by the possessive *my*.

70 **me**. The *me* is the focus here, not an action-oriented *-ing* noun. Also, the noun *king* wasn't created from a verb.

Garage Sale for You

71 | On Monday, May 5, **my** brother cleaned out the garage and gave **our** | 72

neighbors and ~~I~~ me a great opportunity. The merchandise, which, just
73

between **you** and ~~I~~ me is mostly junk, will go on sale tomorrow.
74 | 75

76 | ~~Him~~ **His** taking the initiative to earn a few bucks will put money in

everyone's pocket as well! The gently used videotapes — a few surprises

here for ~~whomever~~ **whoever** looks really carefully at the subtitles — are
77

priced to sell! Buy some for your friends and watch with **them** and **their** pets. | 78
80 | 79

I recommend _For ~~Who~~ **Whom** the Dog Barks_. Other great items include a
81

used refrigerator, given to Mom by **me** and my brother Doug and recently
82

repaired by **our** dad and ~~I~~ me. Only a little freon leaks now.
83 | 84

Come early to 5858 Wisteria Parkway and bring a wallet stuffed with bills,

for it is ~~me~~ **I who** will have to cart away unsold merchandise. I promise a free
85 | 86

balloon to ~~whomever~~ **whoever** buys the most, and **he** or ~~her~~ **she** may blow | 88
87 | 89

it up and pop it right on the spot! As my mom says, "Give ~~she~~ **her** a chance,
90

and everyone will be happy."

---

71 **correct**. _My_ is a possessive pronoun and links the brother to the speaker as strongly as the handcuffs he bought for her birthday last year.

72 **correct**. Another possessive pronoun, attached to the noun _neighbors_.

73 **me**. You need an object pronoun here, receiving the action expressed by the verb _gave_.

74 **correct**. The _you_ is okay (_you_ works for both subject and object jobs).

75 **me**. _I_ is a problem. For some reason the preposition _between_ entices people to plop a subject pronoun where an object pronoun is needed.

76 **His**. The _-ing_ noun _taking_ is the real focus of the sentence, and the possessive pronoun keeps the reader's attention on the taking, not on _him_.

77 **whoever**. The preposition _for_ may have tempted you to opt for an object pronoun, but the verb _looks_ needs a subject, so _whoever_ is best. The object of the preposition, by the way, is the whole expression, _whoever looks_. . . .

78 **correct**. The object pronoun correctly follows the preposition _with_.

79 **correct**. The possessive pronoun _their_ answers the pet-ownership question.

80 **correct**. The subject pronoun *I* pairs with the verb *recommend*.

81 **Whom**. The preposition *for* requires the object pronoun *whom*.

82 **correct**. The preposition *by* takes the object pronoun *me*.

83 **correct**. The possessive pronoun *our* clarifies the parent/child bond here.

84 **me**. *By I?* I don't think so. You need the object pronoun *me*.

85 **I**. The linking verb *is* should be followed by a subject pronoun (*I*), not an object pronoun (*me*).

86 **correct**. The verb *will have* needs a subject, and *who* fits the bill.

87 **whoever**. The verb *buys* takes the subject, *whoever*.

88 **correct**. The verb *may blow* is paired with the subject pronouns *he*.

89 **she**. You need a subject pronoun for the verb *may blow*, so *she* does the job.

90 **her**. The verb *give* needs the object *her*.

Chapter 11

Choosing the Best Pronoun for a Tricky Sentence

In This Chapter

▶ Matching possessive pronouns with *everyone, several,* and other pronouns

▶ Referring to companies and organizations with pronouns

▶ Pairing *who, which,* and *that* with verbs

▶ Avoiding vague pronoun references

Have you figured out that pronouns are the most annoying part of speech in the entire universe? Pronouns are the words that stand in for nouns — words that name people, places, things, and ideas. The language can't do without pronouns, but when it comes to error-potential, they're a minefield just waiting to blow up your speech or writing.

I cover the basics of pronoun use in Chapter 3 and more advanced topics in Chapter 10. In this chapter I hit the big time, supplying information about pronouns that your great-uncle, the one who has a collection of antique grammar books that he actually reads, doesn't even know. If you master everything in this chapter, give yourself a gold pronoun . . . er, star.

Nodding in Agreement: Pronouns and Possessives Come Head to Head

Pronouns substitute for nouns, but in a sincere effort to ruin your life, they also match up with other pronouns. For example, take a look at this sentence: "When Charlie yelled at me, I smacked him and poured glue on his homework." The pronoun *his* refers to the pronoun *him,* which stands in for the noun *Charlie.* This example sentence is fairly straightforward; unfortunately, not all pronoun-pronoun couples get together so easily.

"Everybody is here." Doesn't that comment sound plural? So why do you need the singular verb *is?* Because *everybody* is a singular pronoun. So are *everyone, someone, anyone, no one, somebody, anybody, nobody, everything, something, anything, nothing, each, either,* and *neither.* Chances are your ear for good English already knows that these pronouns belong in the singular box.

If you extend the logic and match another pronoun — such as a possessive — to any of the "every . . .," "some . . .," "any . . .," and other similar pronouns, you may stub your toe. I often hear sentences such as "Everyone needs their lunch pass" — a grammatical felony because the singular *everyone* doesn't agree with the plural *their.* And in the grammar world, agreement (matching up all plurals with other plurals and singulars with other singulars) is a Very Big Deal. To get out of the grammatical penitentiary, substitute *his or her* for *their:* "Everyone needs his or her lunch pass."

Not every pronoun is singular. *Both, several, few,* and *many* are plurals and may match with *their* or other plural words.

Scan the following example sentence and practice exercises and plop a pronoun that makes sense in each blank.

Q. Neither of my aunts has a wart on _____ nose.

A. **her**. The singular pronoun *neither* must pair with another singular pronoun. True, the sentence refers to *aunts,* a plural. But the word *neither* tells you that you're talking about the *aunts* individually, so you have to go with a singular pronoun. Because *aunts* are female, *her* is the word you want.

1. My cousins may be easily found in a crowd because both have warts on _____ noses.

2. My cousin Amy opted for surgery; relieved that the procedure went well, everybody sent _____ best wishes.

3. Many of the get-well cards sported miniature warts on _____ envelopes.

4. A few even had little handwritten messages tucked into _____ illustrations.

5. Because Amy is pleased with the result of her surgery, someone else in her family is going to get _____ nose done also.

6. "Doesn't everyone need more warts on _____ nose?" reasoned Amy.

7. Anybody who disagreed with Amy kept quiet, knowing that _____ opinion wouldn't be accepted anyway.

8. Each of the implanted warts has _____ own unique shape.

9. Several of Amy's new warts model _____ appearance on a facial feature of a famous movie star.

10. Although someone said that _____ didn't like the new warts, the crowd reaction was generally positive.

11. Neither of the surgeons who worked on Amy's nose has opted for a similar procedure on _____ own schnozz.

12. I assume that nothing I say will change your mind about the nose-wart question; _____ will "go in one ear and out the other," as my mother used to say.

13. Aftercare is quite extensive; not one of the warts will continue to look good unless Amy gives _____ a lot of attention.

14. Both Amy and her sister Emily look forward to having _____ portraits painted, warts and all.

15. Many will ask _____ own doctors for cosmetic surgery after this event.

16. A few will opt for _____ own version of "wart enhancement."

17. Not everyone will want the same type of wart on _____ nose.

18. In fact, neither of Elizabeth's daughters will ask for warts on _____ nose, choosing a tasteful cheek placement instead.

19. A few cheek warts have already appeared in the tabloids because many stars want something dramatic for _____ publicity photos.

20. Each of the warts chosen by Elizabeth's daughters has little white spots on _____.

Working for the Man: Pronouns for Companies and Organizations

American Telephone and Telegraph (AT&T), Sears Roebuck & Co., the United Nations, and a ton of other businesses or community groups are waiting for the chance to mess up your pronoun choices. How? They cleverly create names that sound plural, and unsurprisingly, many people pair them up with plural pronouns. However, a moment of logical thinking tells you that each is one business and must therefore be referred to by a singular pronoun. Here's what I mean:

> **Wrong:** Saks Fifth Avenue has put their designer lingerie on sale.

> **Why it is wrong:** I was there last week and the lingerie was full price. Also, the pronoun *their* is plural, but *Saks,* despite the letter *s* at the end of the name, is singular because it's one company.

> **Right:** Saks sometimes puts its designer lingerie on sale.

> **Why it is right:** Now the singular possessive pronoun (its) matches the singular store name (Saks).

In the following example and set of practice exercises, choose the correct pronoun for each sentence. Just to keep you alert, I mixed in a couple of sentences in which the pronoun doesn't refer to a singular company or organization. The same principle applies: Singular matches with singular, and plural matches with plural.

Q. Carrie patronizes Meyer and Frank because (she/they) likes (its/their) shoe department, which has a good supply of her favorite size-13 stiletto heels.

A. **she**, **its**. The first pronoun refers to Carrie, so *she,* a singular, matches nicely. Carrie is not only singular, but also unique when it comes to shoe size. The second refers to the store, which is singular also and thus merits the singular *its.*

21. Carrie, who is not noted for logical thinking, believes that the United Countries Association should sell cookies to feed (its/their) "starving" staffers, even if the staffers have been stuffing (itself/himself or herself/themselves) for years.

22. The World Health Maintenance Association (WHMA) answered Carrie's letter with a suggestion of (its/their) own.

23. "Please work locally to overcome starvation," read the reply. "The WHMA will take care of (its/their) own staff."

24. Carrie, depressed by her failure to launch a cookie drive, immediately visited Mrs. Moo's Cookie World to sample (its/their) merchandise.

25. About 5,000 calories later, Carrie had completely drowned her sorrows and was ready to take on the WHMA again. "The WHMA needs to do a better job with labor relations. (It/They) won't win!" she screamed.

26. Because her mouth was full at the time, Carrie choked on a bit of Macadamia Crunch, which (she/it) had saved for last.

27. "I'll sue Mrs. Moo's Cookie World and all (its/their) subsidiaries," vowed Carrie, after she had been revived by a handsome emergency medical technician.

28. "Don't sue the EMT service," muttered the technician. "(It/They) can never get enough funding."

29. "I'm a supporter of the EMT service," declared Carrie hoarsely because (she/it/they) still had a bit of cookie in (her/its) throat.

30. The technician was so nervous around Carrie that he called the National Institute of Health (NIH) to check (its/their) policy on impacted cookie crumbs.

31. The NIH wrote to the EMT service about the WHMA, and in (its/their) letter the NIH requested additional information.

32. "The NIH cannot speak about individual cookie crumbs, but Mrs. Moo's Cookie World did report that macadamia nuts are (its/their) most popular ingredient," read the letter.

33. Carrie's response was to question the NIH about (its/their) integrity.

34. "I think that Mrs. Moo herself, the founder of Mrs. Moo's Cookie World, has bribed the NIH, and (it/they) will always rule in favor of those who contribute money," said Carrie.

35. Mrs. Moo, distressed at Carrie's accusation, ate 12 cookies to calm herself; (it/they) were delicious.

Decoding Who, That, and Which

Most pronouns are either singular or plural, masculine or feminine or neuter, popular or unpopular, good at math or barely passing arithmetic. Okay, I went a little too far, but you get the point. The characteristics of most pronouns are fixed. But a couple of pronouns change from singular to plural (or back) and from masculine to feminine without a moment's pause. *Who, which,* and *that* take their meaning and characteristics from the sentences in which they appear. Here's what I mean:

> May, who was born in April, wants to change her name. (The *who* is feminine and singular because it replaces the feminine, singular *May.*)

> Her sisters, who were named after their birth months of June and August, support May's changes. (The *who* is feminine and plural because it replaces *sisters.*)

A change in the meaning of *who, which,* or *that* would be an interesting but useless fact except for one issue. Whether a subject pronoun is singular or plural affects what sort of verb (singular or plural) is paired with it. In the preceding sample sentences, the *who* is paired with *was* when the *who* represents *May* and with *were* when the *who* represents *sisters.*

Deciding singular/plural verb issues is especially tough sometimes:

> She is one of the few quarterbacks who (is/are) ready for prime time.

> She is the only quarterback who (is/are) negotiating with the Jets.

Leaving aside the issue of a female quarterback (hey, it could happen!), the key to this sort of sentence is deciding what the pronoun represents. If *who* means *she*, then of course you opt for a singular verb because *she* is a singular pronoun. But if *who* means *quarterbacks*, the verb should be plural, because *quarterbacks* is plural. Logic tells you the answers:

> She is one of the few quarterbacks who **are** ready for prime time.

> She is the only quarterback who **is** negotiating with the Jets.

How many are ready for prime time? A few quarterbacks are ready — you football fans can make the list — and she's one of them. The *who* in the first example clearly stands in for *quarterbacks,* a plural. In the second example just one person is negotiating — *she*. Therefore, *who* is singular and so is the verb paired with it.

Catch as many correct verbs as you can in the following example sentence and practice exercises. I promise that at least one of each pair in parentheses is what you want.

Q. Kristin is one of the many lawyers on the fishing boat who (want/wants) to catch a shark.

A. **want**. How many lawyers want to catch a shark, according to this sentence? One or more than one? The sentence tells you that quite a lot of lawyers are in that category, so the *who* stands in for the group of lawyers. Bingo: A plural verb is needed to match the plural *who*.

36. The shark that Kristin caught was the only one that (was/were) hungry enough to take the odd bait that Kristin offered.

37. The bait that (was/were) on sale at the market when Kristin went shopping was extremely cheap (just like Kristin herself).

38. "I know that there is at least one shark that (likes/like) peanut butter," reasoned Kristin.

39. Kristin's fellow shark fans, who (sails/sail) even in the winter, read a lot about these animals on the Internet.

40. The only one of the shark sites that (doesn't/don't) appeal to Kristin is the one sponsored by the Stop Fishing Society.

41. Could it be that Kristin is one of the shark fans who (believes/believe) the Great White is a vegetarian?

42. Why did Kristin choose a bait that (is/are) completely unappetizing when dunked in salt water?

43. One of the many experienced sailors who (was/were) laughing at Kristin's bait exclaimed, "Peanut butter can't catch anything!"

44. I'm going to take Kristin's shark to the only taxidermist that (is/are) willing to stuff such a catch.

45. In the mouth of the shark he is planning to mount a jar of one of the many brands of peanut butter that (is/are) shark-friendly.

Getting Down to Specifics: Avoiding Improper Pronoun References

Pronoun rules are far more rigid than even the U.S. tax code. The underlying principle, that one pronoun may replace one and only one matching noun, bends only a tiny bit by allowing *they,* for instance, to take the place of more than one name. (*Ida, Mary, and Joan,* for example, may be replaced by *they.*) In common, informal speech and writing, pronouns are sometimes sent to fill other roles. But if you're going for correct, formal English, don't ask a pronoun to violate the rules.

A common error is to ask a pronoun to stand in for an idea expressed by a whole sentence or paragraph. (Pronouns can't replace verbs or noun/verb combos.) The pronouns *that, which,* and *this* are often misused in this way.

> **Wrong:** Jeffrey handed in a late, error-filled report, which annoyed his boss.

> **Why it's wrong:** The pronoun *which* improperly refers to the whole sentence. In formal English the pronoun has to replace one and only one noun.

> **Right:** Jeffrey's report, which annoyed his boss, was late and error-filled. (Now *which* refers to *report,* a noun.)

> **Also right:** The fact that Jeffrey's report was late and error-filled annoyed his boss. (Sometimes the best way to fix one of these sentences is to eliminate the pronoun entirely.)

Another common mistake is to send in a pronoun that approaches, but doesn't match, the noun it's replacing:

> **Wrong:** Jeffrey's sports marketing course sounds interesting, but I don't want to be one.

> **Why it's wrong**: *One* what? *Sports marketing course?* I don't think so. The *one* replaces *sports marketer* (or *sports marketing executive*), but the sentence has no noun to match *one.*

> **Right:** Jeffrey's sports marketing course sounds interesting, but I don't want to enroll in it. (Now *it* replaces *sports marketing* — a better match.)

> **Also right:** Jeffrey is studying to become a sports marketer, but I don't want to be one. (Now *one* replaces *sports marketer.*)

Fix the pronoun problem in the following example sentence and practice exercises. Some are correct as written. When you find one, write "correct" in the blank. Rewrite the clunkers so that every pronoun refers to an appropriate noun. Remember that sometimes you have to dump the pronoun entirely in order to correct the mistake. *Note:* The incorrect sentences have more than one answer; in the following example, I show you two possibilities, but in the answers section of this chapter, I provide only one possible answer.

Q. Jeffrey's dream job features a corner office, three-hour lunches, and frequent "research" junkets to Tahiti, which is unlikely given that he has no skill whatsoever.

_____

_____

A. **Given that he has no skill whatsoever, Jeffrey is unlikely to get his dream job, which features a corner office, three-hour lunches, and frequent "research" junkets to Tahiti.** The preceding sentence is just one possible solution, in which the pronoun *which* takes the place of *job*. Here's another: **The fact that Jeffrey has no skill whatsoever makes his dream job, which features a corner office, three-hour lunches, and frequent "research" junkets to Tahiti, unlikely.** Any sentence that achieves the goal of one noun out, one pronoun in is fine. The original doesn't work because *which* replaces an entire sentence, *Jeffrey's dream job features a corner office, three-hour lunches, and frequent "research" junkets to Tahiti.*

46. Jeffrey jogged for an hour in an effort to work off the pounds he had gained during his last three-hour lunch, but this didn't help.

_____

_____

47. He's always admired the superhero's flat-ab look, but no matter how hard he tries, he can't be one.

_____

_____

48. The 15 sit-ups that were prescribed by his exercise coach didn't help at all.

_____

_____

49. Jeffrey's next fitness effort ended in disaster; that did not discourage him.

_____

_____

50. He simply ignored the arrest warrant and continued to run; this was only a temporary solution.

_____

_____

51. Next, Jeffrey joined a gym, where he recites Shakespeare's sonnets, which help him to stay focused.

_____

_____

52. The great poet inspired Jeffrey to study it also.

_____

_____

53. "No, I did not see the car when I directed my bicycle into the street," testified Jeffrey, "but that wasn't the cause of the accident."

_____

_____

54. "The driver was distracted by his cell phone, which rang at the exact moment I started to ride," explained Jeffrey.

_____

_____

55. The judge was not impressed by Jeffrey's testimony and fined him, and Jeffrey paid it.

_____

_____

56. When Jeffrey paid the fine, the court clerk quoted Shakespeare, which impressed Jeffrey very much.

_____

_____

57. "I see you are a sonneteer," commented Jeffrey as he smiled and gave the clerk a romantic look; she wasn't impressed by this at all.

_____

_____

58. "Please pay your fine and leave the room," she roared, and that flattened Jeffrey's hopes for a Saturday-night date.

_____

_____

59. The clerk never dates anyone from work, which is a wise policy.

_____

_____

60. The clerk quotes poetry because she's hoping to become a literary critic; Jeffrey majored in it in college, so in theory he is a good match for her.

_____

_____

Calling All Overachievers: Extra Practice with Tricky Pronoun Situations

Here's a field trip report (see Figure 11-1), written by a battle-weary teacher after a particularly bad day. Can you find ten pronoun errors that cry out for correction? Circle the mistakes and give a thought to how you would fix them.

Mr. Levi Martin

Associate Professor, English 103

Field Trip Report, 1/18/12

I left school at 10:03 a.m. with 45 freshmen, all of whom were excited about our visit to Adventure Land. The day passed without incident, which was a great relief to me. I sat in the Adventure Land Bar and Grille for five hours while the youngsters visited Space Camp, Pirates' Mountain, and other attractions that are overrated but popular. The group saw me eating and said they wanted one too, but I replied that everyone had their school-issued lunch. This was a disappointment, and several students threw them at me. We got on one of the vans that was overdue for maintenance. The motor whirred loudly, and it scared the van driver. We drove to Makoski Brake and Wheel Repairs because the driver said their expertise was what we needed. Makoski is also the only one of the many repair shops on Route 9 that take credit cards, which was helpful because I had spent all my money in the Adventure Land Bar and Grille.

Figure 11-1:
A field trip report, written by a teacher who doesn't use pronouns correctly (shame!).

Answers to Advanced Pronoun Problems

1 **their**. The plural pronoun *both* matches with the plural possessive pronoun *their*.

2 **his or her**. Technically you can answer "his best wishes" and be grammatically correct, but I always opt for the more inclusive term "his or her." Don't pair the plural *their* with the singular *everyone* because singular and plural don't socialize in the grammar world.

3 **their**. The plural pronoun *many* is a good mate for the plural possessive *their*.

4 **their**. The pronoun *few* is plural, and so is *their*. A fine pair — they may even get married!

5 **his or her**. The singular possessive *his or her* links up nicely with the singular *someone*.

6 **his or her**. Once again you're matching a possessive with the singular pronoun *everyone*.

7 **his or her**. The singular pronoun *anybody* must be paired with a singular possessive pronoun (or two, for gender fairness), so go for *his or her*.

8 **its**. Yes, the sentence refers to warts, but the *each* indicates that you're talking about one wart at a time. The singular *each* matches the singular possessive pronoun *its*.

WARNING!

Don't confuse the possessive pronoun *its* with the shortened form of *it is* (it's). The possessive has no apostrophe.

9 **their**. The pronoun *several* moves you into plural territory, where *their* rules.

10 **he or she**. The pronoun *someone* is singular (notice the *one* inside the word?) and must pair with the singular *he or she*.

11 **his or her**. If you know that the surgeons are both men (or both women), use one of the singular pronouns (either *his* or *her*). Absent gender knowledge, go for the inclusive *his or her* (writing both singular pronouns). No matter what, don't opt for the plural *their* because *neither* is singular.

12 **it**. The singular *nothing* pairs with the singular pronoun *it* in this sentence.

13 **it**. The singular *not one* needs the singular *itself*.

14 **their**. The plural pronoun *both* tells you that the girls are springing for two portraits. It also tells you that you need the plural pronoun *their*.

15 **their**. The pronoun *many* is plural, so *their* is the best choice.

16 **their**. The pronoun *few* is plural and matches with the plural pronoun *their*.

17 **his or her**. The pronoun *everyone*, like all the *-one* pronouns, is singular and must be matched by a singular pronoun. Because the gender is not specified, *his or her* allows for both possibilities.

18 **her**. The pronoun *neither* is singular, and the sentence concerns two females, Elizabeth's daughters. Hence *her*, a singular feminine pronoun, is what you want here.

19 **their**. The plural possessive pronoun *their* refers to *many stars*, a plural.

20 **it**. This sentence is tricky. True, the sentence talks about *warts*, and *warts* is a plural. However, the pronoun *each* is singular and *has* means that the group of warts is being considered one at a time. Therefore you need a singular pronoun, *it*, to match with *each*.

21 **its, themselves**. In the first part of the sentence, the possessive pronoun refers to the organization, the United Countries Association. Because the organization is singular, it should be matched with a singular possessive, *its*. In the second part of the sentence, the pronoun refers to the individual staffers, who like to chow down and party hearty. Because lots of staffers are stuffing, *themselves* is the best choice.

22 **its**. The possessive pronoun refers to the WHMA, a singular organization. The singular pronoun is the one you want.

23 **its**. I know, I know. The word that sounds correct here is *their*. Unfortunately, the correct word is *its,* the singular pronoun that matches the singular organization.

24 **its**. Mrs. Moo's Cookie World is one business, so it must pair with the singular *its*.

25 **It**. Use your logic. Carrie is referring to the WHMA, and thus *it* is appropriate. If she were referring to the staff or to the administration, *they* would work.

26 **she**. The singular feminine pronoun *she* refers to Carrie, a singular female.

27 **its**. The company is singular, so pronouns referring to it must also be singular.

28 **It**. The service is singular (and the technician, I happen to know, is also single). The singular possessive works well here.

29 **she, her**. These two pronouns refer to Carrie, so singular and feminine rule.

30 **its**. The organization's name implies a plural, but in reality a singular entity is referenced, and *its* matches up correctly.

31 **its**. The National Institute of Health, an organization that in real life has never done anything remotely like the actions in this exercise, should be referred to with the singular pronoun *its* in this sentence.

32 **its**. Mrs. Moo's Cookie World is one business, so *its,* the singular pronoun, is best.

33 **its**. To refer to the organization, use the singular pronoun *its*.

34 **it**. The NIH, an organization, takes the singular pronoun *it*.

35 **they**. This pronoun refers to the 12 cookies that Mrs. Moo scarfed down. *Twelve cookies* is a plural, so the plural pronoun *they* makes a match.

36 **was**. The clue here is *the only one*. Not all, or even some, sharks would take Kristin's unusual bait. *Only one was hungry enough*. The pronoun *that* is singular.

37 **was**. The pronoun *that* replaces *bait,* a singular word that must match with the singular *was*.

38 **likes**. Now Kristin is talking about *one shark,* and the pronoun *that* is singular.

39 **sail**. The pronoun *who* refers to *fans,* so the *who* is plural and takes a plural verb, *sail*.

40 **doesn't**. The *only* tells you that the pronoun *that* is singular and is therefore desperate for a singular verb, *doesn't*. Okay, not desperate, but you get the idea.

41 **believe**. She's not the only one; she's one out of a crowd. The people in the crowd *believe*.

42 **is**. The pronoun *that* represents *bait,* so *that* is singular and takes the singular verb *is*.

43 **were.** How many people are doubled over in mirth? Not just one. (Knowing Kristin, I'd guess thousands.) The *who* is plural, as is its verb, *were.*

44 **is.** Just one taxidermist, so singular is the way to go.

45 **are.** Strange as it may sound, more than one brand of peanut butter is shark-friendly (no sharks were harmed in the grinding or bottling operation). Bingo, you need a plural.

46 **Jeffrey jogged for an hour in an effort to work off the pounds he had gained during his last three-hour lunch, without success.** The easiest way to fix the pronoun problem (in the original sentence, *this* incorrectly refers to a complete sentence, not to a single noun) is to eliminate *this.* You can dump *this* with any number of rewrites, including the one given here.

47 **He's always admired the superhero with flat abs, but no matter how hard he tries, he can't be one.** Now the pronoun *one* refers to *superhero.* In the original, the noun *superhero* doesn't appear, just the possessive *superhero's,* which doesn't match the nonpossessive pronoun *one.*

48 **correct.** The pronoun *that* replaces one word: *sit-ups.*

49 **The fact that Jeffrey's next fitness effort ended in disaster did not discourage him.** Eliminate the pronoun and you eliminate the problem, which is the pronoun *that. That* may not refer, as it does in the original sentence, to a whole sentence *(Jeffrey's next fitness effort ended in disaster).*

50 **As a temporary solution, he simply ignored the arrest warrant and continued to run.** The pronoun *this* needs a one-word reference, but in the original, *this* replaces everything that appears before the semicolon. As usual, an easy fix is to rewrite without a pronoun.

51 **correct.** Surprised? The pronoun *which* refers to *sonnets.* One word out and one in: You're okay.

52 **The great poet inspired Jeffrey to study poetry also.** In the original, no one can figure out what *it* means. The solution is to insert a noun *(poetry)* and dump the pronoun.

53 **"No, I did not see the car when I directed my bicycle into the street," testified Jeffrey, "but my distraction wasn't the cause of the accident."** One possible fix is to cut *that* and insert a specific. I've chosen *distraction,* but you may select *blindness, lack of awareness,* or something similar.

54 **correct.** The pronoun *which* refers to *phone,* a legal use.

55 **The judge was not impressed by Jeffrey's testimony and fined him, and Jeffrey paid the $500.** Okay, pick any amount you want, so long as you dump the *it.* Why is *it* illegal? The original sentence has no *fine,* just the verb *fined.* A pronoun replaces a noun, not a verb.

56 **When Jeffrey paid the fine, he was impressed by the court clerk, who quoted Shakespeare.** The problem here is the pronoun *which.* In the original sentence, the *which* refers to the fact that the court clerk spouted sonnets while Jeffrey counted out his money. In my suggested rewrite, I drop the *which* altogether.

57 **"I see you are a sonneteer," commented Jeffrey as he smiled and gave the clerk a romantic look; she was not impressed by Jeffrey's efforts at all.** The original sentence contains a vague pronoun *(this).* You can eliminate this vagueness in a couple of different ways; just write a noun instead of *this* and you're all set.

58 **"Please pay your fine and leave the room," she roared, flattening Jeffrey's hopes for a Saturday night date.** Jeffrey has no reason to hope for a Saturday night date (unless he signs up for some sort of television makeover show). You have plenty of reason to hope for proper pronoun usage. Simply rewrite the sentence to omit the vague pronoun *that.*

59 **The clerk wisely never dates anyone from work.** You can eliminate the vague pronoun *which* in several different ways. Another possible correction: *The clerk's policy never to date anyone from work is wise.*

60 **The clerk quotes poetry because she's hoping to become a literary critic; Jeffrey majored in literary criticism in college, so in theory he is a good match for her.** In reality, they would hit the divorce court within a month, but the problem with the original sentence is the pronoun, not Jeffrey's romance. In the original sentence *it* refers to nothing. Jeffrey didn't major in *literary critic* (the expression in the original); he majored in *literary criticism,* an expression that replaces *it* in the corrected sentence.

Mr. Levi Martin

Associate Professor, English 103

Field Trip Report, 1/18/12

I left school at 10:03 a.m. with 45 freshmen, all of whom were excited about our visit to Adventure Land. The day passed without incident, **which** was a   **61** great relief to me. I sat in the Adventure Land Bar and Grille for five hours while the youngsters visited Space Camp, Pirates' Mountain, and other attractions that are overrated but popular. The group saw me eating and said **62** they wanted **one** too, but I replied that everyone had ~~their~~ **his or her**   **63** school-issued lunch. **This** was a disappointment, and several students threw **64** **them** at me. We got on one of the vans that ~~was~~ **were** overdue for mainte-   **66** **65** nance. The motor whirred loudly, and **it** scared the van driver. We drove to **67** Makoski Brake and Wheel Repairs because the driver said ~~their~~ **its** exper-   **68** tise was what we needed. Makoski is also the only one of the many repair shops on Route 9 that ~~take~~ **takes** credit cards, **which** was helpful because I   **70** **69** had spent all my money in the Adventure Land Bar and Grille.

---

61 In the original sentence, *which* refers to the fact that *the day passed without incident.* The pronoun can't replace an entire sentence. One possible fix: "The fact that the day passed . . . was a great relief to me."

62 *One* what? The pronoun has no noun to refer to, just the verb *eating.* Reword to add some food (". . . saw me eating an ice cream cone") and the *one* will make sense.

63 The pronoun *everyone* is singular, so it must be paired with *his or her,* not *their.*

64 The pronoun *this* needs one noun to replace, not a whole sentence. Eliminate the pronoun with something like "The lunch packs were a . . . at me."

65 In the original, the pronoun *them* refers to nothing. Add "lunch packs" or "sandwiches" and you're in business.

66 The sentence should read "one of the vans that were," not "one of the vans that was." The pronoun *that* is a stand-in for *vans*.

67 What does *it* mean? The motor didn't scare the driver; the whirring sound scared him. But *it* should replace a noun. Fix this problem by saying that "the driver was scared" or a similar statement.

68 *Their* shouldn't refer to a company. Try *its*.

69 This sentence should say that it was "the only one of the many that *takes*." When you get into "only one of ____" territory, you know that the pronoun is singular and needs a singular verb.

70 What does *which* mean? The fact that the repair shop takes credit cards! The pronoun can't replace all those words. Rewrite to eliminate the pronoun with something like "Makoski's acceptance of credit cards was helpful because. . . ."

Chapter 12

Traveling in Time: Tricky Verb-Tense Situations

. . . .

In This Chapter

▶ Choosing the proper tense to summarize speech

▶ Expressing unchangeable facts in the correct verb tense

▶ Putting events in order with verbals

. . . .

I've always been attracted to sci-fi movies in which the heroes move around through the millennia. I probably like fiddling with verb tense for exactly the same reason; standard English verbs allow writers and speakers to time travel. You may not have a chief engineer to warn you when the motor's about to overheat, but you do have this chapter, which allows you to practice some tricky verb-tense situations. For example, did Arthur say that he *has* or *had* a cold? *Did* or *does* Mars qualify as a planet? And what effect do verbals — hybrid forms that are half verb, half another part of speech — have on the timing of events in a sentence? If you're sure of all these issues, drop the book and play a round of miniature golf. If you're not completely certain, try your hand at these exercises.

Telling Tales of the Past

Humans love to gossip, so I'm betting that your lunch table is filled with a ton of stories, many of which include summaries of what others have said or written. Because you're telling (actually, retelling) something that already happened, your base of operations is past tense. Note the past-tense verbs in italics:

> She *caught* Arthur with Stella, but he *told* her that he *was* only tying Stella's bow tie and not nibbling her neck. Then she *said* that Arthur *brought* her a box of candy with a note saying that no one else *had* eyes like hers.

What's wrong with the preceding example? Apart from the fact that Arthur *was* indeed nibbling Stella's neck, nothing. The verb tenses are all in the past because that's where a *summary of speech* resides. So even if she still *has* incomparable eyes, in this paragraph the verb *had* is better. (One important exception to the stay-in-past-tense-for-speech-summary rule is explained in the next section, "The Unchanging Universe: When You're Stuck in the Present.")

A common error is to switch from one tense to another with no valid reason. I often hear statements such as this one (the verbs are italicized):

> So she *sat* home and *waited* for the phone to ring. He finally *called*. Then he *says* that the big dance *is* a waste of time and they *will skip* the whole thing!

Penalty box. If she *sat* and *waited* until he *called* (all past-tense verbs), the next three verbs *(says, is,* and *will skip)* should be in past tense also *(said, was,* and *would skip).*

Take a crack at selecting the right verb from the choices in parentheses — circle your answer. Just to be sure you're paying attention, I sneak in a few verbs that aren't summary of speech and therefore shouldn't be in past tense.

Q. During yesterday's tryouts for the new reality show, *Grammarian Idol Factor,* Roberta (tells/told/will tell) the producer that she (likes/liked/will like) selecting pronouns while dangling 200 feet above the ground.

A. **told, liked.** The first answer is easy. If the tryouts were yesterday, the fact that Roberta lied to the producer (she actually hates pronouns) has to be in past tense. *Told* is past tense. The second part is trickier. She may always "like" selecting pronouns, but in summary of speech, past tense is the way to go (with one exception, which I note in the next section of this chapter).

1. The director of the show, *Grammarian Idol Factor,* explained to the candidates that he (has/had/will have) to select a maximum of 30 contestants.

2. Most of the contestants eagerly replied that they (want/wanted/would want) to make the final 30.

3. Roberta, who (likes/like/had liked) to play hard to get, screamed at the director that he (doesn't/didn't) have the faintest idea how to select the best applicants.

4. One who didn't make the cut, Michael Hooper, told me that Roberta (is/was/had been) the clear winner of the first three challenges — the noun toss, the pronoun shuffle, and the verb race.

5. Michael also whispered something surprising: Roberta (fails/failed/had failed) the psychological screening.

6. Last week when the psychologist (asks/asked) Roberta her feelings about various parts of speech, Roberta said that the linking verbs (do/did) present a problem.

7. "Why (don't/didn't) you like linking verbs?" continued the psychologist.

8. Roberta explained that any form of the verb *to be* (annoys/annoyed) her.

9. "I (try/tried) to avoid any sentence with that sort of verb," added Roberta.

10. She went on to say that adjectives (are/were/had been) her favorite part of speech.

11. The psychologist later reported that he (is/was/had been) worried about Roberta's reaction to punctuation.

12. Roberta apparently said that commas (are/were/had been) "out to get her."

13. She added that exclamation points (threaten/threatened/had threatened) her also.

14. The psychologist complained that quotation marks (hem/hemmed) him in and (make/made) him feel trapped.

15. Roberta and the psychologist disagreed, however, when Roberta said that the semicolon (is/was) the best punctuation mark.

16. The director said that he (doesn't/didn't) know what to make of Roberta's punctuation obsession.

17. He declared that she (is/was) too unstable for a show that relies heavily on question marks.

18. The assistant director, on the other hand, whispered that Roberta (is/was) faking a punctuation phobia just to attract attention.

19. The camera operator added that he (knows/knew) many people who (are/were) truly terrified by commas and apostrophes.

20. In the final report on Roberta, the psychologist mentioned that she (is/was/had been) afraid of punctuation because of a childhood attack by a mad copy editor.

The Unchanging Universe: When You're Stuck in the Present

Verb tenses express the march of time: past, present, and future actions. But some things don't march; they stay in one, unchanging state forever. When you talk about these things, present tense is the only one that makes sense, no matter what else is going on in the sentence. Take a look at these examples:

Wrong: Marty told me that the earth was a planet.

Why it is wrong: What is the earth now, a bagel? The unchanging fact, that the earth is a planet, must be expressed in present tense, despite the fact that all other summarized speech should be in past tense. (See "Telling Tales of the Past," the previous section in this chapter, for more information.)

Right: Marty told me that the earth is a planet.

Choose the correct verb from the parentheses in the following sentences. To complicate your life, I mixed "eternal truths" with changeable information. The eternal truths get present tense no matter what, but with the other stuff . . . you're on your own.

Q. Although Marty knew that 10 plus 10 (equals/equaled) 20, she wrote "15" on the test as a gesture of defiance.

A. **equals**. In our number system (I'm not sure what they do on Mars), 10 added to 10 makes 20. No change is possible, so present tense is what you want here.

21. Marty's job as a schoolteacher won't last very long if she keeps telling her class that each molecule of water (has/had) three oxygen atoms.

22. Science has never been Marty's best subject, but she did explain that water (covers/covered) nine tenths of the planet.

23. I gently confronted her with the fact that land (makes/made) up about a quarter of the earth's surface.

24. Marty sniffed and said that she (has/had) a cold and couldn't think about the earth anyway.

25. We went out for a snack (bagels and cream cheese), and Marty told me that cheese (is/was) a dairy product.

26. "Not the way they make it here," I replied, pointing out that the product (is/was) mostly artificial.

27. Did anyone actually like guar gum, I wondered, and why (is/was) it on my bagel, pretending to be cheese?

28. Marty put on her best science teacher's voice and intoned, "Dairy produce (comes/came) from milk."

29. "Do you know that guar gum (is/was) not naturally found in dairy?" I asked.

30. Marty shook her head and began to compute the tip, muttering that twenty percent of ten dollars (is/was) two dollars.

31. Ten years ago I took Marty to a restaurant that served only peanut butter, which (is/was) made from nuts.

32. Marty used to be a big fan of jelly, though she never liked strawberries because they (have/had) seeds.

33. Marty is such a fanatic about seeds that she once counted all the seeds on a strawberry before she ate it; there (are/were) 45.

34. Marty was very critical of the cuisine, even though she (knows/knew) almost nothing about cooking.

35. Marty at the time was following a vegetarian diet, which (does/did) not include meat.

Tackling the Timeline: Verbals to the Rescue

In Chapter 1 I explain the basic and "perfect" tenses of verbs (past, present, future, past perfect, present perfect, and future perfect). Here I drop you into a vat of boiling grammar as you choose the best tense for some complicated elements called *verbals*. Verbals, as the name implies, have a link with verbs, but they also have a link with other parts of speech (nouns, adjectives, and adverbs). Verbals never act as the verb in a sentence, but they do influence the sense of time that the sentence conveys. The three types of verbals are as follows:

- ✔ **Gerunds** look like the -*ing* form of a verb but function as a noun; that is, a gerund names a person, place, thing, or idea. ("I like *smiling*," commented Alice, who had just had her braces removed. In this sentence, *smiling* is a gerund.)

- ✔ **Infinitives** are what you get when you add "to" to a verb. Infinitives may function as nouns or they may take a descriptive role. ("*To be* safe, Alice packed a few hundred rolls of breath mints." In this sentence, *to be* is an infinitive.)

- ✔ **Participles** are the -*ing* or -*ed* or -*en* form of a verb, plus a few irregulars. They're also the form of the verb that joins up with *has, have,* or *had*. Participles describe, often explaining what action someone is doing, but they never function as the actual verb in a sentence. ("*Inhaling* sharply, Elaine stepped away from the blast of peppermint that escaped from Alice's mouth." In this sentence, *inhaling* is a participle giving information about *Elaine*. The verb is *stepped*.)

All three verbals give time information. The plain form (without *has, have, having,* or *had*) shows action happening at the same time as the action expressed by the main verb in the sentence. The perfect form (with *has, have, having,* or *had*) places the action expressed by the verbal before the action of the main verb.

The tricky part about choosing either the plain or perfect form is to decide whether the events are actually simultaneous, at least in the grammatical sense. First, figure out how important the timeline is. If the events are so closely spaced so as not to matter, go for the plain form. If it matters to the reader/listener that one event followed or will follow another, go for a perfect form.

Circle the correct verbal form from the parentheses in this example. In the practice exercises that follow, get out your time machine and read about a fictional tooth whitener called "GreenTeeth" — sure, the content is strange, but all that you need to worry about is whether you circle the correct verbal form.

Q. (Perfecting/Having perfected) the new product, the chemists asked the boss to conduct some market research.

A. **Having perfected**. The two events occurred in the past, with the chemists' request closer to the present moment. The event expressed by the verbal (a participle, if you absolutely have to know) attributes another action to the chemists. The perfect form (*having* tells you you're in perfect-land) places the act of *perfecting* prior to the action expressed by the main verb in the sentence, *asked*.

36. (Peering/Having peered) at each interview subject, the researchers checked for discoloration.

37. One interview subject shrieked upon (hearing/having heard) the interviewer's comment about "teeth as yellow as sunflowers."

38. (Refusing/Having refused) to open her mouth, she glared silently at the interviewer.

39. With the market research on GreenTeeth (completed/having been completed), the team tabulated the results.

40. The tooth whitener (going/having gone) into production, no further market research is scheduled.

41. The researchers actually wanted (to interview/to have interviewed) 50 percent more subjects after GreenTeeth's debut, but the legal department objected.

42. Additional interviews will be scheduled if the legal department succeeds in (getting/ having gotten) participants to sign a "will not sue" pledge.

43. "(Sending/Having sent) GreenTeeth to the stores means that I am sure it works," said the CEO.

44. (Weeping/Having wept), the interviewers applauded the boss's comment.

45. Next year's Product Placement Awards (being/having been) announced, the GreenTeeth team is celebrating its six nominations and looking for future dental discoveries.

Calling All Overachievers: Extra Practice with Verb Tenses

You need to know how to summarize speech, allow for unchangeable facts, and create a timeline with verbals to edit this accident report, filed by a security guard. Check out the report in Figure 12-1 and circle the proper verbs or verbals in the parentheses.

GMT Industries

Incident Report

Date: 8/29/05   Time: 1:10 a.m.

Place: Loading dock   Guard on duty: P. Samuels

(Proceeding, Having proceeded) from the locker room where *Grammarian Idol Factor* was on television, I noticed smoke (coming, having come) from a doorway that leads to the loading dock. (Knowing, Having known) that no deliveries were scheduled, I immediately became suspicious and took out my two-way radio. I alerted the other guard on duty, M. Faulkner, that trouble might be brewing. Faulkner, not (turning, having turned) off the television, couldn't hear me. Upon (screaming, having screamed) into the radio that I needed him right away, I crept up to the door.

I noticed that the smoke was not hot. As I waited, (touching, having touched) the door to see whether it was getting hot, I sincerely wished (to find, to have found) Faulkner and (to strangle, to have strangled) him for not (replying, having replied) when I called. (Arriving, Having arrived), Faulkner apologized and explained that the adverb competition (is, was, had been) his favorite. He also said that he (has, had) a clogged ear that he (has, had) not been able to clean out, no matter how many toothpicks he (uses, used).

"(Speaking, Had spoken) of heating up," I remarked, "I don't sense any heat from this door." I reminded him that fire (is, was) hot, and where there's smoke (there is, there was) fire. Then Faulkner and I, (hearing, having heard) a buzz from the other side of the door, ran for shelter. I told Faulkner that the buzz (is, was) not from a bomb, but neither of us (being, having been) in the mood to take chances, we headed for the locker room. We did not put the television on again, *Grammarian Idol Factor* (being, having been) over for more than ten minutes, but we did plug in a CD as we waited for the police to arrive, (calling, having called) them some time before. Therefore we didn't hear the director yell, "Cut!" In no way did we intend (to disrupt, to have disrupted) the film crew's work or (to ruin, to have ruined) the dry ice that caused the "smoke." (Respecting, Having respected) Hollywood for many years, Faulkner and I wish Mr. Scorsese only the best with his next film.

Figure 12-1:
Sample accident report with a lot of verbal indecision.

Answers to Advanced Verb Tense Problems

 1 **had**. The tip-off is the verb *explained,* which tells you that you're summarizing speech. Go for the past tense *had.*

2 **wanted**. *Replied* is a clue that you're summarizing speech, so *wanted,* the past tense, is best. The last choice, by the way, imposes a condition (he *would* do something under certain circumstances). Because the sentence doesn't impose a condition, that choice isn't appropriate.

3 **likes, didn't**. The first choice has nothing to do with summary of speech and is a simple statement about Roberta. The present tense works nicely in this spot. The second choice *is* a speech summary (well, a *scream* summary, but the same rule applies), so the past-tense verb *didn't* fills the bill.

4 **was**. The sentence tells you that *Michael Hooper told.* The past tense works here for summary of speech.

5 **failed**. You can arrive at the answer in two separate ways. If Michael *whispered,* the sentence is summarizing what he said. Another way to look at this sentence is to reason that Michael is telling you something that already happened, not something happening in the present moment. Either way, the past tense *failed* is best.

6 **asked, did**. The first answer comes from the fact that the psychological test was in the past. The second is summary of speech (Roberta's words) and calls for past tense.

7 **don't**. Give yourself a pat on the back if you got this one. The quotation marks indicate that the words are exactly what the psychologist said. The speech isn't summarized; it's quoted. The present tense makes sense here because the tester is asking Roberta about her state of mind at the current moment.

8 **annoyed**. Straight summary of speech here, indicated by the verb *explained.* Therefore, past tense is the one you want.

9 **try**. This statement isn't a summary, but rather a direct quotation from Roberta. She's speaking about her current actions, so present tense fits.

10 **were**. Roberta's comments are summarized, not quoted, so past tense is appropriate.

11 **was**. The psychologist may still be worried (I would be, if I were treating Roberta!), but the summary of what he said should be in simple past tense.

12 **were**. The parentheses contain two past-tense verbs, *were* and *had been.* The *had* form is used to place one event further in the past than another, a situation that isn't needed here, when you're simply summarizing what someone is saying and not placing events in order. Go for simple past tense.

13 **threatened**. Roberta's remark about exclamation points is summarized speech calling for past tense.

14 **hemmed, made**. The psychologist's comments should, like all summarized speech, be reported in simple past tense.

15 **was**. I like semicolons too, though I hesitate to say that they're the best. Whatever I say about them, however, must be summarized in simple past tense.

16 **didn't**. "The director said" is your cue to chime in with simple past tense, because you're reporting his speech.

17 **was**. "He declared" tells you that you're reporting what he said. Thus, past tense is the way to go.

18 **was**. The word *whispered* is the key here because it indicates summarized speech, which calls for simple past tense.

19 **knew**, **were**. Your intuition may point you toward present tense in this sentence because the camera operator may still be hanging around with people who can't handle punctuation marks. However, summarized speech needs past tense.

20 **was**. Regardless of how long Roberta's fearful state lasts, go for past tense to indicate summarized speech.

21 **has**. The composition of a molecule doesn't change, no matter how wrong Marty is about the number of oxygen atoms (the actual number is two). Present tense is called for here.

22 **covers**. Marty has apparently tried to change the amount of water on the planet (from three quarters to nine tenths), but in reality the amount of water is constant and thus merits present tense.

23 **makes**. The amount of land doesn't change; go with present tense.

24 **had**. Colds come and go; they aren't unchangeable conditions. The summary of speech rule doesn't change. Past tense is what you want. (See the section, "Telling Tales of the Past," earlier in this chapter, for more detail.)

25 **is**. For once, Marty is correct. Cheese *is* a dairy product and can't change into anything else. For an eternal truth, present tense is correct.

26 **was**. Product composition can change, and the speaker is summarizing what was said. Past tense makes sense.

27 **was**. The guar gum's location on the bagel doesn't fall into the eternal truth category, and the speaker is talking about the past. The past-tense verb *was* is the one you want.

28 **comes**. The definition of dairy doesn't change, so present tense works best here.

29 **is**. This directly quoted remark refers to something that doesn't change. Guar gum doesn't appear in dairy products unless someone's been tampering with Mother Nature. Present tense works for an unchangeable fact.

30 **is**. Math doesn't change, so present tense is appropriate here.

31 **is**. Peanut butter is always made from nuts; the definition can't change, so present tense is best here.

32 **have**. What do strawberries have now? Press conferences? Because strawberries and seeds are linked for eternity, go for present tense.

33 **were**. One particular strawberry had 45 seeds, but another strawberry may have a different number. Because this sentence expresses a changeable and not an eternal truth and because the sentence as a whole is in past tense, past tense is appropriate for the last verb as well.

34 **knew**. Marty (contrary to the opinion of every single one of her teachers) can learn, so this statement expresses a fact that may change. The past tense works best here because the sentence is talking about a previous time.

35 **does**. Vegetarian diets never include meat. The definition is set, so present tense is needed here.

36 **Peering**. Here the two actions take place at the same time. The researchers check out the subjects' teeth and check for trouble. The perfect form (with *having*) is for actions at different times.

37 **hearing**. Once again, two actions take place at the same time. Go for the plain form.

38 **Refusing**. The "not in this universe will I open my mouth" moment is simultaneous with an "if looks could kill" glare, so the plain form is best.

39 **having been completed**. The plain form *completed* would place two actions (the completing and the tabulating) at the same time. Yet common sense tells you that the tabulating follows the completion of the research. The perfect form (with *having*) places the completing before the tabulating.

40 **having gone**. The decision to stop market research is based on the fact that it's too late; the tooth whitener, in all its glory, is already being manufactured. Because the timeline matters here, and one action is clearly earlier, the perfect form is needed.

41 **to interview**. The *have* form places the action of interviewing *before* the action expressed by the main verb in the sentence. But the legal department objected first. Dump the *have* form.

42 **getting**. Three actions are mentioned in this sentence: scheduling, succeeding, and getting. The first action is placed in the future, so don't worry about it. The last two actions take place at the same time, because the minute somebody signs a legal paper, the attorneys are successful. As it expresses a simultaneous action, the plain form of the verbal (without *having*) is appropriate.

43 **Sending**. The CEO's statement places two things, sending and being sure, at the same time. Bingo: The plain form is best.

44 **Weeping**. The interviewers are all choked up as they clap their hands and hope for a very big raise. Plain form works because the two things happen at the same time.

45 **having been**. The celebration and "time to get back to work" movement take place at the same time as the announcement. No perfect tense is needed.

GMT Industries

Incident Report

Date: 8/29/05   Time: 1:10 a.m.

Place: Loading dock   Guard on duty: P. Samuels

46 **Proceeding** from the locker room where *Grammarian Idol Factor* was on television,
47 I noticed smoke **coming** from a doorway that leads to the loading dock. **Knowing** **48**
that no deliveries were scheduled, I immediately became suspicious and took out
my two-way radio. I alerted the other guard on duty, M. Faulkner, that trouble might
be brewing. Faulkner, not **having turned** off the television, couldn't hear me. Upon
49
50 **screaming** into the radio that I needed him right away, I crept up to the door.

I noticed that the smoke was not hot. As I waited, **touching** the door to see
51
whether it was getting hot, I sincerely wished **to find** Faulkner and **to strangle** him
52 **53**
for not **replying** when I called. **Arriving**, Faulkner apologized and explained that
54 **55**
56 the adverb competition **was** his favorite. He also said that he **had** a clogged ear
57
58 that he **had** not been able to clean out, no matter how many toothpicks he **used**. **59**

60 "**Speaking** of heating up," I remarked, "I don't sense any heat from this door." I
61 reminded him that fire **is** hot, and where there's smoke **there is** fire. Then Faulkner **62**
63 and I, **hearing** a buzz from the other side of the door, ran for shelter. I told Faulkner
64 that the buzz **was** not from a bomb, but neither of us **being** in the mood to take **65**
chances, we headed for the locker room. We did not put the television on again,
Grammarian Idol Factor **having been** over for more than ten minutes, but we did
66 plug in a CD as we waited for the police to arrive, **having called** them some time **67**
before. Therefore we didn't hear the director yell, "Cut!" In no way did we intend
68 **to disrupt** the film crew's work or **to ruin** the dry ice that caused the "smoke." **69**
70 **Having respected** Hollywood for many years, Faulkner and I wish Mr. Scorsese
only the best with his next film.

---

46 The proceeding and the noticing took place at roughly the same time, so the plain form is the one you want here.

47 The noticing and the coming of the smoke were more or less simultaneous, so go for the plain form here. The perfect form would place one action earlier than another, which is contrary to the intended meaning.

48 The suspicions arose from the knowledge that no deliveries were scheduled, so the knowing and the act of suspecting are simultaneous, calling for the plain verbal.

49 This sentence emphasizes the order of events. Because the television was not turned off first, Faulkner couldn't hear. The perfect form works to show an earlier action (not turning off the television).

50 The screaming and the creeping are simultaneous; go for the plain form.

51 The touching of the door and the waiting are simultaneous, calling for a plain (no sprinkles added) verbal.

52 The narrator *wished to find* Faulkner (everyone's looking for him, including his bookie), and the wishing and finding are more or less simultaneous. Plain form doesn't set up any special order of events.

53 The plain infinitive *to strangle* is appropriate because the narrator *wished to find and to strangle* Faulkner all at the same time. The actions are presented equally, not in time order.

54 The calling and replying are presented as simultaneous acts, so go for plain, not perfect.

55 The apologizing and the arriving are going on at the same time; a plain form is therefore best.

56 This verb expresses summarized speech, so past tense is what you want.

57 Another speech summary is expressed by this verb, so go for past tense.

58 In summarizing speech, always opt for past tense.

59 All these verbs fall into the category of summarized speech and thus take the past tense.

60 The *I* in the sentence is *speaking* now, so the plain form is needed.

61 Fire is always hot, so present tense works here.

62 This unchangeable fact (fire is never without smoke) calls for present tense.

63 These two cowards took off at exactly the same time they heard a buzz — no time lag here! The perfect form would indicate two consecutive events, but these events were simultaneous and thus need the plain form.

64 Summarized speech, indicated by *told*, calls for past tense.

65 *Being* keeps the speakers in the moment. The writer is not placing the mood before another action. Go for plain form.

66 The perfect form is appropriate because the speaker is putting events in order. First, the show ends. Second, they put on a CD.

67 In hopes of saving his job, the writer emphasizes the order of events, using the perfect form to place the calling of the police earlier on the timeline.

68 The intending and the disrupting are simultaneous, so plain form is best.

69 Plain form works here because the intending and the ruining occur at the same time.

70 Here the writer is emphasizing a longstanding respect for the film world. The perfect form extends the respectful feeling into the past.

Chapter 13

Are You and Your Verbs in the Right Mood?

*N*o, they're not pregnant or in the midst of midlife crises; nevertheless, verbs do have mood swings. One minute they're *indicative,* the regular, plain-vanilla, just-the-facts sort of verb. (The dishes *are* dirty. No one *has washed* them. Little colonies of mold *established* themselves all over the sink a couple of days ago.) Suddenly they're issuing orders in *imperative* mood. (*Wash* the dishes. *Stop* whining. *Don't think* your allowance is off limits!) And when you least expect a change, *subjunctive* pops up. (If I *were* rich enough to hire a maid, I wouldn't ask for your dishwashing help. I'm not a millionaire, so I request that 7 p.m. *be* the official dishwashing hour.)

Got the idea? Of the three verb moods, you're probably the most familiar with indicative. Every statement of fact is in indicative mood, as are nearly all the sentences in this book. The imperative mood gives commands, usually to an understood *you* who doesn't appear in the sentence. The subjunctive, the one designed to give you a headache, shows up in condition-contrary-to-fact and in certain command/wish sentences. In this chapter I take you through all three, with a little extra attention on the hard one, also known as the subjunctive.

Stating the Obvious: Indicative Mood

Just about everything I *say* about verbs in this book actually *applies* to indicative verbs, which, as the name implies, *indicate* facts. Indicative mood *is* the one you *use* automatically, stating action or being in any tense and for any person. *Do* you *want* to see some samples of indicative verbs? No problem. Every verb in this paragraph *is* in indicative mood. I *have placed* all the verbs in italics so you *can locate* them easily.

Indicative verbs change according to the time period you're talking about (the tense) and, at times, according to the person doing the action. I cover these issues in Chapters 1 and 2.

If you're in the mood, circle the indicative verb that works best in each of the following sentences. The verb choices are in parentheses.

Q. Mr. Adams (holds/held) a performance review every June.

A. **holds**. Both choices are indicative, but the present tense works better. The clue is the expression *every June*.

1. Each employee (is/was) summoned to Adams' office for what he calls "a little chat."

2. All the workers (know/will know) that the "chat" is all on Adams' side.

3. Adams (likes/like) to discuss baseball, the economy, and the reasons no one (will/would) receive a raise.

4. "(Is/Was) business good these days?" he always says.

5. He always (mentions/will mention) that he may have to make personal sacrifices to save the company.

6. Sacrifices! He (means/meant) that he (earns/will earn) only a million instead of two million next year!

7. Maybe he (replaced/will replace) the linen napkins in the executive dining room with paper.

8. After the chat, the employees always (go/will go) out for some conversation of their own.

9. (Does/Do) they review Adams' performance in the most candid way?

10. Everyone (believe/believes) that the company needs new leadership.

Taking Command: Imperative Mood

I studied a couple of foreign languages in college, and I remember a major headache arriving right around the time I tried to learn the imperative mood. Each verb had a bunch of rules on how to form commands — plus irregulars! English is much kinder than those other languages. In English, the command, also known as the imperative mood, is the same whether you're talking to one person or 20, to a peasant or to a queen. The English command form is the infinitive minus the *to*. In other words, the unchanged, plain form of the verb. Negative commands are slightly different. They take the infinitive-minus-*to* and add *do not*, as in *do not snivel, do not blink,* and *do not blubber*.

Some examples, with the imperative verb italicized:

> *Stop* sniveling, Henry.
>
> *Pull* yourself together and *meet* your new in-laws.
>
> *Do* not *mention* our engagement.
>
> *Prepare* to die if they find out we're getting married!

Fill in the blanks with commands for poor Henry, who is meeting his prospective in-laws. The base verb you're working with appears in parentheses at the end of each sentence.

O. _____ quietly on the couch, Henry, while I fetch Daddy. *(to sit)*

A. **Sit**. The command is formed by dropping the *to* from the infinitive.

11. Henry, _____ my lead during the conversation. *(to follow)*

12. If Mom talks about Paris, _____ your head and _____ interested. *(to nod/to look)*

13. Dad hates bad accents, so _____ French. *(to speak, negative command)*

14. _____ them to show you slides of last year's trip to Normandy. *(to ask)*

15. _____ asleep during the slide show, if you can help it! *(to fall, negative command)*

16. _____ some of Mom's potato salad, even if it's warm. *(to eat)*

17. _____ about unrefrigerated mayonnaise and the risk of food poisoning. *(to talk, negative command)*

18. When she ignores you and serves the potato salad anyway, just _____ an appointment with your doctor and _____ quiet. *(to make/to keep)*

19. _____ them good night and _____ them for a lovely evening. *(to wish/ to thank)*

20. _____ that we won't visit them very often after the wedding. *(to remember)*

Telling Lies or Being Passive: Subjunctive Mood

The subjunctive is a very big deal in some languages; whole terms were devoted to it in my college Spanish class. Fortunately for you, in English the subjunctive pops up only rarely, in two situations: condition-contrary-to-fact and indirect commands.

Condition-contrary-to-fact means that you're talking about something that isn't true.

> If I *were* famous, I would wear sunglasses to hide my identity. (The verb *were* is subjunctive.)

> *Had* I *known* the secret password, I would have passed the bouncer's test and entered the club.

> If I *had* not punched the police office, I would have avoided jail.

Notice that the subjunctive changes some of the usual forms. In indicative, the pronoun *I* is paired with *was* (see the section on indicative mood earlier in this chapter for more detail). The switch to *were* in the first sample sentence tells you that you're in fantasy land. Referring to the first sample sentence, I must confess that I'm not famous, though I do wear sunglasses. In the second and third sample sentences, the *had* does more than its usual indicative job, which is to place events earlier in the past than other past-tense events. (See Chapter 1 for more details on this use of *had*.) Instead, in a subjunctive sentence the *had* also means that I didn't know the secret password, the bouncer muttered something about "getting in when it snows in July," and I was forced to go the 19th Precinct instead of dancing with sports stars and supermodels.

Condition-contrary-to-fact sentences always feature a *would* form of the verb. In standard English, the *would* form never appears in the part of the sentence that is untrue.

Subjunctive verbs also express commands indirectly, as in these sentences, in which the subjunctive verb is italicized:

> The bouncer requested that he *remove* himself from the line as soon as possible.

> The club owner declared that guests wearing unfashionable clothes *be* denied entry.

Subjunctive, indirect commands are formed by dropping the *to* from the infinitive. In the first sample sentence, the pronoun *he* normally (that is, in indicative mood) pairs with *removes*. In subjunctive, the infinitive *to remove* loses the *to* and becomes *remove*. In the second sample, *guests* pairs with *be*, which is created by dropping *to* from the infinitive *to be*. The indicative form would be *guests are*.

Write the correct verb in the blank for each exercise in this section. The verb you're work-ing with appears in parentheses after each sentence. Just to keep you honest, I tucked in a few sentences that don't require subjunctive. Keep your eyes open.

0. If Ellen _____ for her turn at the wheel, she wouldn't have wrapped her car around that telephone pole. *(to prepare)*

A. **had prepared**. The *had* creates a subjunctive here, because Ellen didn't prepare for her road test. Instead, she went to a drive-in movie, as a passenger.

21. The motor vehicle tester asked that Ellen _____ ready for her exam at 9 a.m. *(to be)*

22. The test would have gone better if Ellen _____ a morning person. *(to be)*

23. "If it _____," explained the instructor, "you will be required to take the test as soon as the roads are plowed." *(to snow)*

24. If the snow plow _____ the entire route, Ellen would have passed. *(to cover)*

25. Unfortunately, the supervisor of the snow-removal crew declared that the highways _____ cleaned first. *(to be)*

26. Terrified of ice, Ellen requested that the examiner _____ her test. *(to postpone)*

27. If he _____, Ellen would have taken the test on a sunny, warm day. *(to refuse, negative form)*

28. If Ellen _____ about the examiner, the motor vehicle department would have investigated. *(to complain)*

29. If an examiner _____ unfair, the motor vehicle department schedules another test. *(to be)*

30. The department policy is that if there _____ a valid complaint, they dismiss the examiner promptly. *(to be)*

31. If Ellen _____ the test fives times already, she would have been more cheerful about her grade. *(to take, negative form)*

32. If in the future Ellen _____ to another district, she may have more luck. *(to go)*

33. Not every county, for example, cares if the driver _____ into a tree. *(to skid)*

34. If only Ellen _____ to Smithsburg, she would have a license already. *(to travel)*

35. Smithsburg requires that a driver _____ "reasonable competency" and nothing more. *(to demonstrate)*

Calling All Overachievers: Extra Practice with Moody Verbs

If you master the three moods (cranky, irritable, ready to bite someone's head off), try your hand at this exercise. The progress report in Figure 13-1 has some serious mood problems. Check out the underlined verbs, circle the ones that are correct, and cross out and correct the ones that are in the wrong mood.

Progress Report: Coffee Break Control

From: Ms. Bell, Coffee Break Coordinator

To: Ms. Schwartz, Department Head

Re: Coffee Break Control

July 31, 2006

As you <u>know</u>, I <u>were</u> now in charge of implementing the new directive that every employee <u>submits</u> to a coffee-residue test. If a test <u>were</u> given at a time when coffee-sipping <u>were</u> not <u>authorized</u> and the results <u>were</u> positive, the policy <u>require</u> that the worker "<u>donates</u>" a pound of coffee to the break room.

<u>Do not asked</u> me to describe the union's reaction to this directive. If I <u>would tell</u> you what the shop steward <u>would have said</u>, you <u>had blushed</u>. All I <u>would say</u> is that the steward <u>were</u> not happy.

<u>Would</u> you <u>have known</u> about the reaction before issuing the directive, you <u>would have had reconsidered</u>. One more thing: the coffee stains on my shirt, if they <u>were to come</u> out, should not make you <u>thought</u> that I <u>were drinking</u> coffee outside of the official break time. These stains <u>result</u> from coffee being thrown at me.

Figure 13-1:
This progress report contains some verbs that are in the wrong mood.

Answers to Verb Mood Problems

1 **is**. The sentence speaks of an on-going situation, so present tense is best.

2 **know**. The workers have been through this "chat" many times, so the act of knowing isn't in the future but in the present.

3 **likes**, **will**. The present-tense form for talking about someone (*Adams*, in this sentence) is *likes*. The future-tense verb *will* explains that in the coming year, as always, employees will be shopping in the bargain basement.

4 **Is**. The expression *these days* is a clue that you want a present-tense verb that talks about something or someone.

5 **mentions**. If an action *always* occurs, present tense is the best choice.

6 **means**, **will earn**. The boss is talking about the future (the clue is *next year*). The talking takes place in the present (so you want *means*), but the earning is in the future (hence, *will earn*).

7 **will replace**. The *maybe* creates a hypothetical situation, wondering what the boss *will* do in the future.

8 **go**. An on-going situation calls for present tense.

9 **Do**. The subject *they* calls for the plural form.

10 **believes**. Although *everyone* sounds like a plural, it's actually a singular pronoun requiring a singular verb.

11 **follow**. The command is formed by stripping the *to* from the infinitive.

12 **nod**, **look**. Drop the *to* and you're in charge, commanding poor Henry to act interested even if he's ready to call off the engagement rather than listen to one more story about French wine.

13 **don't speak** or **do not speak**. The negative command relies on *do*.

14 **Ask**. Poor Henry! He has to ask, which in command form is *ask*.

15 **Do not fall**. Take *to* from the infinitive and add one *do* and you have a negative command.

16 **Eat**. Henry's in for a long evening, given the command *Eat*, which is created by dropping *to* from the infinitive.

17 **Don't talk** or **Do not talk**. The negative command needs *do* or it dies.

18 **make**, **keep**. Drop the *to* from each infinitive and you're in imperative mood.

19 **Wish**, **thank**. The imperative verbs are created by subtracting *to* from the infinitives.

20 **Remember**. Somehow I doubt that Henry will forget this fact, but to order him, take *to* from the infinitive.

21 **be**. The subjunctive is needed for this indirect command, expressed by the verb *asked*.

22 **were**. Ellen likes to sleep until mid-afternoon. As she's not a morning person, the subjunctive verb *were* expresses condition-contrary-to-fact. The verb *were* is better than *had been* because Ellen still *is* not a morning person, and *had been* brings in the past.

23 **snows**. Surprise! This one isn't subjunctive. The instructor is talking about a possibility, not a condition that didn't occur. The normal indicative form, *snows,* is what you want.

24 **had covered**. The plow didn't finish (the clue here is *would have passed*), so subjunctive is needed.

25 **be**. An indirect command is created by the verb *declared*. The subjunctive *be* fits nicely.

26 **postpone**. The indicative (the normal, everyday form) of *to postpone* is *postpones,* when the verb is paired with *examiner*. Here the indirect command created by *requested* calls for the subjunctive *postpone*.

27 **had not refused**. The examiner stood firm: Take the test or die. Thus the first part of this sentence is condition-contrary-to-fact and calls for the subjunctive.

28 **had complained**. Ellen said nothing, as revealed by the conditional *would have investigated* in the second part of the sentence. Subjunctive is the way to go!

29 **is**. Did I get you here? The possibility expressed in the *if* portion of the sentence calls for a normal, indicative verb *(is)*. Stay away from subjunctive if the statement may be true.

30 **is**. The first part of this sentence is not condition-contrary-to-fact. It expresses a possibility and thus calls for the normal, indicative verb *(is)*.

31 **had not taken**. She has taken it five times, so the statement isn't true and needs a subjunctive.

32 **goes**. Here the sentence expresses a possibility. She may go and she may have more luck. Stay away from subjunctive if the sentence may be true.

33 **skids**. As in sentence 32, this one talks about something that is true (or may be true). Go for the normal indicative and give the subjunctive a rest.

34 **had traveled**. She didn't travel, and she (thank goodness) doesn't have a license. This condition-contrary-to-fact sentence needs the subjunctive.

35 **demonstrate**. The verb *requires* tips you off to the fact that subjunctive is appropriate for the indirect command.

Progress Report: Coffee Break Control

From: Ms. Bell, Coffee Break Coordinator

To: Ms. Schwartz, Department Head

Re: Coffee Break Control

July 31, 2006

36 As you **know**, I ~~were~~ **am** now in charge of implementing the new directive

37 that every employee ~~submits~~ **submit** to a coffee-residue test. If a test

38 ~~were~~ **is** given at a time when coffee-sipping ~~were~~ **is** not **authorized** and the **40**

39 results ~~were~~ **are** positive, the policy ~~require~~ **requires** that the worker **42**

41 "~~donates~~" "**donate**" a pound of coffee to the break room.

43 **Do not** ~~asked~~ **ask** me to describe the union's reaction to this directive. If I

44 ~~would tell~~ **were to tell** you what the shop steward ~~would have~~ **said**, you **46**

45 ~~had blushed~~ **would blush**. All I ~~would say~~ **will say** is that the steward **48**

47 ~~were~~ **was** not happy.

49 ~~Would~~ **Had** you ~~have~~ **known** about the reaction before issuing the directive,

50 you **would have** ~~had~~ **reconsidered**. One more thing: the coffee stains on

51 my shirt, if they ~~were to~~ **come** out, should not make you ~~thought~~ **think** that I **53**

52 ~~were drinking~~ **drink** coffee outside of the official break time. These stains

54 **result** from coffee being thrown at me.

55

36 Correct.

37 The indicative is called for here because the sentences expresses a truth, not a condition-contrary-to-fact or a command.

38 This part of the sentence expresses an indirect command, *that every employee submit*. The indicative verb that matches the singular subject *every employee* is *submits*, but the subjunctive form *(submit)* is needed here.

39 A normal indicative verb works here because possibility exists.

40 The indicative *is* works best in this sentence, which expresses a real possibility and not a condition-contrary-to-fact.

41 Because the possibility exists, the indicative is called for.

42 This statement is simply a fact, so the indicative is needed.

43 The second part of the sentence is an indirect command (the employee "donate") and needs the subjunctive.

44 The imperative mood, the command, calls for the infinitive minus the *to*. As this is a negative command, *do not* is added. In the original, the *-ed* at the end of *ask* is wrong.

45 The writer is *not* telling, so a subjunctive verb form is needed to express a condition-contrary-to-fact.

46 The report referred to concerns what was actually *said*. Indicative rules!

47 In a sentence expressing a condition-contrary-to-fact, the "untrue" portion should be subjunctive, with the "would" statement in the other part of the sentence. This sentence reverses the proper order (and plops a correct indicative verb, *said,* in the middle). Another possible correction: *Had I told you . . . you would blush*.

48 A plain indicative verb is needed for this statement.

49 The original has a subjunctive *(were)* but indicative is called for in this simple statement.

50 The sentence expresses an untruth, so you need subjunctive. The corrected sentence reads "Had you known about the reaction. . . ."

51 The original has two "would" statements. The "would" doesn't belong in the "untrue" portion of the sentence. Replace the first with a *had* statement and you're in business: *Had you known . . . you would have reconsidered*.

52 This sentence doesn't express a condition-contrary-to-fact. Instead, it talks about a possibility. Go with indicative, not subjunctive.

53 Stay in the indicative present here, not past.

54 Indicative present is needed here.

55 Correct.

Part IV
All You Need to Know about Descriptions and Comparisons

The 5th Wave   By Rich Tennant

COLLECTIVE NOUNS

A LEAK OF PLUMBERS

A FLURRY OF METEOROLOGISTS

A SUCK OF VACUUM CLEANER SALESMEN

A FLATULENCE OF GASTROENTEROLOGISTS

In this part . . .

Listen to a little kid and you hear language at its most basic: *Tommy want apple. Mommy go store? No nap!* These "sentences" — nouns and verbs and little else — communicate effectively, but everyone who's passed the sandbox stage needs a bit more. Enter descriptions and comparisons. Also enter complications, because quite a few common errors are associated with these elements.

In this part you can practice your navigation skills, steering around such pitfalls as the choice between adjectives, adverbs, and articles. (*Sweet* or *sweetly? Good* or *well? A* or *an?* Chapter 14 explains all.) This part also tackles the placement of descriptions (Chapter 15) and the proper way to form comparisons (Chapters 16 and 17). Mastering all these topics lifts you out of the sandbox and places you permanently on the highest grammatical levels.

Chapter 14

Writing Good or Well: Adjectives and Adverbs

In This Chapter

▶ Choosing between adjectives and adverbs

▶ Managing tricky pairs: *good/well* and *bad/badly*

▶ Selecting *a, an,* or *the*

Do you write *good* or *well* — and what's the difference? Does your snack break feature *a apple* or *an apple* or even *the apple?* If you're stewing over these questions, you have problems . . . specifically, the problems in this chapter. Here you can practice choosing between two types of descriptions, adjectives and adverbs. This chapter also helps you figure out whether *a, an,* or *the* is appropriate in any given situation.

Distinguishing Between Adjectives and Adverbs

In your writing or speaking, of course, you don't need to stick labels on adjectives and adverbs. But you do need to send the right word to the right place in order to get the job done, the job being to communicate your meaning to the reader or listener. (You also need to punctuate strings of adjectives and adverbs correctly. For help with that topic, check out Chapter 5.) A few wonderful words (*fast, short, last,* and *likely,* for example) function as both adjectives and adverbs, but for the most part, adjectives and adverbs are *not* interchangeable.

Adjectives describe nouns — words that name a person, thing, place, or idea. They also describe pronouns, which are words that stand in for nouns (*other, someone, they,* and similar words). Adjectives usually precede the word they describe, but not always. In the following sentence, the adjectives are italicized:

> The *rubber* duck with his *lovely orange* bill sailed over the *murky bath* water. (*Rubber* describes *duck; lovely* and *orange* describe *bill; murky* and *bath* describe *water.*)

An adverb, on the other hand, describes a verb, usually telling how, where, when, or why an action took place. Adverbs also indicate the intensity of another descriptive word or add information about another description. In the following sentence, the adverbs are italicized:

> The alligator snapped *furiously* as the duck *violently* flapped his wings. (*Furiously* describes *snapped; violently* describes *flapped.*)

TIP

Most adverbs end in *-ly,* but some adverbs vary, and adjectives can end with any letter in the alphabet, except maybe *Q* or *Z.* If you're not sure which form is an adjective and which is an adverb, check the dictionary. Most definitions include both forms with handy labels telling you what's what.

Here I hit you with a description dilemma: which word is correct? The parentheses contain both an adjective and an adverb. Circle your selection.

Q. The water level dropped (slow/slowly), but the (intense/intensely) alligator-duck quarrel went on and on.

A. **slowly, intense**. How did the water drop? The word you want from the first parentheses must describe an action, so the adverb *slowly* wins the prize. Next up is a description of a *quarrel,* a thing, so the adjective *intense* does the job.

1. The alligator, a (loyal/loyally) member of the Union of Fictional Creatures, (sure/surely) resented the duck's presence near the drainpipe.

2. "How dare you invade my (personal/personally) plumbing?" inquired the alligator (angry/angrily).

3. "You don't have to be (nasty/nastily)!" replied the duck.

4. The two creatures (swift/swiftly) circled each other, both looking for a (clear/clearly) advantage.

5. "You are (extreme/extremely) territorial about these pipes," added the duck.

6. The alligator retreated (fearful/fearfully) as the duck quacked (sharp/sharply).

7. Just then a (poor/poorly) dressed figure appeared in the doorway.

8. The creature whipped out a bullhorn and a sword that was (near/nearly) five feet in length.

9. When he screamed into the bullhorn, the sound bounced (easy, easily) off the tiled walls.

10. "Listen!" he ordered (forceful/forcefully). "The alligator should retreat to the sewer and the duck to the shelf."

11. Having given this order, the (Abominable/Abominably) Snowman seemed (happy/happily).

12. The fight in the bathtub had made him (real/really) angry.

13. "You (sure/surely) can't deny that we imaginary creatures must stick together," explained the Snowman.

14. Recognizing the (accurate/accurately) statement, the duck apologized to the alligator.

15. The alligator retreated to the sewer, where he found a (lovely/lovingly) lizard with an urge to party.

16. "Come (quick/quickly)," the alligator shouted to the duck.

17. The duck left the tub (happy/happily) because he thought he had found a new friend.

18. The alligator also celebrated because he had discovered an enemy (dumb/dumbly) enough to enter the sewer, the alligator's turf.

19. "You go (first/firstly)," murmured the gator, as the duck entered a (particular/particularly) narrow tunnel.

20. The duck waddled (wary/warily), beginning to suspect danger.

21. "You look (worried/worriedly)," said the alligator.

22. The duck was (silent/silently), too frightened to quack.

23. Fortunately, the Snowman had also decided to explore the (winding/windingly) tunnel.

24. The Snowman sounded (angry/angrily) as he scolded the gator.

25. "I've had it!" he screamed. "I'm sealing these (filthy/filthily) pipes for once and for all!"

How's It Going? Choosing Between Good/Well and Bad/Badly

For some reason, the "judgment" adjective and adverb pairs (*good* and *well, bad* and *badly*) cause a lot of trouble. Here's a quick guide on how to use them. *Good* and *bad* are adjectives, so they have to describe nouns (people, places, things, or ideas). *Well* and *badly* are adverbs used to describe action. They also attach to other descriptions. In the expression *a well written essay,* for example, *well* is attached to the word *written,* which describes *essay.*

Well can be an adjective in one particular circumstance: health. When someone asks how you are, the answer (I hope) is *I am well* or *I feel well.* You can also — and I hope you do — feel *good,* especially when you're talking about your mental state, though this usage is a bit more informal. Apart from health questions, however, *well* is a permanent member of the adverb team. In fact, if you can insert the word *healthy* in a particular spot, *well* works in the same spot also.

Check out these judgment words in action:

I gave a good report to the boss this morning. (The adjective *good* describes the noun *report.*)

In my opinion, the report was particularly well written. (The adverb *well* attaches to the verb *written.*)

Truffle, a bad dog, snarfed up an entire bag of kibble this morning. (The adjective *bad* describes the noun *dog.*)

Truffle slept *badly* after his kibble-fest. (The adverb *badly* describes the verb *slept.*)

When a description follows a verb, danger lurks. You have to decide whether the description gives information about the verb or about the person/thing who is doing the action or being. If the description attaches to the verb, go for an adverb. If it attaches to the person/thing (the subject, in grammatical terms), opt for the adjective.

Put on your judge's robes and circle the right word in each set of parentheses.

Q. Truffle's trainer works (good/well) with all types of dogs, especially those that don't outweigh him.

A. **well**. How does the trainer work? The word you need must be an adverb because you're giving information about an action (work), not a noun.

26. Truffle barks when he's run (good/well) during his daily race with the letter carrier, Adam Arbel.

27. The letter carrier likes Truffle and feels (bad/badly) about beating him.

28. Truffle, on the other hand, tends to bite the poor guy whenever the race doesn't turn out (good/well).

29. Truffle's owner named him after a type of chocolate candy she likes very (good/well).

30. The slightly deaf letter carrier thinks high-calorie snacks are (bad/badly).

31. He eats organic sprouts and wheat germ for lunch, though his meal tastes (bad/badly).

32. Truffle once caught a corner of Arbel's lunch bag and chewed off a (good/well) bit.

33. Resisting the urge to barf, Truffle ate (bad/badly), according to his doggie standards.

34. Truffle, who didn't feel (good/well), barked quite a bit that day.

35. Tired of the din, his owner confiscated the kibble and screamed, "(Bad/Badly) dog!"

Mastering the Art of Articles

Three little words — *a, an,* and *the* — pop up in just about every English sentence. Some-times (like my relatives) they show up where they shouldn't. (I probably just blew my Thanksgiving invitation.) Technically, these three words are adjectives, but they belong to the subcategory of articles. As always, forget about the terminology. Just use them properly!

Here's how to tell the difference:

- ✔ *The* refers to something specific. When you say that you want *the book,* you're implying one particular text, even if you haven't named it. *The* attaches nicely to both singular and plural words.

- ✔ *A* and *an* are more general in meaning, and they work only with singular nouns. If you want *a book,* you're willing to read anything, or at least to browse the bookshelves a bit. *A* precedes words beginning with consonants, and *an* comes before words beginning with vowels. In other words, you want *a book* but *an encyclopedia.*

If you want a general term but you're talking about a plural, try *some* or *any* instead of *a* or *an,* because these last two articles can't deal with plurals.

Write an article covering the Miss Grammar Pageant — oops, wrong type of article. Write the correct article in each blank in the sentences that follow.

Q. When Lulu asked to see _____ wedding pictures, she didn't expect Annie to put on _____ twelve-hour slide show.

A. **the**, **a**. In the first half of the sentence, Lulu is asking for something specific. Also, *wedding pictures* is a plural expression, so *a* and *an* are out of the question. In the second half of the sentence, something more general is appropriate. Because *twelve* begins with the consonant *t, a* is the article of choice.

36. Although Lulu was mostly bored out of her mind, she did like _____ picture of Annie's Uncle Fred that caught him snoring in the back of the church.

37. _____ nearby guest, one of several attempting to plug up their ears, can be seen poking Uncle Fred's ribs.

38. At Annie's wedding, Uncle Fred wore _____ antique bow tie that he bought in _____ department store next door to his apartment building.

39. _____ clerk who sold _____ tie to Uncle Fred secretly inserted _____ microphone and _____ miniature radio transmitter.

40. Uncle Fred's snores were broadcast by _____ obscure radio station that specializes in embarrassing moments.

41. Annie, who didn't want to invite Uncle Fred but was forced to do so by her mother, placed _____ buzzer under his seat.

42. Annie's plan was to zap him whenever he snored too loudly; unfortunately, Fred chose _____ different seat.

43. Lulu's sneeze set off the buzzer, whereupon she jumped a foot into _____ air.

44. One of _____ two flower girls, distracted by Lulu's movement, dropped _____ basket of roses that she was supposed to scatter in _____ center aisle.

45. Reverend Foster shortened _____ ceremony in _____ effort to avoid even more trouble.

Calling All Overachievers: Extra Practice with Descriptors

Show off the knowledge you gained from the sections in this chapter by finding the mistakes in this excerpt from a dress catalogue (see Figure 14-1). Twenty descriptive words are underlined, but only some of them are wrong. Look for adjectives trying to do an adverb's job (and vice versa) or the wrong sort of articles. When you find an error, correct it. If the description is okay, leave it alone.

Dollars' Clothing: Fashions That Work

A–D. <u>Surprising</u> <u>comfortably</u> suits for work and leisure. <u>Easily</u>-to-clean polyester in <u>real</u> varied colors goes from the <u>office</u> grind to the <u>extreme</u> <u>bright</u> club scene without a pause!

A. <u>Fast</u> track jacket. Stun your co-workers with <u>a</u> <u>astonishingly</u> elegance of <u>deeply</u> eggplant. <u>Gently</u> curves follow <u>an</u> <u>real</u> natural outline to accentuate your figure. The <u>silkily</u> lining, in <u>delightful</u> loud shades of orange, gives <u>a</u> <u>strong</u> message: I am woman! Hear me roar!

B. <u>Softly</u>, woven pants coordinate with <u>a</u> jacket described above — and with everything in your wardrobe. In eggplant, orange, or eggplant-orange plaid.

Figure 14-1:
Sample dress-catalogue exercise.

Answers to Adjective and Adverb Problems

1 **loyal, surely.** What kind of member is the alligator? A *loyal* member. Because you're describing a noun *(member)*, you need the adjective *loyal*. In the second part of the sentence, the adverb *surely* explains how the duck's presence was *resented*. *Resented* is a verb and must be described by an adverb.

2 **personal, angrily.** In the first part of the sentence, *personal* describes a thing *(plumbing)*. How did the alligator inquire? *Angrily.* The adverb tells about the verb, *inquire*.

3 **nasty.** The adjective *nasty* describes *you*. Of course I don't mean you-the-reader. You earned my undying affection by buying this book. I would never call you nasty!

4 **swiftly, clear.** The adverb *swiftly* describes the action of *circling*. The adjective *clear* explains what kind of *advantage* the creatures were seeking.

5 **extremely.** The adverb *extremely* clarifies the intensity of the descriptive word *territorial*. (If you absolutely have to know, *territorial* is an adjective describing *you*.)

6 **fearfully, sharply.** Both of these adverbs tell how the actions *(retreated* and *quacked)* were performed.

7 **poorly.** The adverb *poorly* gives information about the descriptive word *dressed*.

8 **nearly.** This was a tough question, and if you got it right, treat yourself to a spa day. The expression *five feet* is a description of the *sword*. The adverb *nearly* gives additional information about the description *five feet in length*.

9 **easily.** The adverb *easily* describes the verb *bounced*.

10 **forcefully.** The adverb *forcefully* tells how he *ordered,* a verb.

11 **Abominable, happy.** You can cheat on the first part of this one just by knowing the name of the possibly imaginary monster that supposedly stalks the Himalayas, but you can also figure it out with grammar. A *snowman* is a thing (or a person) and thus a noun. Adjectives describe nouns, so *abominable* does the trick. In the second half you need an adjective to describe the *snowman,* who was *happy.* You aren't describing the action of *seeming,* so an adverb is inappropriate.

12 **really.** This sentence presents a common mistake. The word *angry* is a description; you need an adverb to indicate its intensity, and *really* fills the bill.

13 **surely.** That horse in the fifth race might be a *sure thing,* because *thing* is a noun and you need an adjective to describe it. But the verb *deny* must be described by an adverb, so *surely* is the one you want.

14 **accurate.** *Statement* is a noun because it's a thing. The adjective *accurate* attaches nicely to *statement.*

15 **lovely.** A *lizard* is a noun, which may be described by the adjective *lovely* but not the adverb *lovingly.* Incidentally, *lovely* isn't an adverb, despite the fact that it ends with *-ly.*

16 **quickly.** The adverb *quickly* describes the verb *come.*

17 **happy.** This sentence presents a puzzle. Are you talking about the duck's mood or the way in which he left the tub? The two are related, of course, but the mood is the primary meaning, so the adjective *happy* is the better choice. *Happy,* by the way, describes *duck.*

18 **dumb**. The adjective *dumb* is attached to *enemy*. Most, but not all, adjectives are in front of the words they describe, but in this case the adjective follows the noun.

19 **first, particularly**. The handy, adaptable word *first* functions as both an adjective (*first* prize) and an adverb. In this sentence it's an adverb telling about the verb *go*. The second answer is also an adverb, attached to the descriptive word *narrow*.

20 **warily**. To describe the verb *waddled,* the adverb *warily* is best.

21 **worried**. The description isn't talking about the action of *looking* but rather describing *you*. The pronoun *you* may be described only by an adjective, so *worried* wins the prize here.

22 **silent**. This adjective describes the noun *duck*. The verb in between is a linking verb, which may be thought of as a giant equal sign linking (how clever are these grammar terms!) the noun and its description.

23 **winding**. As the Beatles once sang, you have to travel "a long and winding road" to this answer. The adjective *winding* is attached to the noun *tunnel*.

24 **angry**. The adjective *angry* tells you about the Snowman. You're not describing the action *(sounded)* but instead the person doing the action *(the Snowman)*. In this sentence, the verb *sounded* is a stand-in for *was,* which is a linking verb that connects what precedes and follows it *(Snowman and angry)*.

25 **filthy**. If you're describing *pipes,* a thing and therefore a noun, you need an adjective, which in this case is *filthy*.

26 **well**. The adverb *well* tells you how Truffle *has run*.

27 **bad**. This sentence illustrates a common mistake. The description doesn't tell you anything about Truffle's ability to *feel* (touching sensation). Instead, it tells you about the letter carrier's state of mind. Because the word is a description of a person, not of an action, you need an adjective, *bad*. To feel *badly* implies that you're wearing mittens and can't *feel* anything through the thick cloth.

28 **well**. The adverb *well* is attached to the action *to turn out* (to result).

29 **well**. How does she like chocolate truffles? Almost as much as I do! Also, she *likes* them *well*. The adverb is needed because you're describing the verb *likes*.

30 **bad**. The description *bad* applies to the *snacks,* not to the verb *are*. Hence, an adjective is what you want.

31 **bad**. The description tells you about his *meal,* a noun (also a truly terrible combination of foods). You need the adjective *bad*.

32 **good**. The adjective *(good)* is attached to a noun *(bit)*.

33 **badly**. Now you're talking about the action *(ate),* so you need an adverb *(badly)*.

34 **well**. The best response here is *well,* an adjective that works for health-status statements. *Good* will do in a pinch, but *good* is better for psychological or mood statements.

35 **Bad**. The adjective *bad* applies to the noun *dog*.

36 **the**. The sentence implies that one particular picture caught Annie's fancy, so *the* works nicely here. If you chose *a,* no problem. The sentence would be a bit less specific but still acceptable. The only true clinker is *an,* which must precede words beginning with vowels — a group that doesn't include *picture*.

37 **A.** Because the sentence tells you that several guests are nearby, *the* doesn't fit here. The more general *a* is best.

38 **an** or **the**, **the**. In the first blank you may place either *an* (which must precede a word beginning with a vowel) or *the*. In the second blank, *the* is best because it's unlikely that Fred is surrounded by several department stores. *The* is more definitive, pointing out one particular store.

39 **The, the, a, a.** Lots of blanks in this one! The first two seem more particular (one clerk, one tie), so *the* fits well. The second two blanks imply that the clerk selected one from a group of many, not a particular microphone or transmitter. The more general article is *a*, which precedes words beginning with consonants.

40 **an**. Because the radio station is described as *obscure*, a word beginning with a vowel, you need *an*, not *a*. If you inserted *the*, don't cry. That article works here also.

41 **a**. The word *buzzer* doesn't begin with a vowel, so you have to go with *a*, not *an*. The more definite *the* could work, implying that the reader knows that you're talking about a particular buzzer, not just any buzzer.

42 **a**. He chose any old seat, not a particular one, so *a* is what you want.

43 **the**. There's only one air, so *the*, which is more specific, is what you need.

44 **the, a, the**. In the first and third blanks in this sentence, you're discussing particulars, so *the* fills the bill. In the middle blank, the more general article works well.

45 **the, an**. Because only one wedding ceremony is in question here, *the* does the job for the first blank. In the second blank, he's making *an effort*. The vowel in *effort* requires *an*, not *a*.

Dollars' Clothing: Fashions That Work

46 **47** **48** **49** **50** **52** **51**

A–D. ~~Surprising~~ **Surprisingly** ~~comfortably~~ **comfortable** suits for work and leisure. ~~Easily~~ **Easy**-to-clean polyester in ~~real~~ **really** varied colors goes from the **office** grind to the ~~extreme~~ **extremely** **bright** club scene without a pause!

53 **54** **55** **56** **57** **59** **58** **61** **60** **63** **62**

A. **Fast** track jacket. Stun your co-workers with ~~a~~ **the** ~~astonishingly~~ **astonishing** elegance of ~~deeply~~ **deep** eggplant. ~~Gently~~ **Gentle** curves follow ~~an~~ ~~a~~ ~~real~~ **really** natural outline to accentuate your figure. The ~~silkily~~ **silky** lining, in ~~delightful~~ **delightfully** loud shades of orange, gives **a strong** message: I am woman! Hear me roar!

64 **65**

B. ~~Softly~~ **Soft**, woven pants coordinate with ~~a~~ **the** jacket described above — and with everything in your wardrobe. In eggplant, orange, or eggplant-orange plaid.

46 The description *comfortable* must be intensified by the adverb *surprisingly*, not by the adjective *surprising*.

47 The adjective *comfortable* describes the noun *suits*.

48 *Polyester* is a noun, so it must be described by an adjective. *Easy*, which is part of the combo description *easy-to-clean*, attaches nicely to the noun.

49 The description *varied* is intensified by the adverb *really*.

50 In this sentence *office* is an adjective describing *grind*, a noun here.

51 The adverb *extremely* intensifies the descriptive word *bright*.

52 The adjective *bright* describes the *club scene*, a noun.

53 That wonderful word *fast* may be either an adjective or an adverb. Here it functions as an adjective describing *track*.

54 A particular sort of elegance is being discussed, so the definitive *the* is called for.

55 *Elegance* is a noun, so the adjective *astonishing* is the best description.

56 *Eggplant* is a color, which is a thing and therefore a noun. To describe a noun, the adjective *deep* is needed.

57 To describe the noun *curves*, go for the adjective *gentle*, not the adverb *gently*.

58 *An* can only precede words beginning with vowels, and *real* begins with a consonant.

59 *Natural* is a descriptive word, so it must itself be described by an adverb, *really*.

60 The noun *lining* is described by the adjective *silky*.

61 The adverb *delightfully* attaches to another description, *loud*. Descriptions are always described by adverbs, not by adjectives.

62 The article *a* is the one you need to precede a word beginning with a consonant.

63 The adjective *strong* describes the noun *message*.

64 Did I fool you here? True, you may have thought that *softly* described *woven* in this sentence, but the meaning indicates otherwise. You're not talking about how the cloth was woven. Instead, you have two separate words (the comma clues you in on this) describing the noun *pants. Soft* is an adjective, appropriate for noun descriptions.

65 Clearly you're talking about one particular item, the extremely ugly jacket described as item A. Hence *the*, which goes well with particulars, is better than the more general *a*.

Chapter 15

Going on Location: Placing Descriptions Correctly

● ●

In This Chapter
▶ Placing *even, only, almost,* and similar words
▶ Avoiding misplaced, dangling, or confusing descriptions

● ●

My out-of-town friends always tell me that I can buy a ten-room mansion for the price of a closet in New York City. My standard reply is that location is everything. That statement is as true for descriptive words as it is for home prices. Plop one in the wrong spot, and your meaning may sink like a stone.

First, some definitions: Descriptions in English may be composed of one word or, if you like to pour it on, twenty or more. Regardless of length or form, descriptive elements fall into one of two huge categories. They belong in the *adjective* bin if they describe people, places, things, or ideas (in grammar terms, nouns or pronouns). The *adverb* family claims them if they describe verbs (action or being words) or other descriptions. Flip to Chapter 14 for a host of practice exercises with basic adjectives and adverbs.

The general principle guiding the placement of descriptions is simple: Descriptive words should clearly relate to what they describe. Some sentences give you a bit more leeway than others. Move a descriptive word an inch and the meaning still comes across. But a few words require precision.

In this chapter you can practice that precision and, like a real estate agent, concentrate on location, location, location.

Little Words Mean a Lot: Situating "Even," "Only," and Similar Words

The other day I saw a tee shirt that made me want to turn my grammar book into a guided missile. The shirt declared that *My Grandma went to NYC and only bought me this lousy tee shirt.* Why, as a founding member of Grammarians Anonymous, was I upset? Because the descriptive term *only* was misplaced. The sentence as written means that Grandma did nothing at all in NYC except buy one tee shirt — no theater, no walk in Central Park — just tee-shirt buying.

Little words — *only, even, almost, just, nearly,* and *not* — will torpedo the meaning of your sentence if you put them in the wrong spot. Each of these descriptions should precede the word being described. Take a look at these examples:

Even Mary knows that song. (Mary generally sticks to talk radio, but the song is so popular that she recognizes it.)

Mary knows *even* that song. (Mary has 56,098 CDs. She knows every musical work ever written, including the one that the sentence is referring to.)

Got the idea? Now take a look at the following sentences. If you find a misplaced description, rewrite the sentence as it should be. If everything is fine and dandy, write "correct" in the blank.

0. My Uncle Fred only pays taxes when he's in the mood or when the IRS serves an arrest warrant.

_____

_____

A. **My Uncle Fred pays taxes only when he's in the mood or when the IRS serves an arrest warrant.** The *only* has to move because it makes a comment on the conditions that make Fred pay up (his mood and the times when the IRS puts him in the mood). This description should precede the conditions it talks about. The *only* is not a comment on *pays,* so it's out of place in the original.

1. Because she was celebrating an important birthday, Ms. Jonge only gave us ten hours of homework.

_____

_____

2. The first task nearly seemed impossible: to write an essay about the benefits of getting older.

_____

_____

3. After I had almost written two pages, my instant message beeped and I put my pen down.

_____

_____

4. I even figured that Ms. Jonge, the meanest teacher on the planet, would understand the need to take a break.

_____

_____

5. I made a cup of coffee, but because I'm dieting, I only ate one doughnut and ignored the other three that were silently shouting, "Eat me."

_____

_____

6. My friend Eloise nearly gained three pounds last week just from eating glazed doughnuts.

_____

_____

7. Eloise, my brother, and I love doughnuts, but all of us do not eat them; Eloise can't resist.

_____

_____

8. Eloise even draws the line somewhere, and she seldom munches a chocolate sprinkle outside of homework time.

_____

_____

9. After I had sent a text message to Eloise, I returned to my homework and found I only had five tasks left.

_____

_____

10. Not all the work was boring, and I actually liked the history assignment.

_____

_____

11. I had to read two chapters about an empire that almost covered half the known world.

_____

_____

12. The conquerors even invaded countries that had superb defense systems.

_____

_____

13. The next day I was surprised to hear Ms. Jonge comment that she had almost assigned seven chapters before changing her mind.

_____

_____

14. "I nearly love all children, except those who fight or scribble on their homework, and I wanted to celebrate my birthday with a homework holiday," she said.

_____

_____

15. I was startled to hear that Ms. Jonge considers ten hours of homework a holiday, but I know that she only wants what's best for us.

_____

_____

It Must Be Here Somewhere! Misplaced Descriptions

If you're at a car dealership and want to buy *a new car from a sales associate with snow tires,* you're in the right place. Unfortunately, the description — *with snow tires* — is not, because its current placement attaches it to *sales associate* and thus indicates a car guy whose feet have been replaced by big round rubber things, not a vehicle you can drive confidently through a storm.

This section deals with long descriptions (for the grammar obsessed: prepositional phrases, verbals, and clauses) that sometimes stray from their appointed path. I cover short descriptions — simple adjectives and adverbs — in Chapter 14. To keep your descriptions legal, be sure that they're very close to the word they describe.

Except for a few place or time descriptions, nearly every multiword description directly follows the word it describes, as in these sentences:

> I want to buy a car *with snow tires* from a sales associate. (The description *with snow tires* describes *car.*)

> The bread *that Lulu baked yesterday* is as hard as the rock of Gibraltar. (*That Lulu baked yesterday* refers to *bread.*)

> The leaf *shimmering in the sunlight* bothers Jeff's light-sensitive eyes. (The expression *shimmering in the sunlight* describes the *leaf.*)

These descriptions quickly become absurd if they move slightly. (Imagine the sentence, *The bread is as hard as the rock of Gibraltar that Lulu baked yesterday.* See what I mean?)

When you move a misplaced description, take care not to make another error. For example, if I change *I placed a stone in my pocket that I found in the playground* to *I placed a stone that I found in the playground in my pocket,* I have a problem. In the original sentence, I found the pocket in the playground. In the changed sentence, I have a playground in my pocket. The solution is to place a description at the beginning of the sentence: *In my pocket I placed a stone that I found in the playground.*

Check out the following sentences. If all the descriptions are where they should be, write "correct" in the blank. If anything is misplaced, rewrite the sentence in the blanks provided, dropping the description into the right spot. *Tip:* In addition to moving descriptions, you may have to reword here and there in order to create a sentence that makes sense.

Q. Even before she passed the road test, Julie bought a leather license holder that was given only twice a month.

_____

_____

A. **Even before she passed the road test that was given only twice a month, Julie bought a leather license holder.** The license holder is available all the time in a leather goods store, but the test shows up only twice a month. Move the description closer to *test* and you're all set.

16. Julie passed the eye examination administered by a very near-sighted clerk with flying colors.

_____

_____

17. The written test inquired about maneuvers for cars skidding on ice.

_____

_____

18. Another question inquired about defensive driving, which required an essay rather than a multiple-choice response.

_____

_____

19. About a week after the written portion of the exam, the Department of Motor Vehicles sent a letter giving Julie an appointment for the road test lacking sufficient postage.

_____

_____

20. Julie asked her sister to drive her to the testing site before the letter arrived.

_____

_____

21. Julie's examiner, a nervous man whose foot kept slamming onto an imaginary brake pedal, constantly wrote notes on an official form.

_____

_____

22. The first page contained details about Julie's turning technique, which was single-spaced.

_____

_____

23. Julie hit only two pedestrians and one tree in the middle of a crosswalk.

_____

_____

24. The examiner relaxed soon after Julie's road test in his aunt's house in Florida.

   _____

   _____

25. Julie wasn't surprised to hear that she had failed her first road test, but the pedestrians' lawsuit was a shock because the examiner had fainted when the speedometer hit 80.

   _____

   _____

Hanging off a Cliff: Dangling Descriptions

The most common structure in an English sentence is subject (the person or thing you're talking about) and verb (a statement of being or action about the subject), in that order. This structure is a good workhorse to carry your meaning to the reader, but it's a bit boring if overused. To spice up your writing, you may begin some sentences with extra information — introductory descriptions that may resemble verbs but not actually be verbs. (In official grammar terminology, they're verbals. Verbals can show up elsewhere in the sentence; in this section I'm just dealing with those that introduce sentences.) Usually a comma separates these introductory statements from the main portion of the sentence. Here are a couple of examples, with the introductory description italicized:

> *Dazzled by the reflection from Tiffany's new diamond ring,* Lulu reached for her sunglasses. (The introductory description gives more information about *Lulu.*)

> *To block out all visible light,* Lulu's glasses have been coated with a special plastic film. (The introductory description gives more information about the *glasses.*)

A variation of this sort of introduction is a statement with an implied subject:

> *While wearing these glasses,* Lulu can see nothing at all and thus constantly walks into walls. (The implied statement is *While Lulu is wearing these glasses.*)

All these introductory elements must follow one important rule: The subject of the sentence must be what the introduction describes. In the preceding examples, *Lulu* is the one who is *dazzled, Lulu's glasses* are what *blocks out light,* and *Lulu* is the one who is *wearing* the sunglasses.

A common error is to detach the introduction from the subject, resulting in a sentence with flawed logic, what grammarians call a *dangling modifier* or simply a *dangler.* (English thoughtfully supplies you with plenty of room for error. Here I deal with faulty descriptions at the beginning of a sentence. If you want to avoid misplaced descriptions elsewhere in the sentence, check out the preceding section on misplaced description.) Here are some dangers:

> *Perched on her nose,* the stop sign was invisible to Lulu's eyes.

> *Before buying them,* the glasses carried a clear warning, which Lulu ignored.

In the first preceding sentence the *stop sign* is on *her nose* — not a pretty picture and also not what the writer is trying to say. In the second sample sentence, the expansion of the sentence would read *Before the glasses were buying them.* Illogical! These corrections tie up the danglers:

Perched on her nose, Lulu's glasses made the stop sign invisible.

Before buying them, Lulu read a warning about the glasses and chose to ignore it.

Check out these sentences for danglers and rewrite if necessary. If everything is securely attached, write "correct" in the blank. Your rewritten sentence may differ from the suggested answer. No problem, as long as the introductory information refers to the subject.

O. After waiting for a green light, the crosswalk filled with people rushing to avoid Lulu and her speeding skateboard.

_____

_____

A. After waiting for a green light, people rushed into the crosswalk to avoid Lulu and her speeding skateboard. In the original sentence, the *crosswalk* is *waiting for a green light.* The rewritten sentence has the *people waiting* for an escape hatch from the sidewalk, where Lulu is riding blind, thanks to her non-see-through sunglasses.

26. To skateboard safely, kneepads help.

_____

_____

27. Sliding swiftly across the sidewalk, a tree smashed into Lulu.

_____

_____

28. Although bleeding from a cut near her nose ring, a change of sunglasses was out of the question.

_____

_____

29. To look fashionable, a certain amount of sacrifice is necessary.

_____

_____

30. While designing her latest tattoo, a small camera attached to the frames of her glasses seemed like a good idea.

_____

_____

31. Covered in rhinestones, Lulu made a fashion statement with her glasses.

_____

_____

32. Discussed in the fashion press, many articles criticized Lulu's choice of eyewear.

_____

_____

33. Coming to the rescue, Tiffany swiped the offending glasses and lectured Lulu on the irrelevance of such fashion statements.

_____

_____

34. To pacify Tiffany and the pedestrians' lawyers, the glasses eventually went into the trash can.

_____

_____

35. Being reasonable, Lulu opted for a wraparound stainless steel helmet with UV protection.

_____

_____

Dazed and Confused: Vague Descriptions

If you've read the previous sections in this chapter, you already know that the general rule governing descriptions is that they should be near the word they're describing. If you place a description an equal distance from two words it may describe, however, you present a puzzle to your reader. Not a good idea! Check out this beauty:

> Protesting successfully scares politicians.

Which word does _successfully_ describe? _Protesting_ or _scares?_ You can't tell. Now look at these corrections:

> Successful protests scare politicians.

> Protests scare politicians successfully.

Which one should you use? It depends on what you want to say. The point is that each of these sentences is clear, and clarity is a great quality in writing, if not in politics.

Check out the following sentences and decide whether they're clear or unclear. If they're clear, write "correct" in the blanks. If not, rewrite them.

_Q._ The senator speaking last week voted against the Clarity Bill.

_____

_____

A. **The senator speaking voted against the Clarity Bill last week.** Or, **The senator who spoke last week is the one who voted against the Clarity Bill.** You may find still other variations. As long as your sentence indicates whether *last week* is attached to *speaking* or *voted*, you're fine.

36. Running a red light once earned a stiff fine.

_____

_____

37. Backing away from the traffic cop swiftly caused a reaction.

_____

_____

38. The ticket he got last summer was a blot on his spotless driving record.

_____

_____

39. The judge said when the case came to trial he would punish the drivers severely.

_____

_____

40. The warden of the driving-infraction division soon arrived on the scene.

_____

_____

41. Speaking to the driver forcefully made the point.

_____

_____

42. The driver charged with reckless driving recently went to court.

_____

_____

43. The driver education course redesigned a year ago won an award.

_____

_____

Calling All Overachievers: Extra Practice Placing Descriptions

Breathing deeply, check out this yoga instruction manual (see Figure 15-1), which, my lawyer begs me to mention, does *not* describe real postures that a normal human body can achieve. Do *not* try these positions at home, but *do* look for ten errors caused by vague, misplaced, or dangling descriptions. After you find the clunkers, correct them — cross out misplaced words, insert words by using carats, and revise sentences in the margins of this book. *Note:* The errors have several possible corrections, but in the answers section, I show only one correction for each error.

Figure 15-1:
Sample
instruction
manual
exercise.

Yoga and Y'all: An Excerpt

If you only learn one yoga posture, this should be it. Beginners can even do it. To form the "Greeting Turtle Posture," the mat should extend from knees to armpits freshly laundered and dried to fluffiness. While bending the right knee up to the nose, the left ankle relaxes. You should almost bend the knee for a minute before straightening it again. Throw your head back now extending each muscle to its fullest, only breathing two or three times before returning the head to its original position. Tucking the chin close to the collarbone, the nose should wiggle. Finally, raise the arms to the sky and bless the yoga posture that is blue.

Answers to Description Placement Problems

1 **Because she was celebrating an important birthday, Ms. Jonge gave us only ten hours of homework.** The implication of this sentence is that she could have given twenty hours. Because the number of hours is the issue, the *only* belongs in front of *ten hours,* not in front of *gave.*

2 **The first task seemed nearly impossible: to write an essay about the benefits of getting older.** If it *nearly seemed,* it did not *seem* — just approached that state. But that's not what you're trying to say here. Instead, the task approached *impossible* but stopped just short, still in the realm of possibility. Thus the *nearly* describes *impossible* and should precede that word.

3 **After I had written almost two pages, my instant message beeped and I put my pen down.** How many pages did you write? That's what the sentence discusses. When the *almost* is in the right place, you have about a page and a half or a bit more. In the original sentence, you have nothing at all on paper because the sentence says that the speaker *had almost written* (had approached the action of writing but then stopped).

4 **I figured that even Ms. Jonge, the meanest teacher on the planet, would understand the need to take a break.** Clearly the sentence compares this particular teacher with all others, so the *even* belongs in front of her name.

5 **I made a cup of coffee, but because I'm dieting, I ate only one doughnut and ignored the other three that were silently shouting, "Eat me."** This sentence compares the number of doughnuts eaten (one) with the number available (four). The *only* belongs in front of the number, not in front of the action (ate).

6 **My friend Eloise gained nearly three pounds last week just from eating glazed doughnuts.** One word — *just* — is in the appropriate place, but *nearly* must be moved. The *nearly* tells you that the gain was a bit less than three, and the *just* tells you the reason (snarfing down doughnuts).

7 **Eloise, my brother, and I love doughnuts, but not all of us eat them; Eloise can't resist.** To correct this sentence you have to play around with the verb a little, because you don't need the *do* in the new sentence. Here's the logic: If Eloise eats the doughnuts and the rest keep their lips zipped, *not all* but *some* eat doughnuts. The original sentence illogically states that no one eats and then goes on to discuss Eloise's gobbling.

8 **Even Eloise draws the line somewhere, and she seldom munches a chocolate sprinkle outside of homework time.** The *even* shouldn't precede *draws* because two actions aren't being compared. Instead, *Eloise* is being singled out.

9 **After I had sent a text message to Eloise, I returned to my homework and found I had only five tasks left.** The sentence comments on the amount of remaining homework (*only five tasks,* not six or seven). Hence the *only* properly precedes *five tasks.*

10 **correct.** Some work made you yawn and some didn't. Logic tells you that *not all* is what you want.

11 **I had to read two chapters about an empire that covered almost half the known world.** If the chapters *almost covered,* they didn't *cover* at all, they just approached the act of covering. If the empire covered *almost half,* it spread over maybe 40 to 45 percent *of the known world,* a much more logical meaning.

12 **The conquerors invaded even countries that had superb defense systems.** They're willing to go up against the best (countries with superb defenses), and that's where the *even* belongs. In front of the verb, you get an implied comparison of action (*even invaded,* didn't just threaten).

13   **correct**. In this one Ms. Jonge _almost assigned_ but then changed her mind. She didn't assign, say, the first five chapters and half of the sixth.

14   **"I love nearly all children, except those who fight or scribble on their homework, and I wanted to celebrate my birthday with a homework holiday," she said.** Whom does she love? _Nearly all,_ with some notable exceptions. If _nearly love_ is what she does, then she feels affection that never reaches the level of love. Because the sentence compares _all children_ with _all children_ minus a few clinkers, the _nearly_ belongs in front of _all._

15   **I was startled to hear that Ms. Jonge considers ten hours of homework a holiday, but I know that she wants only what's best for us.** If she _only wants,_ she doesn't do anything else — just _wants._ But this sentence implies a comparison between _only what's best for us_ and water torture. Thus the _only_ belongs in front of _what's best for us._

16   **With flying colors, Julie passed the eye examination administered by a very near-sighted clerk.** You can easily see what's wrong with the original sentence. Fixing it can be tricky. If you move _with flying colors_ so that it follows _examination,_ you solve one problem and create another because then the _colors_ are _administered by a very near-sighted clerk._ You can place _with flying colors,_ as I have, at the beginning of the sentence or, if you wish, after _passed._ In either spot the description is close enough to the verb to tell you how _Julie passed,_ and that's the meaning you want.

17   **correct**. The two descriptions, _written_ and _for cars skidding on ice,_ are close to the words they describe. _Written_ describes _test_ and _for cars skidding on ice_ describes _maneuvers._

18   **Another question, which required an essay rather than a multiple-choice response, inquired about defensive driving.** Defensive driving techniques don't include essays, but test questions do. The description belongs after _question_ because that's the word being described.

19   **About a week after the written portion of the exam, the Department of Motor Vehicles sent a letter lacking sufficient postage and giving Julie an appointment for the road test.** The _letter_ is described by _lacking sufficient postage,_ so that description must follow _letter._ I inserted _and_ after _postage_ to clarify that the letter, not the postage, gave Julie her appointment. The _and_ attaches both expressions _(lacking sufficient postage, giving Julie an appointment for the road test)_ to the same word, _letter._ Another possible correction drops _lacking sufficient postage_ and inserts _postage-due_ before _letter._

20   **Before the letter arrived, Julie asked her sister to drive her to the testing site.** This sentence mentions two actions: _asked_ and _drive._ The time element, _before the letter arrived,_ tells you when Julie asked, not when she wanted her sister to drive. The description should be closer to _asked_ than to _drive_ because _asked_ is the word it describes.

21   **correct**. The description is where it should be. The information about the examiner's foot is near _nervous man,_ and he's the one with the fidgety foot.

22   **The first page, which was single-spaced, contained details about Julie's turning technique.** The _page_ is described by _single-spaced,_ not Julie's three-point turn, which always sends her into a skid.

23   **Julie hit only two pedestrians in the middle of a crosswalk and one tree.** Common sense tells you that the tree isn't in the crosswalk, but the pedestrians are. The description _in the middle of a crosswalk_ should follow the word it describes, in this case, _pedestrians._

24   **The examiner relaxed in his aunt's house in Florida soon after Julie's road test.** I'm sure he needed a break! The relaxing took place _in his aunt's house in Florida._ The road test took place on Route 9. Move the description closer to the word it describes.

25 **Because the examiner had fainted when the speedometer hit 80, Julie wasn't surprised to hear that she had failed her first road test, but the pedestrians' lawsuit was a shock.** The *because* statement should be closer to *was not surprised,* as that expression is being described. You may have been tempted to move *because the examiner had fainted when the speedometer hit 80* to the spot after *test.* Bad idea! If you put the *because* information after *test,* it looks as if she failed *because the examiner had fainted.* Yes, the examiner fainted, but the *because* information relates to Julie's lack of surprise and thus needs to be near *was not surprised.*

26 **To skateboard safely, you may find kneepads helpful.** In the original sentence, no one is skateboarding. A person must be inserted into the sentence. I've chosen *you,* but *skaters, people,* and other terms are also okay, as long as some sort of potential skater is in the sentence.

27 **Sliding swiftly across the sidewalk, Lulu smashed into a tree.** Lulu should be the one doing the *sliding,* not the tree, but the original sentence has the tree sliding across the sidewalk.

28 **Although Lulu was bleeding from a cut near her nose ring, a change of sunglasses was out of the question.** The original sentence has *a change of sunglasses bleeding.* The easiest way to correct a sentence with the wrong implied subject is to insert the real subject, which is *Lulu.* Another correct revision: **Although bleeding from a cut near her nose ring, Lulu said that a change of sunglasses was out of the question.** Now Lulu is doing the bleeding, a common state for her.

29 **To look fashionable, one must sacrifice a certain amount.** Who is looking fashionable? In the original sentence, no one. Add a person: *one, you, everybody,* or something similar.

30 **While designing her latest tattoo, Lulu thought it would be a good idea to attach a small camera to the frames of her glasses.** Lulu has to be doing the designing, but in the original sentence, *a small camera* is *designing her latest tattoo.* Another way to correct this sentence is to insert *Lulu* into the first part of the sentence, making her the subject: *While Lulu was designing . . . .*

31 **Covered in rhinestones, Lulu's glasses made a fashion statement.** Lulu's glasses are covered in rhinestones, not Lulu herself. *Lulu's glasses* must be the subject of the sentence.

32 **Discussed in the fashion press, Lulu's choice of eyewear was criticized in many articles.** What was discussed? The eyewear, not the articles.

33 **correct**. Tiffany's *coming to the rescue,* so the sentence is fine.

34 **To pacify Tiffany and the pedestrians' lawyers, Lulu eventually threw the glasses into the trash can.** The *glasses* can't *pacify,* but *Lulu* can.

35 **correct**. Okay, it's a stretch to see *Lulu* as *reasonable,* not to mention the discomfort of a *stainless steel helmet,* but grammatically this sentence is correct.

36 Several corrections are possible. Two examples: **A single red-light infraction earned a stiff fine. Running a red light earned a stiff fine at one time.** The problem word is *once,* which must be more clearly attached to either *running* or *earned.* Here you have to reword and drop the *once* in order to be perfectly clear whether you're talking about *at one time* or *a single time,* both of which are meanings of *once.*

37 Several corrections are possible. Two examples: **Backing swiftly away from the traffic cop caused a reaction. Backing away from the traffic cop caused a swift reaction.** Here *swiftly* causes problems unless it is moved closer to *backing* or, changed to *swift,* it describes *reaction.*

38 **correct**. It's hard to imagine that anyone would hear this sentence and attach *last summer* to *was.* This one passes the clarity test.

39 Several corrections are possible. Two examples: **When the case came to trial, the judge said that he would punish the drivers severely. The judge said that he would punish the drivers severely when the case came to trial.** The problem with the original is subtle but nevertheless worthy of attention. The expression *when the case came to trial* may be when the judge made his statement or when the judge intended to wallop the drivers. Move the expression and clarity reigns.

40 **correct**. The description *soon* can describe only *arrived*. The word preceding the description, *division,* doesn't logically attach to a time element, so the sentence is okay as written.

41 Several corrections are possible. Two examples: **Speaking forcefully to the driver made the point. Speaking to the driver made the point forcefully.** The problem with the original is that *forcefully* could describe either *speaking* or *made*. To clarify the meaning, you have to move *forcefully* closer to one of those words.

42 Several corrections are possible. Two examples: **The driver recently charged with reckless driving went to court. The driver charged with reckless driving went to court recently.** *Recently* is a description that, like all descriptions, likes to nestle next to the word it describes. If you place it between two possible descriptions, it has a nervous breakdown.

43 Several corrections are possible. Two examples: **The redesigned driver education course won an award a year ago. The driver education course was redesigned a year ago and has won an award.** The problem with the original sentence is that *a year ago,* placed between *redesigned* and *won,* could describe either. Fixing this one is a bit tricky; you have to reword to express a clear meaning.

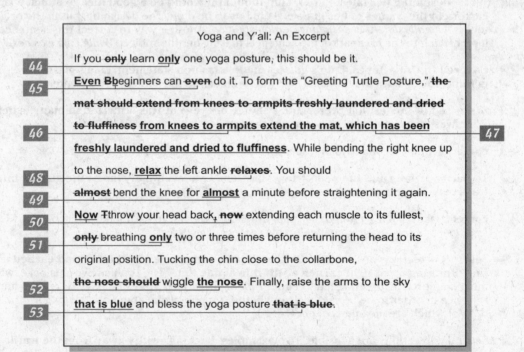

Yoga and Y'all: An Excerpt

44 If you ~~only~~ learn **only** one yoga posture, this should be it.

45 **Even B**~~b~~eginners can ~~even~~ do it. To form the "Greeting Turtle Posture," ~~the~~

~~mat should extend from knees to armpits freshly laundered and dried~~

46 ~~to fluffiness~~ **from knees to armpits extend the mat, which has been** **47**

freshly laundered and dried to fluffiness. While bending the right knee up

to the nose, **relax** the left ankle ~~relaxes~~. You should

48

49 ~~almost~~ bend the knee for **almost** a minute before straightening it again.

50 **Now T**~~t~~hrow your head back**,** ~~now~~ extending each muscle to its fullest,

51 ~~only~~ breathing **only** two or three times before returning the head to its

original position. Tucking the chin close to the collarbone,

52 ~~the nose should~~ wiggle **the nose**. Finally, raise the arms to the sky

53 **that is blue** and bless the yoga posture ~~that is blue~~.

44 The description *only* applies to the number, not to the act of learning.

45 The description *even* is attached to *beginners* to show how easy this posture is.

46 The sentence begins with a verb form (To form the "Greeting Turtle Posture"), so the subject of the sentence must be the person who is supposed to do this ridiculous exercise. In the corrected sentence, an understood "you" fills that need.

47 The laundry description belongs to *mat,* not to *armpits,* though I do think fluffy armpits are nice.

48 In the original sentence the subject of *bending* is implied, not stated, so by default, the other subject in the sentence (*the left ankle*) takes that role. But the *left ankle* can't bend the right knee, so the logic is flawed. Changing the second half of the sentence to "relax the left ankle" makes the subject you (understood), and "you" works as the understood subject you want for the first half of the sentence. Another possible solution: Change the first half of the sentence to "While you are bending. . . ."

49 The description *almost* applies to *minute,* not to *bending*.

50 In the original sentence *now* is equidistant from *throw* and *extending,* creating a vague statement. Moving the description clarifies the meaning. Once you move *now,* add a comma between *back* and *extending* to help the reader separate these two actions.

51 The description *only* applies to the number of times one should breathe, not to the number of actions one should be doing.

52 The introductory verb form must be an action done by the subject, and the *nose* can't *tuck the chin.* The understood subject *you* can *tuck the chin.*

53 The color description belongs to *sky,* not to *yoga posture.* Another, more concise correction is to delete "that is blue" and simply say, "blue sky."

Chapter 16

For Better or Worse: Forming Comparisons

In This Chapter

▶ Creating the comparative and superlative forms of adjectives and adverbs

▶ Dealing with irregular comparisons

▶ Identifying absolutes that may not be compared

Does Nellie have a *bigger* ice cream cone? Whose cold is *worse?* Do you think Tom Cruise is the *most attractive, strongest,* and *richest* star in Hollywood? If human beings weren't so tempted to compare their situations with others', then life — and grammar — would be a lot easier.

Comparisons may be expressed by one word *(higher, farther,* or *sooner)* or two words *(more beautiful, most annoying,* or *least sensible).* Sometimes many words are needed *(taller than any other Lincoln impersonator* or *as much electricity as Con Edison).* I deal with extended comparisons in Chapter 17. In this chapter you get to practice creating and placing one- or two-word comparisons that make your meaning come through loud and clear (Oops! What I meant was *more loudly* and *more clearly).*

Visiting the -ER (And the -EST): Creating Comparisons

Adjectives (words that describe people, places, things, or ideas) and adverbs (describing actions, states of being, or other descriptions) are the basis of comparisons. Regular unadorned adjectives and adverbs are the base upon which two types of comparisons may be made: the *comparative* and the *superlative.* Comparatives *(dumber, smarter, neater, more interesting, less available,* and the like) deal with only two elements. *Superlatives (dumbest, smartest, neatest, most interesting, least available,* and so forth) identify the extreme in a group of three or more. To create comparisons, follow these guidelines:

✔ **Tack *-er* onto the end of a one-syllable descriptive word to create a comparative form showing a greater or more intense quality.** For descriptions of more than one syllable, the *-er* may sound awkward. Generally, comparatives of long words are created by tacking *more* onto the description. For a comparative that shows inferiority, use *less.*

✔ **Glue *-est* to one-syllable words to make a superlative that expresses superiority.** *Most* does the trick for most longer words. Superlatives expressing inferiority are created with the word *least.*

✔ **Check the dictionary if you're not sure of the correct form.** The entry for the plain adjective or adverb normally includes the comparative and superlative forms, if they're single words. If you don't see a listing for another form of the word, take the *less/more, least/most* option.

As you may have guessed, a few comparatives and superlatives are irregular. I discuss these in the next section, "Going from Bad to Worse (and Good to Better): Irregular Comparisons."

Ready for some comparison shopping? Insert the comparative or superlative form, as needed, into the blanks for each question. The base word is in parentheses at the end of the sentence.

Q. Helen is the _____ of all the women living in Troy, New York. *(beautiful)*

A. **most beautiful** or **least beautiful**. The sentence compares *Helen* to other women in Troy, New York. Comparing more than two elements requires the superlative form. Because *beautiful* is a long word, *most* and *least* create the comparison. Which should you choose? The answer depends on your opinion of Helen's looks. Personally, ever since the do-it-yourself face-lift, I'm going with *least*.

1. Helen, who manages the billing for an auto parts company, is hoping for a transfer to the Paris office, where the salaries are _____ than in New York but the night life is _____. *(low, lively)*

2. Helen's boss claims that she is the _____ of all his employees. *(efficient)*

3. His secretary, however, has measured everyone's output of P-345 forms and concluded that Helen is _____ than Natalie, Helen's assistant. *(slow)*

4. Natalie prefers to type her P-345s because she thinks the result is _____ than handwritten work. *(neat)*

5. Helen notes that everyone else in the office writes _____ than Natalie, whose penmanship has been compared to random scratches from a blind chicken. *(legibly)*

6. Helen has been angry with Natalie ever since her assistant declared that Helen's coffee was _____ than the tea that Natalie brought to the office. *(drinkable)*

7. Helen countered with the claim that Natalie brewed tea _____ than the office rules allow, a practice that makes her _____ than Helen. *(frequently, productive)*

8. The other auto-parts workers are trying to stay out of the feud; they know that both women are capable of making the work day _____ and _____ than it is now. *(long, boring)*

9. The _____ moment in the argument came when Natalie claimed that Helen's toy duck "squawked _____ than Helen herself." *(petty, annoyingly)*

10. I bought the duck for Helen myself, and it was the _____ toy in the entire store! *(expensive)*

11. Knowing about Helen's transfer request, I asked for a duck that sounded _____ than the average American rubber duck. *(international)*

12. The clerk told me my request was the _____ he had ever encountered. *(silly)*

13. I replied that I preferred to deal with store clerks who were _____ than he. *(snobby)*

14. Anyway, Helen's transfer wasn't approved, and she is in the _____ mood imaginable. *(nasty)*

15. We all skirt Natalie's desk _____ than Helen's, because Natalie is even _____ than Helen about the refusal. *(widely, upset)*

16. Natalie, who considers herself the _____ person in the company, wanted a promotion to Helen's rank. *(essential)*

17. Larry, however, is sure that he would have gotten the promotion because he is the _____ of all of us in his donations to the Office Party Fund. *(generous)*

18. "Natalie bakes a couple of cupcakes," he commented _____ than the average Mack truck, "and the boss thinks she's executive material." *(forcefully)*

19. "I, on the other hand, am the _____ of the three clerks in my office," he continued. *(professional)*

20. When I left the office, Natalie and Larry were arm wrestling to see who was _____. *(strong)*

Going from Bad to Worse (and Good to Better): Irregular Comparisons

A couple of basic descriptions form comparisons irregularly. Irregulars don't add -er or more/less to create a comparison between two elements. Nor do irregulars tack on -est or most/least to point out the top or bottom of a group of more than two, also known as the superlative form of comparisons. (See the preceding section, "Visiting the -ER (And the -EST)," for more information on comparatives and superlatives.) Instead, irregular comparisons follow their own strange path, as you can see in Table 16-1.

Table 16-1	Forms of Irregular Comparisons	
Description	*Comparative*	*Superlative*
Good or well	Better	Best
Bad or ill	Worse	Worst
Much or many	More	Most

Take a stab at this section's practice exercises, but don't go to the -ER if your aim is faulty and you put the wrong form of the description (which you find in parentheses at the end of each sentence) in the blank. Just read the explanation in the answers section of the chapter and move on.

Q. Edgar's scrapbook, which contains souvenirs from his trip to Watch Repair Camp, is the _____ example of a boring book that I have ever seen. *(good)*

A. **best**. Once you mention the top or bottom experience of a lifetime, you're in the superlative column. Because *goodest* isn't a word, *best* is the one you want.

21. Edgar explains his souvenirs in _____ detail than anyone would ever want to hear. *(much)*

22. Bored listeners believe that the _____ item in his scrapbook is a set of gears, each of which Edgar can discuss for hours. *(bad)*

23. On the bright side, everyone knows that Edgar's watch repair skills are _____ than the jewelers' downtown. *(good)*

24. When he has the flu, Edgar actually feels _____ when he hears about a broken watch. *(bad)*

25. Although he is only nine years old, Edgar has the _____ timepieces of anyone in his fourth grade class, including the teacher. *(many)*

26. The classroom clock functions fairly well, but Ms. Appleby relies on Edgar to make it run even _____. *(well)*

27. Edgar's scrapbook also contains three samples of watch oil; Edgar thinks Time-Ola Oil is the _____ choice. *(good)*

28. Unfortunately, last week Edgar let a little oil drip onto his lunch and became sick; a few hours later he felt _____ and had to call the doctor. *(ill)*

29. "Time-Ola Oil is the _____ of all the poisons," cried the doctor. *(bad)*

30. "But it's the _____ for watches," whispered Edgar. *(good)*

Words That Are Incomparable (Like You!)

Because you bought this book, I'm assuming that you (like me) are *perfect*. Therefore you can't be compared to anything or anyone else because the word *perfect* — as well as *unique, round, circular, right, mistaken,* and a few other terms — is an absolute. Logic, which pops up from time to time in English grammar, is the basis for this rule. If you reach an absolute state, you can't be more or less absolute. Therefore an expression such as *more circular* or *really unique* is a no-no. You can, however, approach an absolute, being, for example, *nearly perfect* (okay, I admit that's a better term for me) or *almost round*.

Words for direction and shape tend to be absolutes. You can turn *left* and but not *lefter* or *more left*. Nor can you be the *squarest* or *most square* of them all, at least when you're discussing a four-sided figure.

Check out the following sentence pairs and circle the correct sentence. Just to keep you awake, I throw in some pairs in which both sentences are wrong or both sentences are right. (For those sentences, just write "both wrong" or "both right" in the margin.)

Q. Sentence A: The design of that vase is quite unique, and I expect to pay big bucks for it.

Sentence B: The design of that vase is unique, and I expect to pay big bucks for it.

A. **Sentence B.** The vase is either one-of-a-kind or not, an idea that sentence B expresses. If you want anything less than unique, use the word *rare* or *uncommon,* as in *the design of the vase is quite uncommon, and I expect to pay big bucks for it.*

31. Sentence A: The base of your vase is round, but mine is rounder.

Sentence B: The base of your vase is round, but mine is almost round.

32. Sentence A: The antiques dealer said that the top of the vase is circular, but he's probably mistaken.

Sentence B: The antiques dealer said that the top of the vase is nearly circular, but he's mistaken.

33. Sentence A: To find a better antiques dealer, drive west for about an hour.

Sentence B: To find a better antiques dealer, drive more west for about an hour.

34. Sentence A: That dealer sells Victorian-era buttons that are some of the most unique gift items you can imagine.

Sentence B: That dealer sells Victorian-era buttons that are some of the most unusual gift items you can imagine.

35. Sentence A: The reasonably circular shape of the buttons is surprising, given that the buttons are so old.

Sentence B: The very circular shape of the buttons is surprising, given that the buttons are so old.

36. Sentence A: The dealer obtained the buttons from an extremely elderly widow.

Sentence B: The dealer obtained the buttons from an elderly widow.

37. Sentence A: The widow claimed that she would sell her antiques only when the time was very right.

Sentence B: The widow claimed that she would sell her antiques only when the time was just right.

38. Sentence A: Last week I bought a button that was almost perfect.

Sentence B: Last week I bought a button that was surprisingly perfect.

39. Sentence A: I thought I could sell it over the Internet for a huge profit, but my plans were more mistaken than I had assumed.

Sentence B: I thought I could sell it over the Internet for a huge profit, but my plans were very mistaken.

40. Sentence A: My sister confiscated the button, claiming that it was uniquely suited to her personal style.

Sentence B: My sister confiscated the button, claiming that it was uncommonly suited to her personal style.

Calling All Overachievers: Extra Practice with Bad Comparisons

Political campaign literature is heavy with comparisons — Why Seymour and not Sally? How much more often did Seymour vote for tax increases, compared to Sally? — but not all the comparisons are correct. (I'm talking grammar here, not politics.) Run your eyeballs over the campaign leaflet in Figure 16-1. It's for a completely fictitious race between two fifth-graders hoping for higher office, specifically, President of Grade Six. Locate and correct ten errors in comparisons. To correct the errors, you may have to rewrite an entire sentence or phrase.

Vote for Sally!

She will be the most unique president our grade hasever had!

Here is Sally's campaign platform:

✓ Our cafeteria is dirtier than the cafeterias of William Reed School, Mercer Prep, and Riverton.

✓ Sally is gooder at organizing school events than her opponent.

✓ Sally will collect dues most efficiently than Seymour.

✓ Seymour is very wrong when he says that Sally spends dues money on herself.

✓ The principal likes Sally's ideas because compared to Seymour's, hers are best.

✓ Seymour is most frequently absent, and the class should choose the candidate who will attend all school events.

✓ Sally's plan for the school field will make it more square and add really unique bleachers.

✓ Seymour's face is unattractiver than Sally's, and you'll have to look at him all day if he is president.

Figure 16-1:
Faux political campaign literature riddled with errors.

Answers to Comparison Problems

1 **lower**, **livelier**. The comparative form is the way to go because two cities are being compared, Paris and New York. One-syllable words such as *low* form comparatives with the addition of *-er*. Most two-syllable words rely on *more* or *less,* but *lively* is an exception. If you aren't sure how to form the comparative of a particular word, check the dictionary.

2 **most efficient**. In choosing the top or bottom rank from a group of three or more, go for superlative. *Efficient*, a long word, takes *most* or *least.* In the context of this sentence, *most* makes sense.

3 **slower**. Comparing two elements, in this case *Helen* and *Natalie,* calls for comparative form. The one-syllable word takes *-er.*

4 **neater**. Here the sentence compares typing to handwriting, two elements, so the comparative is correct. The one-syllable word turns comparative with the addition of *-er.*

5 **more legibly**. Once you read the word *everyone,* you may have thought that superlative (the form that deals with comparisons of three or more) was needed. However, this sentence actually compares two elements (Natalie and the group composed of everyone else). *Legibly* has three syllables, so *more* creates the comparative form.

6 **less drinkable**. In comparing *coffee* and *tea,* go for the comparative form. Both *more drinkable* and *less drinkable* are correct grammatically, but Helen's anger more logically flows from a comment about her coffee's inferiority.

7 **more frequently**, **less productive**. The fight's getting serious now, isn't it? Charges and counter-charges! Speaking solely of grammar and forgetting about office politics, each description in this sentence is set up in comparison to one other element (how many times Natalie brews tea versus how many times the rules say she can brew tea, Natalie's productiveness versus Helen's). Because you're comparing two elements and the descriptions have more than one syllable, go for a two-word comparative.

8 **longer**, **more boring**. When you compare two things (how long and boring the day is now and how long and boring it will be if Natalie and Helen get angry), go for the comparative, with *-er* for the short word and *more* for the two-syllable word.

9 **pettiest**, **more annoyingly** or **less annoyingly**. The argument had more than two moments, so superlative is what you want. The adjective *petty* has two syllables, but *-est* is still appropriate, with the letter *y* of *petty* changing to *i* before the *-est.* The second blank compares two (the duck and Helen) and thus takes the comparative. I'll let you decide whether Natalie was insulting Helen or the duck. Grammatically, either form is correct.

10 **most expensive** or **least expensive**. A store has lots of toys, so to choose the one that will cost the most or least (I'll let you decide how cheap the narrator is), go for superlative. Because *expensive* has three syllables, tacking on *most* or *least* is the way to go.

11 **more international**. Comparing two items (the sound of the duck you want to buy and the sound of the "average American rubber duck") calls for comparative, which is created with *more* because of the length of the adjective *international.*

12 **silliest**. Out of all the requests, this one is on the top rung. Go for superlative, which is created by changing the *y* to *i* and adding *-est.*

13 **less snobby**. Two elements (*he* and *a group of store clerks,* with the group counting as a single item) are being compared here, so comparative is needed. The add-on *less* does the job.

14 **nastiest**. I can imagine many moods, so the extreme in the group calls for the superlative. The final *y* changes to *i* before the *-est*.

15 **more widely**, **more upset**. Employee habits concerning two individuals *(Natalie and Helen)* are discussed here; comparative does the job.

16 **most essential**. Natalie is singled out as the extreme in a large group. Hence superlative is the one that fits here. Three-syllable words need *most* to form the superlative.

17 **most generous**. *All* includes more than two (*both* is the preferred term for two), so superlative rules. Go for the two-word form because *generous* has three syllables.

18 **more forcefully**. This sentence compares his force to the force of a truck. Two things in one comparison gives you comparative form, which is created by *more* for long words.

19 **most professional**. Choosing one out of three calls for superlative. (One out of two is comparative, as in *more professional*.)

20 **stronger**. Natalie and Larry are locked in a fight to the death (okay, to the strained elbow). Two elements being compared requires comparative. Because *strong* is a single syllable, tacking on *-er* does the trick.

21 **more**. Two elements are being compared here: the amount of detail Edgar uses and the amount of detail people want. When comparing two elements, the comparative form rules.

22 **worst**. The superlative form singles out the extreme (in this case the most boring) item in the scrapbook.

23 **better**. The sentence pits Edgar's skills against the skills of one group *(the downtown jewelers)*. Even though the group has several members, the comparison is between two elements — Edgar and the group — so comparative form is what you want.

24 **worse**. Two states of being are in comparison in this sentence, Edgar's health before and after he hears about a broken watch. In comparing two things, go for comparative form.

25 **most**. The superlative form singles out the extreme, in this case Edgar's timepiece collection, which included even a raw-potato clock until it rotted.

26 **better**. The comparative deals with two states — how the clock runs before Edgar gets his hands on it and how it runs after.

27 **best**. To single out the top or bottom rank from a group of more than two, go for superlative form.

28 **worse**. The sentence compares Edgar's health at two points (immediately after eating the oil spill and a few hours after that culinary adventure). Comparative form works for two elements.

29 **worst**. The very large group of poisons has two extremes, and Time-Ola is one of them, so superlative form is best.

30 **best**. The group of watch oils also has two extremes, and Time-Ola is one of them, so once again you need superlative.

31 **Sentence B**. Because *round* is absolute, the term *rounder* isn't standard English.

32 **Sentences A and B**. Two absolutes are in question here: *circular* and *mistaken*. The words tacked on to the absolutes (*probably* in Sentence A and *nearly* in Sentence B) don't express a degree of circularity or mistakenness. Instead, *probably* expresses an opinion about whether or not the absolute term applies, and *nearly* expresses an approach to the absolute.

33 **Sentence A**. You can't go *more west*. The direction is absolute.

34 **Sentence B**. Because *unique* is an absolute term, *most unique* is illogical. *Unusual,* on the other hand, isn't absolute, so *most* may be attached.

35 **neither**. The shape is either *circular* or not. The *reasonably* in sentence A is a no-no, as is the *very* in sentence B.

36 **Sentences A and B**. I tried to trick you here by sneaking in a non-absolute, *elderly.* You can be *very, extremely, really,* and *not-so elderly,* depending upon your birth certificate and your degree of truthfulness.

37 **Sentence B**. *Right* is an absolute, so you're either *right* or *wrong,* not *very right* or *wronger.* You can, however, be *just right,* implying that you have reached the absolute state.

38 **Sentences A and B**. *Perfect* is an absolute, but *almost* expresses an approach to the absolute (legal) and *surprisingly* deals with the opinion of the speaker, not with a degree of perfection (also legal).

39 **neither**. *Mistaken* is an absolute, so *more* and *very* are wrong. (Not *wronger,* or *very wrong,* because *wrong* is also an absolute.)

40 **Sentences A and B**. If the button is *uniquely suited,* nothing else in the universe is *suited* in the same way. No problem. *Uncommonly* means that more than one item may be suited, but this button fits to a rare degree. Also no problem.

Vote for Sally!

41 She will be ~~the most unique~~ **a unique** president ~~our grade has ever had~~!

Here is Sally's campaign platform:

42 ✓ Our cafeteria is ~~dirtier than~~ **dirtiest compared to** the cafeterias of William Reed School, Mercer Prep, and Riverton.

43 ✓ Sally is ~~gooder~~ **better** at organizing school events than her opponent.

44 ✓ Sally will collect dues ~~most~~ **more** efficiently than Seymour.

45 ✓ Seymour is ~~very~~ **wrong** when he says that Sally spends dues money on herself.

46 ✓ The principal likes Sally's ideas because compared to Seymour's, hers are ~~best~~ **better**.

47 ✓ Seymour is ~~most~~ **more** frequently absent, and the class should choose the candidate who will attend all school events.

48 ✓ Sally's plan for the school field will make it **more nearly** square

49 and add ~~really~~ unique bleachers.

50 ✓ Seymour's face is ~~unattractiver~~ **more unattractive** than Sally's, and you'll have to look at him all day if he is president.

41 *Unique* is an absolute and can't be compared.

42 In comparing more than two elements, use the superlative *(dirtiest)*.

43 *Better* is an irregular comparison. *Gooder* isn't a word in standard English.

44 In comparing two items (the way Sally gets the money from her classmates and the way Seymour does), go for comparative, not superlative form.

45 *Wrong* is an absolute and may not be compared.

46 The comparative form *(better)* works for a two-element comparison.

47 The implied comparison here is between two attendance records, so comparative form is what you want.

48 *Square* is an absolute and may not be compared. You may, however, state how close to the absolute a particular form is.

49 The absolute term *unique* may not be compared.

50 A three-syllable word becomes comparative or superlative with the addition of *more/less* or *most/least*.

Chapter 17

Apples and Oranges: Improper Comparisons

In This Chapter

▶ Avoiding incomplete or illogical comparisons

▶ Handling double comparisons

You can't compare apples and oranges, according to the old saying, but that error is only one of many common comparison mistakes. Sitting in the bleachers at Yankee Stadium, I once heard a fan compare the Yankee shortstop, Derek Jeter, to "the Yankee players." The imaginary umpire I conjured up, the one who knows the rules of grammar as thoroughly as the rules of baseball, immediately screamed, "Foul! You should have compared Jeter to 'the *other* Yankee players.'" (The real me kept her mouth shut. My reputation for nerdiness is bad enough as it is.)

Chapter 16 explains one- or two-word comparisons; this chapter takes you through more complicated situations, including illogical comparisons like the Jeter comment and incomplete comparisons. You can also practice double comparisons, a sentence construction for people who like to hedge their bets. As they say in Yankee Stadium, play ball!

No One Likes to Feel Incomplete, and Neither Do Comparisons

By definition, a comparison discusses two elements in relation to each other or singles out the extreme in a group and explains exactly what form the extremism takes. For example, *She throws more pies than I do* or *Of all the clowns, she throws the most pies.* A comparison may also examine something in relation to a standard, as in *Her comment was so sugary that I had to take an extra shot of diabetes medication.*

A comparison may be any of these things, but what it may *not* be is partially absent. If someone says, "The snapper is not *as* fresh" or "The sea bass is *most musical,*" you're at sea. As fresh as what? Most musical in comparison to whom? You have no way of knowing.

Of course, in context these sentences may be perfectly all right:

> I considered the snapper but in the end went with the flounder. The snapper is not as fresh.

In the preceding example, the reader understands that the second sentence is a continuation of the first. Also, some words in a comparison may be implied, without loss of meaning. Take a look at this sentence:

The snapper makes fewer snotty comments than a large-mouth bass *does.*

The italicized word in the preceding sentence may be left out — and frequently is — without confusing the reader. And that's the key: The reader must have enough information to understand the comparison.

So may also mean *therefore,* in which case it doesn't pair with *that.* In informal speech, *so* may also be the equivalent of *very,* as in *I was so tired.* In formal English, however, *so* should be paired with *that* when it creates a comparison.

Read the following sentence; see whether you can catch an incomplete comparison. If the sentence is correct, write "correct" in the blank. If not, rewrite the sentence to complete the comparison. You may come up with thousands of possible answers, a further illustration of why incomplete comparisons make for poor communication. I give two suggested answers for the example, but only one suggested answer for the exercises that follow, because I can't cover everything. Check your answer by determining whether your comparison is clear and complete.

0. "There are more fish in the sea," commented the grouper as she searched for her posse.

_____

_____

A. **"There are more fish in the sea than you know," commented the grouper as she searched for her posse.** Or, **"There are more fish in the sea than on a restaurant menu," commented the grouper as she searched for her posse.** The key here is to define the term *more. More than* what? If you answer that question, you're fine.

1. The trout, who is wealthier, spends a lot of money on rap CDs.

_____

_____

2. The octopus has almost as much money but prefers to keep the trout at arm's length.

_____

_____

3. Mermaids are the most adept at financial planning, in my experience.

_____

_____

4. On the other hand, mermaids are less competent at purchasing shoes.

_____

_____

5. Not many people realize that mermaid tail fins are so sensitive.

_____

_____

6. Whales are as fashion-challenged at shoe and accessory selection.

_____

_____

7. This whole under-the-sea theme has become more boring.

_____

_____

8. The marine jokes are so uninteresting.

_____

_____

9. I will work harder at formulating new ideas.

_____

_____

10. You can always boycott this chapter if you find the comedy less than satisfying.

_____

_____

Being Smarter Than Yourself: Illogical Comparisons

If I say that my favorite Yankee, Derek Jeter, is _cuter than the Yankee players_ or _better at turning double plays than the Yankees,_ I'm making an error that's a lot worse than Derek's occasional wild throw into the stands. Why? Because Derek is one of the players on the Yankees. According to the logic of those statements, Derek would have to be _cuter_ or _better_ than himself. The solution is simple. Insert _other_ or _else_ or a similar expression into the sentence. Then Derek becomes _cuter than anyone else on the team_ or _better at turning double plays than the other Yankees._

Don't insert _other_ or _else_ if the comparison is between someone in the group and someone outside the group. I can correctly say that _Derek is cuter than the Red Sox players_ because Derek isn't a Red Sox player and he _is_ cute.

Another form of illogic that pops up in comparisons is overkill: the use of both _-er_ and _more_ or _less_ or _-est_ and _most_ or _least._ You can be either _sillier_ or _more silly,_ but not _more sillier._

Time for some comparison shopping. Check out the following sentences. If the comparison is logical, write "correct" in the blank. If the comparison is faulty, rewrite the sentence in the space provided. Because some sentences may be corrected in more than one way, your answer may differ from mine. Just be sure that your answers are logical.

0. The average pigeon is smarter than any animal in New York City.

_____

_____

A. **The average pigeon is smarter than any other animal in New York City.** Pigeons are animals, and pigeons flap all over New York. (I've even seen them on subway cars, where they wait politely for the next stop before waddling onto the platform.) Without the word *other,* pigeons are smarter than themselves. Penalty box! The insertion of *other* repairs the logic.

11. Despite the fact that they don't use Metrocards, subway pigeons are no worse than any rider.

_____

_____

12. Spotting a pigeon waiting for the subway door to open is no odder than anything you see on an average day in New York.

_____

_____

13. On a midtown corner I once saw a woman shampooing her hair in the rain, an experience that was more weirder than anything else I've seen in my life.

_____

_____

14. Singing a shower song with a thick New York accent, she appeared saner than city residents.

_____

_____

15. A tourist gawking through the window of a sightseeing bus was more surprised than New Yorkers on the street.

_____

_____

16. Is this story less believable than what you read in this book?

_____

_____

17. You may be surprised to know that it is more firmly fact-based than the material in this chapter.

_____

_____

18. Tourists to New York probably go home with stranger stories than visitors to big cities.

_____

_____

19. New Yorkers themselves, of course, make worse tourists than travelers from large metropolitan areas.

_____

_____

20. New Yorkers are more likely to become impatient than residents of small towns.

_____

_____

Double Trouble: A Sentence Containing More Than One Comparison

Do you have trouble making up your mind? Well, yes and no. Does this statement sound like something you'd say? If so, you probably employ double comparisons. Some examples:

> The new sculpture is as fragile as the old one, if not more fragile.

> Eleanor is almost as annoying as Sarah, if not equally annoying.

> Carrie's speech on tariff reduction was as complicated as, if not more complicated than, Jessica's oration.

The preceding examples are correct because each falls into one of two categories:

✔ **The first comparison is completed before the second begins.** The first two sentences in the preceding example set follow this pattern.

✔ **The beginning of both comparisons may be logically completed by the phrase at the end of the sentence.** The third sample sentence in the preceding set falls into this category. The first comparison in that sentence begins with the statement _as complicated as_. Tack that statement to the conclusion of the comparison, _Jessica's oration,_ and you have a complete and logical comparison: _as complicated as Jessica's oration._ The second comparison begins with _more complicated than_ and is completed by the same statement, _Jessica's oration._ Thus the second comparison is complete: _more complicated than Jessica's oration._ Because both comparisons are completed by the same phrase, the sentence is correct.

The most common mistake in double comparisons is to omit part of the first comparison:

Wrong: Carrie's speech on tariff reduction was as complicated, if not more complicated than, Jessica's oration.

Why it's wrong: Each comparison must be completed by the same phrase at the end of the sentence. In the preceding sample sentence, the first comparison is *not* completed by the phrase at the end of the sentence. The way it is now, the first comparison reads *as complicated Jessica's oration*. The word *as* is missing.

Right: Carrie's speech on tariff reduction was as complicated as, if not more complicated than, Jessica's oration.

Also right: Carrie's speech on tariff reduction was as complicated as Jessica's oration, if not more complicated.

Double comparisons are so annoying that you may be tempted to make up your mind and go for one statement only. I applaud that decision. But if you must give two alternatives, be sure that each is correct. Here's an example and a practice set of exercises. If you find an error, rewrite the sentence. *Note:* More than one correction is possible with this sort of error. Just pick one way to rewrite.

Q. Celeste put as many people — if not even more people — to sleep as Elizabeth, even though Celeste's speech was five minutes shorter.

A. **Celeste put as many people to sleep as Elizabeth, if not even more than Elizabeth, even though Celeste's speech was five minutes shorter.** The two comparisons should be logically completed by the same phrase, but in the original sentence, the second comparison is faulty. The first comparison, *Celeste put as many people to sleep as Elizabeth,* is okay. The second comparison in the original sentence, *If not even more people to sleep as Elizabeth,* is illogical. The word *than* is missing. The corrected version supplies two complete comparisons.

21. Celeste described every, or even more than, the provisions of the Snooty-Harvey Tariff Law.

_____

_____

22. Elizabeth concentrated on one of the most, if not the most important, provisions of the law.

_____

_____

23. Celeste's choice of subject matter was equally, if not more important, than Elizabeth's.

_____

_____

24. Elizabeth insisted on the same amount, or even more time, as Celeste.

_____

_____

25. Celeste's demand for a bowl of pink jellybeans during the lecture was as ridiculous, if not more ridiculous, than Elizabeth's request for green gummy bears.

_____

_____

Calling All Overachievers: Extra Practice with Improper Comparisons

Figure 17-1 is an excerpt from a completely fictitious review of an imaginary restaurant, which I designed to give you a thorough review of the rules of comparisons. Be on the lookout for undercooked sausage, incomplete or illogical comparisons, snobby waiters, and messed-up double comparisons. You should find ten mistakes in comparisons and about a million reasons not to eat at this establishment. Correcting the errors may involve adding, removing, or rearranging quite a few words. *Note:* Often more than one correction is possible. I supply one answer for each error in the following section, but your answer may differ slightly and still be correct.

Pembroke Diner: You Won't Go Broke, but You Won't Eat Well Either

A recent meal at the Pembroke Diner on 48th Street was most distressing. First of all, the tables are as close together, if not closer together, than bus riders during rush hour. I truly did not want to hear my neighbors' conversation about their grandchildren, who are, they claim, so smart. Nor did I want to chew each bite of steak for ten minutes because the steak was tougher than any meat I've eaten in my life. The wine list of the Pembroke is the least interesting. I am, I admit, a wine snob, but even people who drink wine only once a year will have a hard time finding something that is as watery, if not more watery, than the house red. I was surprised to realize that I was less impressed than the diners munching happily in the restaurant. Surely the Pembroke can do better! The potato was much more raw and more expensive. I recommend that you find a place with better food. The Pembroke must revise its menu and its habits immediately, or the restaurant will be so unpopular.

Figure 17-1:
A poorly written restaurant review.

Answers to Complicated Comparison Problems

1   **The trout, who is wealthier than the president of a Swiss bank, spends a lot of money on rap CDs.** The problem with the original is that you can't tell what or who is being compared to the trout. The missing element of the comparison must be supplied.

2   **The octopus has almost as much money as the trout but prefers to keep the trout at arm's length.** The original sentence begins the comparison nicely *(almost as much money as)* and then flubs the ending *(almost as much money* as what? as who?). Supply an ending and you're fine.

3   **Mermaids are the most adept at financial planning of all marine mammals, in my experience.** The original comparison doesn't specify the group in which mermaids excel. Your answer must provide context.

4   **On the other hand, mermaids are less competent at purchasing shoes than other mammals.** In the original, the reader is left to wonder about the basis of comparison. In the corrected sentence, the mermaids are compared to other mammals. Now the comparison is complete.

5   **Not many people realize that mermaid tail fins are as sensitive as a duck's foot.** The original sentence contains an incomplete comparison. As sensitive as what? Who knows? The suggested answer finishes the comparison by supplying another sensitive object.

6   **Whales are as fashion-challenged at shoe and accessory selection as mermaids.** It doesn't matter how you finish the comparison so long as you finish it. In the suggested answer I plugged in *mermaids,* but I could just as easily have placed myself or someone else. Your call.

7   **This whole under-the-sea theme has become more boring than a lecture on the economics of pen nibs.** Finish the comparison with your favorite example of excruciating boredom.

8   **The marine jokes are so uninteresting that I may never go to the beach again.** The *so* statement must be completed by some sort of *that* statement.

9   **correct.** Let me explain. Normally a comparison *(harder,* in this sentence) must be placed in context. In this sentence, however, the context is implied *(harder* than I did before).

10   **correct.** The phrase *less than satisfying* compares the comedy to an ideal state (satisfying). The comparison is complete.

11   **Despite the fact that they don't use Metrocards, subway pigeons are no worse than any other rider.** The context makes clear that pigeons sometimes ride the subways. (I'm not kidding about this one, honest! I have seen the little feathered guys on my train.) Without the *other,* pigeons are no worse than themselves, an impossible situation.

12   **Spotting a pigeon waiting for the subway door to open is no odder than anything else you see on an average day in New York.** The *else* serves an important purpose in this sentence; it shows the reader that the pigeon waiting for the subway is being compared to *other* events in New York City. Without the *else,* the sentence is irrational because then the sentence means that seeing pigeons in New York is no odder than what you see in New York.

13   **On a midtown corner I once saw a woman shampooing her hair in the rain, an experience that was weirder than anything else I've seen in my life.** *More weirder* is overkill. Drop the *more* and you're all set.

14. **Singing a shower song with a thick New York accent, she appeared saner than other city residents.** If she's got a New York accent, she's a city resident. Without the word *other,* you're saying that she's saner than herself. Not possible!

15. **correct**. The tourist isn't a city resident, so he or she may be compared to *New Yorkers on the street* without the word *other.*

16. **Is this story less believable than the rest of what you read in this book?** The story is in the book, and it can't be compared to itself. The phrase *the rest of* differentiates the story but preserves the logic. You may also correct this one by writing *less believable than any others you read in this book.*

17. **You may be surprised to know that it is more firmly fact-based than the other material in this chapter.** Your correction must indicate, in any of several ways, that this story is being compared to the rest of the dumb jokes I placed in this chapter. The expressions *other, rest,* or *anything else* can do the job.

18. **Tourists to New York probably go home with stranger stories than visitors to other big cities.** New York is a big city, but the original sentence implies otherwise. The insertion of *other* solves the problem.

19. **New Yorkers themselves, of course, make worse tourists than travelers from other large metropolitan areas.** New York is a *large metropolitan area,* and the original indicates that it isn't. Trouble! Insert *other* and you're all set.

20. **correct**. New Yorkers are compared to *residents of small towns,* and that comparison is legal

21. **Celeste described every provision of the Snooty-Harvey Tariff Law, and even more.** The original sentence muddles two comparisons, braiding them together inappropriately. The first comparison is incomplete. If you untangle it, you get *Celeste described every the provisions of the Snooty-Harvey Tariff Law.* You can easily see that the untangled comparison doesn't make sense. The second comparison is in better shape. Untangled it reads *Celeste described even more than the provisions of the Snooty-Harvey Tariff Law.* One complete and one incomplete comparison isn't a good idea. The corrected version presents two complete ideas.

22. **Elizabeth concentrated on one of the most important, if not the most important, provisions of the law.** Or, **Elizabeth concentrated on one of the most important provisions of the law, if not the most important.** The original is faulty because the first comparison cannot be completed logically by the words supplied in the sentence. In the original sentence, the first comparison reads *one of the most provisions of the law.* Penalty box! The word *important* is missing. The two corrections supply *important.*

23. **Celeste's choice of subject matter was equally important, if not more important than Elizabeth's.** In the original sentence, the first comparison is incomplete: *equally Elizabeth's.* In the rewritten version, each separate comparison makes sense. Comparison one: *equally important.* Comparison two: *more important than Elizabeth's.*

24. **Elizabeth insisted on the same amount of time as Celeste, or even more time than Celeste.** In the original sentence the second comparison is incomplete as written. The *than* is missing. In the corrected version each of the two comparisons works separately. Comparison one: *the same amount of time as Celeste.* Comparison two: *more time than Celeste.*

25. **Celeste's demand for a bowl of pink jellybeans during the lecture was as ridiculous as Elizabeth's request for green gummy bears, if not more ridiculous.** In the original sentence the first comparison is incomplete because it contains only one *as.* If you untangle it from the second comparison, you hear what's missing: *Celeste's demand for a bowl of pink jellybeans during the lecture was as ridiculous than Elizabeth's request for green gummy bears.* The corrected version contains two complete comparisons.

Pembroke Diner: You Won't Go Broke, but You Won't Eat Well Either

A recent meal at the Pembroke Diner on 48th Street was ~~most distressing~~ **the most distressing experience I've had since becoming a restaurant critic**. First of all, the tables are ~~as close together, if not closer together, than bus riders during rush hour~~ **as close together as bus riders during rush hour, if not closer**. I truly did not want to hear my neighbors' conversation about their grandchildren, who are, they claim, **so smart that no IQ test can measure them**. Nor did I want to chew each bite of steak for ten minutes because the steak was tougher than **any other meat** I've eaten in my life. The wine list of the Pembroke is **the least interesting of all the restaurants in the universe that serve wine**. I am, I admit, a wine snob, but even people who drink wine only once a year will have a hard time finding something that is ~~as watery, if not more watery, than the house red~~ **as watery as the house red, if not more watery**. I was surprised to realize that I was less impressed than **the other diners** munching happily in the restaurant. Surely the Pembroke can do better! The potato was much **more raw than an uncooked steak** and **more expensive than filet mignon**. I recommend that you find a place with better food. The Pembroke must revise its menu and its habits immediately, or the restaurant will be **so unpopular that it will go out of business**.

26   The expression *most distressing* must be placed in context. Your answer probably differs from mine, but as long as it indicates the context, you're okay.

27   If you're doubling a comparison, each separate comparison must be complete.

28   A *so* statement must be accompanied by a *that* statement in order to complete the comparison.

29   Steak is a meat, so the word *other* must be inserted.

30   Your completion may be different from mine, but the context of *least interesting* must appear.

31   Each element of a double comparison must be complete.

32   The critic is clearly a diner, and he or she cannot be *less impressed* than him- or herself. Insert *other* and the logic is saved.

You can correct this comparison in about a zillion ways. I've provided one possibility, but anything you come up with is fine so long as the comparison is complete.

34 This comparison must be completed. I supply an answer, but don't worry if yours is different. Just be sure it's complete.

35 The *so* statement can't make a comparison all by itself; a *that* statement must be appended.

Part V
Writing with Style

The 5th Wave   By Rich Tennant

"C'mon Fogelman-talk! And I don't want to hear any of your nonparallel sentence structures, incomplete sentences, or dangling participles!"

In this part . . .

Completing the exercises in this part is the equivalent of designing clothes for one of the famous Parisian fashion houses. If you can make it through this material, you've arrived at the top. The topics in this part include more than grammar; and when you master them, your writing will be as stylish as a supermodel.

Chapter 18 tackles parallelism, the grammar term for order and balance in a sentence. (In fashion terms, how not to wear rain boots with an evening gown.) Chapter 19 lets you practice adding variety to sentences, so you don't end up wearing the same outfit . . . er, structuring every sentence the same way. Chapter 20 concerns the little errors (like wearing something that isn't black in New York City) that sabotage your writing.

Chapter 18

Practicing Parallel Structure

Math teachers have all the luck. Not only can they play with compasses and protractors, but they also get to draw little circles and squares and parallel lines. English has parallels too, but in grammar, parallels are created with words, not with pencils and rulers. No fun at all!

Grammatical parallelism may not be party material, but it's essential to good writing. Parallelism refers to order and balance, the quality a sentence has when it flows smoothly. No parallel sentence starts out in one direction (toward, say, Grandma's house) only to veer suddenly off the road (perhaps to a biker convention two states away). This chapter provides a road map and some practice drives to keep your sentences on track.

Geometry Invades English: Parallelism Basics

When a sentence is parallel, everything performing the same function in the sentence has the same grammatical identity. If you have two subjects, for example, and one is an infinitive *(to ski),* the other one will be an infinitive also *(to fracture).* You can't mix and match; *to ski* and *fracturing* shouldn't show up as paired (or part of tripled or quadrupled or whatever) subjects. Check these sentences out:

> **Nonparallel:** Roberta didn't enjoy paying full price for a lift ticket and that the cashier treated her rudely.

> **Parallel:** Roberta didn't enjoy paying full price for a lift ticket and being treated rudely by the cashier.

In checking for parallelism, don't worry about terminology. Just read the sentence aloud and listen: Parallel sentences sound balanced, but nonparallel sentences sound lopsided.

Keep your balance while you check out the following sentences. Decide whether or not they're parallel. If they are, write "correct" in the blank after each sentence. If they're nonparallel, correct the sentence in the blanks provided.

0. Sliding down Thunder Mountain, artfully spraying snow across his rival's face, and to get the best seat in the ski lodge were Robert's goals for the afternoon.

_____

_____

A. **Sliding down Thunder Mountain, artfully spraying snow across his rival's face, and getting the best seat in the ski lodge were Robert's goals for the afternoon.** The sentence has three subjects. The first two subjects are verb forms ending in *-ing* (gerunds, in official grammar terminology), but the third is an infinitive (the *to* form of a verb). Mismatch! My suggested answer makes all three subjects into gerunds. Here's another possibility: To slide down Thunder Mountain, to spray snow artfully across his rival's face, and to get the best seat in the ski lodge were Robert's goals for the afternoon. Now all are infinitives, and the sentence is parallel.

1. The ski pants that Robert favors are green, skin-tight, and made of stretch fabric.

_____

_____

2. When he eases into those pants and zipping up with great difficulty, Robert feels cool.

_____

_____

3. In this ski outfit, Robert can breathe only with great difficulty and loudly.

_____

_____

4. The sacrifice for the sake of fashion is worth the trouble and how he feels uncomfortable, Robert says.

_____

_____

5. Besides, sliding down the mountain and coasting to a full stop is easier in clothing that resembles a second skin.

_____

_____

6. Robert has often been known to object to secondhand clothing and how some equipment is used.

_____

_____

7. "With a good parka or wearing a warm face mask I'm ready for anything," he says.

_____

_____

8. He adds, "The face mask is useful on the slopes and doing double duty in bank robberies."

_____

_____

9. The ski pants can also be recycled, if they are ripless and without stains.

_____

_____

10. However, robbing a bank and to mug someone on the street is more difficult in ski pants.

_____

_____

11. Robbers need speed and to be private, but they also need pockets.

_____

_____

12. Stashing stolen money and where to put an unwanted ski mask are important issues.

_____

_____

13. Robert, who is actually quite honest and not having the inclination to rob anyone, nevertheless thinks about crime and fashion.

_____

_____

14. He once wrote and had even edited a newsletter called *Crimes of Fashion*.

_____

_____

15. Skiing and to pursue a career in law enforcement are Robert's dreams.

_____

_____

Avoiding Unnecessary Shifts in Tense, Person, and Voice

My driving instructor (my husband) patiently explained to me at least 1,000 times that shifting at the wrong time was bad for (a) the engine and (b) his nerves. I did my best, though the grinding noise that echoed through the car wasn't always my teeth.

Sentences should stay in gear also, unless the meaning requires a shift. Every sentence has tense (the time of the action or state of being), person (who's talking or being talked about), and voice (active or passive). A sentence has a parallelism problem when one of those qualities shifts unnecessarily from, say, present to past tense, or from first person (the *I* form) to third (the *he* or *they* form). Nor should a sentence drift from singular to plural without good reason. For help with verbs, check out Chapters 1 and 2. Pronoun tips are in Chapters 3 and 11.

Some shifts are crucial to the meaning of the sentence. If *I hit you* and then *he hits me,* the shift from one person to another is part of what I'm trying to say. That sort of sentence is fine. What's not parallel is a statement like *I hit him because you always want to be aggressive in tight situations,* where the *you* is a stand-in for *I* or *everyone.*

Hop in for a test ride. Check out the following sentences. If everything's okay, write "correct" in the blank after each sentence. Rewrite the nonparallel sentences so they're correct.

Q. Miranda read her introduction, and then the slides of our trip to Morocco were shown by me.

_____

_____

A. **Miranda read her introduction, and then I showed the slides of our trip to Morocco.** The original sentence unwisely shifts from active voice (*Miranda read*) to passive (*slides . . . were shown*). Verdict: Stripped gears, caused by a lack of parallelism.

16. If anyone has studied biology, you know that a person must learn the names of hundreds, if not thousands, of organisms.

_____

_____

17. Who gave those names, and why?

_____

_____

18. The Amoeba Family provides a good example of the process, so its name will be explained.

_____

_____

19. You may not know that the first example of this single-celled organism would have the name Amy.

_____

_____

20. When you split them in half, the new organisms name themselves.

_____

_____

21. The right half of Amy was still called Amy by herself, but the left half now called herself Bea.

_____

_____

22. The next time Amy and Bea split, you have four new organisms.

_____

_____

23. No one can imagine a conference between four single-celled organisms unless they witnessed it.

_____

_____

24. Amy Right Half favored a name that people will notice.

_____

_____

25. Amy Left Half thought about the choice for so long that her swimming was neglected.

_____

_____

26. Bea Right Half, a proto-feminist, opted for "Amy-Bea," because she wants to honor both her parents.

_____

_____

27. Everyone always pronounced "Amy-Bea" very fast, and soon "Amoeba" was their preferred spelling.

_____

_____

28. Single-celled organisms should have simple names that can be remembered by biology students.

_____

_____

29. Bea Left Half, by the way, will change her name to Amy-Bea when she reached the age of seventeen days.

_____

_____

30. You know what a teenager is like; they always have to assert their identities.

_____

_____

Matchmaking 101: Either/Or, Not Only/But Also, and Similar Pairs

Like dating couples, some words that join ideas (conjunctions, in grammar-speak) arrive in pairs. Specifically, _either/or, neither/nor, not only/but also,_ and _both/and_ work as teams. Also like daters, these conjunction pairs tend to drift apart. Your job is to keep them together by ensuring that they link parallel elements. All you have to do is check that the elements being linked by these words have the same grammatical identity (two nouns, two noun-verb combos, two adjectives, or two whatevers). Check out the following examples, in which the linked elements are underlined and the conjunctions are italicized:

> **Nonparallel:** Gertrude was _not only_ <u>anxious</u> to achieve fame _but also_ <u>she wanted</u> to make a lot of money.

> **Parallel:** _Either_ by going <u>to the moon</u> _or_ by swimming <u>across the Pacific</u>, Gertrude is determined to become famous.

The linked elements in the parallel example are both prepositional phrases. (You don't really need to know the grammatical term.) If you say the underlined sections aloud, your ear tells you that they match. In the nonparallel sentence, the first element is just a description, but the second contains a subject-verb combo that could stand alone as a complete sentence. Clearly these two aren't going to make it through dinner and a movie. Nor can you correct the problem by deleting _she_ from the nonparallel sentence, because then you're pairing a description with a verb. Divorce court looms!

A good way to check parallelism in this sort of sentence is to underline the elements, as I do in the preceding example sentences. Then you can focus on whether or not they match.

Parallel or nonparallel? Take a look at the following sentences. If they're parallel, write "correct" in the blanks. If they aren't, correct them.

0. The bird both swooping over my head and the surprise in the garbage pail startled me.

_____

_____

A. Both the bird that swooped over my head and the surprise that I found in the garbage pail startled me. In the original sentence, *swooping over my head* and *surprise in the garbage pail* don't match. The first element has a verb *(swooping),* and the second doesn't. The corrected version matches *bird that swooped* to *surprise that I found.*

31. When she traveled to the biker convention, Lola intended to show off both her new Harley and to display her new tattoo.

_____

_____

32. Either Lulu would accompany Lola or stay home to work on a screenplay about bikers.

_____

_____

33. Neither Lulu plans ahead nor Lola.

_____

_____

34. Lola not only writes screenplays about bikers but about alien invasions also.

_____

_____

35. Lulu both is jealous of Lola's writing talent and the award for "best cycle" on Lola's trophy wall.

_____

_____

36. Lola scorns not only awards but also refuses to enter most contests.

_____

_____

37. Neither the cycling award nor the trophy for largest tattoo has significance for Lola.

_____

_____

38. Lulu, on the other hand, both wants the cycling award and the trophy.

_____

_____

39. Not only did Lulu bribe the judges, but also ran a full-page ad bragging about herself.

_____

_____

40. The judges were either unimpressed with Lulu's efforts or liked Lola better.

_____

_____

Calling All Overachievers: Extra Practice with Parallels

Look for any parallelism problems in this letter to an elected official from an unfortunate citizen (see Figure 18-1). You should find ten mistakes in parallelism, various shifts, and conjunction pairs. When you find a mistake, correct it.

Dear Mr. Mayor:

I do not like complaining or to be a nuisance, but if a person is persecuted, they should be heard. As you know, the proposed new highway not only runs through my living room but into my swimming pool as well. When I spoke to the Department of Highways, the clerk was rude and that he took my complaint lightly. He said I should either be glad the road didn't touch the breakfast nook or the kitchen. I demand that the issue be taken seriously by you. I have written to you three times already, and you will say that you are "working on the problem." I am angry and in the mood to take legal action. Moving the highway or to cancel it entirely is the only solution. I expect you to cooperate and that you will fire the clerk.

Sincerely,

Joshua Hickman

Figure 18-1:
A disgruntled citizen writes a letter that is unparalleled.

Answers to Parallelism Problems

1 **The ski pants that Robert favors are green, skin tight, and stretchy.** The original sentence links two adjectives *(green* and *skin-tight)* with a verb form *(made of stretch fabric).* Two adjectives + one verb form = penalty box. The corrected version relies on three adjectives *(green, skin-tight,* and *stretchy)* to describe Robert's favorite pants. (In case you're wondering why he finds it hard to get a date, think about his wardrobe.)

2 **When he eases into those pants and zips up with great difficulty, Robert feels cool.** The original sentence isn't parallel because the *and* joins two verbs *(eases* and *zipping)* that don't match. In the corrected version, *and* links *eases* and *zips.* In fact, these verb forms are so well suited to each other that they planned a date for Saturday night. Another possible correction: *Easing into those pants and zipping up with great difficulty, Robert feels cool.* Now *easing* parallels *zipping.*

3 **In this ski outfit, Robert can breathe only with great difficulty and loudness.** The original sentence matches up *difficulty* (a noun) and *loudly* (a description). These two are headed for the divorce court. The correction pairs two nouns *(difficulty* and *loudness).*

4 **The sacrifice for the sake of fashion is worth the trouble and discomfort, Robert says.** The clunker (the original sentence) joins a noun, *trouble,* and a whole clause (that's the grammar term for a subject/verb combo), *how he feels uncomfortable.* Not parallel! The correction links two nouns, *trouble* and *discomfort.*

5 **correct.** The sentence yokes two *-ing* forms *(sliding* and *coasting).* Verdict: legal.

6 **Robert has often been known to object to secondhand clothing and used equipment.** You're okay with two nouns *(clothing* and *equipment).* You're not okay with a noun *(clothing)* and a clause *(how some equipment is used),* which is what you had in the original sentence.

7 **"With a good parka or a warm face mask, I'm ready for anything," he says.** The *or* in the original sentence links *with a good parka* and *wearing a warm face mask.* The second term includes a verb form *(wearing),* and the first doesn't, so you know that the parallelism is off. In the correction, *parka* and *face mask* are linked. Because they're both nouns, the parallelism works.

8 **The face mask is useful on the slopes and does double duty in bank robberies.** The original sentence isn't parallel because *is useful* and *doing* don't match. The corrected sentence pairs *is* and *does,* two verbs, so it's fine.

9 **The ski pants can also be recycled, if they are ripless and clean.** *Ripless* is an adjective, but *without stains* is a phrase. Penalty box! The corrected version has two adjectives *(ripless* and *clean).*

10 **However, bank robbery and simple street muggings are more difficult in ski pants.** In the correction I match two nouns *(robbery* and *muggings),* but you could also go for two infinitives *(to rob a bank* and *to mug someone).* Just be sure the two subjects have the same grammatical identity.

11 **Robbers need speed and privacy, but they also need pockets.** The original sentence falls off the parallel tracks because *speed* is a noun and *to be private* is an infinitive. The correction joins two nouns, *speed* and *privacy.*

12 **How to stash stolen money and where to put an unwanted ski mask are important issues.** In the correction, the subjects are both clauses; that is, they're both expressions containing subjects and verbs. (Think of a clause as a mini-sentence that can sometimes, but not always, stand alone.) Two clauses = legal pairing. The original sentence derails because the first subject *(stashing stolen money)* is a gerund, and the second is based on an infinitive *(to put).*

13 **Robert, who is actually quite honest and not inclined to rob anyone, nevertheless thinks about crime and fashion.** The original sentence links a plain-vanilla-no-sprinkles description *(honest)* with an *-ing* verb form *(not having the inclination to rob anyone)*. No sale. The answer matches two descriptions, *honest* and *inclined*.

14 **He once wrote and edited a newsletter called *Crimes of Fashion*.** The answer matches two past tense verbs, *wrote* and *edited*. The original matched a past *(wrote)* and a past perfect *(had edited)* without any valid reason for a different tense, so it wasn't parallel.

15 **To ski and to pursue a career in law enforcement are Robert's dreams.** Pair two infinitives *(to ski* and *to pursue)* and you're fine. Or, pair *skiing* and *pursuing* for an alternate correct answer.

16 **If you've studied biology, you know that a person must learn the names of hundreds, if not thousands, of organisms.** The original sentence shifts from *anyone* (third person) to *you* (second person). The correction stays in second. Another possible fix pairs *anyone* with *he or she knows* — all third-person forms.

17 **correct**. Two questions. No shifts, no problem.

18 **The Amoeba Family provides a good example of the process, so I will explain its name.** The original sentence shifts unnecessarily from active *(provides)* to passive *(will be explained)*. The corrected sentence stays in active voice. True, it contains a shift from third person (talking about the Amoeba Family) to first, but that shift is justified by meaning.

19 **You may not know that the first example of this single-celled organism was named Amy.** The original sentence shifts inappropriately from present tense *(may not know)* to conditional *(would have)*. The tenses in the correction make more sense; the first part is present and the second past, because you *may not know* right now about something that happened previously. The shift is there, but it's justified by meaning. The correction has another shift, also justified, from active *(may not know)* to passive *(was named)*. Because the person giving the name is unknown, the passive must be used.

20 **When they split in half, the new organisms name themselves.** The question sentence is non-parallel because it moves from the second person *you* to the third person *organisms*. The correction stays in third person (talking about someone), with *they* and *organisms*.

21 **The right half of Amy still called herself Amy, but the left half now called herself Bea.** In the original, the extra *by* in the first half of the sentence unbalances the sentence. The correction eliminated the problem by making both parts of the sentence active.

22 **The next time Amy and Bea split, they formed four new organisms.** Parallel statements should stay in one person, in this case third person, talking about *Amy, Bea,* and *they*.

23 **No one can imagine a conference between four single-celled organisms unless he or she witnesses it.** The issue here is singular/plural pronouns. The original sentence begins with the singular *no one* and then shifts illegally to *they,* a plural. The correction begins with singular *(no one* again) and stays singular *(he or she)*.

24 **Amy Right Half favored a name that people would notice.** The first verb in the original is past, but the second shifts illogically to the future. Penalty box. In the correction, the past tense *favored* is matched with a conditional *(would notice),* but that change is logical because Amy is attaching a condition to her choice of name.

25 **Amy Left Half thought about the choice for so long that she neglected her swimming.** Why change from active *(thought)* to passive *(was neglected)?* Two actives work better.

26 **Bea Right Half, a proto-feminist, opted for "Amy-Bea," because she wanted to honor both her parents.** The original sentence has a meaningless tense shift, from past *(opted)* to present *(wants)*. The correction stays in past tense *(opted, wanted)*.

27 **Everyone always pronounced "Amy-Bea" very fast, and soon "Amoeba" was the preferred spelling.** The original sentence shifts from singular *(everyone)* to plural *(their)*. The answer avoids the problem by dropping the second pronoun entirely.

28 **Single-celled organisms should have simple names that biology students can remember.** The shift from active in the original *(should have)* to passive *(can be remembered)* isn't a good idea. The verbs in the correction *(should have, can remember)* stay active, jogging for at least an hour a day.

29 **Bea Left Half, by the way, will change her name to Amy-Bea when she reaches the age of seventeen days.** The original contains an illogical tense shift. The first verb is future *(will change)* and the second is past *(reached)*, placing the sentence in some sort of time warp and out of the realm of parallel structure. In the correction, both actions are in the future *(will change, when she reaches)*.

30 **You know what teenagers are like; they always have to assert their identities.** The corrected sentence stays in plural *(teenagers, they)*, but the original improperly shifts from singular *(a teenager)* to plural *(they)*.

31 **When she traveled to the biker convention, Lola intended both to show off her new Harley and to display her new tattoo.** The paired conjunction here is *both/and.* The correction pairs two infinitives *(to show off* and *to display),* in contrast to the original sentence, which joins a noun *(her new Harley)* and an infinitive *(to display her new tattoo)*.

32 **Lulu would either accompany Lola or stay home to work on a screenplay about bikers.** The elements joined by *either/or* in the original sentence don't match. One is a subject-verb combo *(Lulu would accompany)* and one just a verb *(stay)*. The new version links two verbs *(accompany and stay)*.

33 **Neither Lulu nor Lola plans ahead.** The corrected sentence links two nouns *(Lulu, Lola)* with the *neither/nor* conjunction pair. The original sentence fails the parallelism test because it links a subject-verb *(Lulu plans)* with a noun *(Lola)*.

34 **Lola writes screenplays not only about bikers but about alien invasions also.** The original isn't parallel because the first element joined by *not only/but also* includes a verb *(writes)* but the second doesn't. The new version joins two prepositional phrases.

35 **Lulu is jealous of both Lola's writing talent and the award for "best cycle" on Lola's trophy wall.** Here you're working with *both/and.* In the original sentence *both* precedes *is,* a verb, but no verb follows the *and.* In the correction, each half of the conjunction pair precedes a noun *(talent, award)*.

36 **Lola not only scorns awards but also refuses to enter most contests.** The conjunction pair, *not only/but also,* links two verbs in the answer sentence *(scorns, refuses)*. The original sentence joins a noun, *awards,* to a verb, *scorns.* Mismatch!

37 **correct**. The *neither/nor* combo precedes two nouns in the sentence *(award, trophy)*. Verdict: parallel.

38 **Lulu, on the other hand, wants both the cycling award and the trophy.** In the original sentence, *both* comes before a verb *(wants),* but *and* precedes a noun *(trophy)*. Penalty box. The new version does better, linking two nouns *(award, trophy)*.

39   **Not only did Lulu bribe the judges, but she also ran a full-page ad bragging about herself.** The two conjunctions *(not only/but also)* link subject-verb combos in the corrected version *(did Lulu bribe, she ran)*, but in the original these conjunctions link a subject-verb and a verb *(did Lulu bribe, ran)*. Verdict: Five to ten in the grammar penitentiary.

40   **Either the judges were unimpressed with Lulu's efforts or they liked Lola better.** The *either/ or* pair in the corrected sentence connects two complete sentences *(the judges were unimpressed* and *they liked Lola better)*. In the original, a description *(unimpressed)* incorrectly follows *either*, but a verb *(liked)* follows *or*.

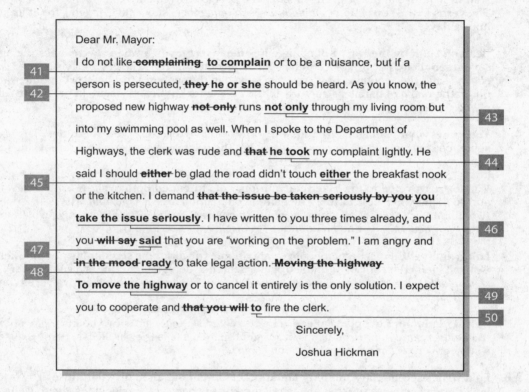

Dear Mr. Mayor:

I do not like ~~complaining~~ **to complain** or to be a nuisance, but if a person is persecuted, ~~they~~ **he or she** should be heard. As you know, the proposed new highway ~~not only~~ runs **not only** through my living room but into my swimming pool as well. When I spoke to the Department of Highways, the clerk was rude and ~~that~~ **he took** my complaint lightly. He said I should ~~either~~ be glad the road didn't touch **either** the breakfast nook or the kitchen. I demand ~~that the issue be taken seriously by you~~ **you take the issue seriously**. I have written to you three times already, and you ~~will say~~ **said** that you are "working on the problem." I am angry and ~~in the mood~~ **ready** to take legal action. ~~Moving the highway~~ **To move the highway** or to cancel it entirely is the only solution. I expect you to cooperate and ~~that you will~~ **to** fire the clerk.

Sincerely,

Joshua Hickman

41   You may change *complaining* to *to complain,* as I did, or you may change *to be* to *being.* Either way makes a parallel sentence.

42   *A person* is singular, but *they* is plural. I change *they* to the singular *he or she,* but if you want to keep *they,* you may scrap *a person* and insert *people* instead.

43   Each part of the *not only/but also* pair should precede a prepositional phrase.

44   The *and* may link *was* and *took,* two verbs, but not a verb *(was)* and a subject-verb combo *(he took)*. Another way to correct this sentence is to select an adjective to replace *he took my complaint lightly* — *dismissive, flippant, disrespectful,* or a similar word. Then the verb *was* precedes two adjectives, *rude* and *dismissive,* perhaps.

45   After the correction, each half of the conjunction pair *either/or* precedes a noun. In the original, the *either* comes before a verb *(be)* and the *or* before a noun.

46 The original sentence switches from active *(I demand)* to passive *(be taken . . . by you)*. The corrected version avoids the shift.

47 The original shifts from present perfect tense *(have written)* to future *(will say)* for no good reason. The correction is in past tense, but that tense is justified by the meaning of the sentence.

48 *Angry* is an adjective, but *in the mood* is a phrase. *Ready,* an adjective, makes the sentence parallel.

49 Either two infinitives (my correction) or two *-ing* forms *(Moving* and *canceling)* are acceptable here, but not one of each.

50 Two infinitives *(to cooperate, to fire)* are legal, as are two subject-verb combinations *(that you will cooperate* and *that you will fire)* but not one of each.

Chapter 19

Spicing Up and Trimming Down Your Sentences

As I write this, the rain beats down on my window. How glad I am not to be outside! Smiling, I type away, dry and cozy.

Compare the above paragraph to the next paragraph:

I am writing. The rain beats down on my window. I am glad that I am not outside. I am smiling. I type away. I am dry and cozy.

Okay, admit it. The first version is better. Why? Because variety is not only the spice of life but the spice of writing as well. In this chapter you practice adding variety to your sentences by altering the underlying structure and combining ideas. You also get some scissor practice by cutting repetitive or awkward expressions.

Beginning with a Bang: Adding Introductory Elements

The spine of most English sentences is subject-verb: *Mary walks, Oliver opens,* and so forth. Most sentences also have some sort of completion, what grammarians call a complement or an object: *Mary walks the dog, Oliver opens the peanut butter.*

Even when you throw in some descriptions, this basic skeleton is boring if it's the only structure you ever use. The easiest and most effective way to change the basic pattern is to add an introductory element, which is italicized in the following examples:

Sticking her finger in the jar, Agnes curdled the peanut butter. (The introductory verb form tells something Agnes did.)

Despite the new polish on her nails, Agnes was willing to eat without a fork. (The introductory phrase gives information about Agnes's willingness to get down and dirty with the peanut butter.)

When she was full, Agnes closed the jar. (The introductory statement has a subject and a verb, *she was,* and in grammar terms is a clause. Once again, you get more information about Agnes.)

As always in grammar, you don't need to clutter your mind with definitions. Just try some of the patterns, but be sure to avoid a common error: The subject of the main part of the sentence must be the one doing the action or in the state of being described by the introductory verb form. Check out Chapter 15 for more information on this sort of error.

Put boredom behind you by combining the two statements in each question, making one of the statements an introductory element. *Note:* Several answers are possible for each exercise. Your answer may differ from the one I provide in the answers section and still be correct. Check to see that you express the same ideas as the original statements and that the action or state of being expressed by the introductory verb form relates to the subject of the main portion of the sentence.

Q. The boss wants the memo immediately. Oliver stops cleaning his teeth and starts typing.

_____

_____

A. **Realizing that the boss wants the memo immediately, Oliver stops cleaning his teeth and starts typing.** This is just one of many possibilities. You may also begin with a statement like **Now that Oliver knows that the boss wants the memo immediately, he stops cleaning his teeth and starts typing.**

1. Jesse is considering retirement. Jesse's mortgage holder thinks that Jesse should work at least 100 more years.

_____

_____

2. The bank wants Jesse to work hard. Jesse's debt is quite large.

_____

_____

3. Jesse wants to drink martinis on a tropical island. Jesse also wants to keep his house.

_____

_____

4. Jesse's entire plan is impractical. An especially unrealistic part lets Jesse drink martinis all day.

_____

_____

5. The bank manager speaks to Jesse in a loud voice. She points out that Jesse has $.02 in his savings account.

_____

_____

6. The bank manager angers easily. Jesse brings out the worst in her.

_____

_____

7. Jesse considered robbing the bank. Jesse is an honest man.

_____

_____

8. The bank manager eventually decided to rob the bank. She drank martinis on a tropical island.

_____

_____

Smoothing Out Choppy Sentences

The term _subordinate_ doesn't refer to the poor slob who has to make coffee and open letters for the boss. Instead, a _subordinate_ is the part of the sentence that, while still containing a subject and a verb, occupies a position of lesser importance in relation to the rest of the sentence. In the world of grammar, which is _not_ a tourist destination, the full name is _subordinate clause_. Try not to remember that fact. Do remember that subordinate clauses may fall at the beginning, middle, or end of the sentence.

Some examples, with the subordinate in italics:

The box, _which Ellen was told never to open,_ practically screamed, "Look inside!"

After she had pried up the lid, Ellen ran screaming down the hall.

Ellen is planning to repair _whatever was damaged if she ever manages to replace the lid._ (This one has two subordinates, _whatever was damaged_ and _if she . . . the lid._)

As you see, subordination is useful for tucking one idea into another. If you have a lot of short sentences strung together, subordination can make your writing less choppy.

Take a shot at inserting ideas. Combine the ideas in these exercises into one sentence per question, using subordinate clauses.

Q. Ellen's boss held a press conference. The boss issued a statement about "the incident."

_____

_____

A. **Ellen's boss held a press conference at which he issued a statement about "the incident."** More than one answer is possible here. Here's another: **Ellen's boss, who held a press conference, issued a statement about "the incident."**

9. Joseph Shmo is a prize-winning reporter. He asked the boss a number of questions.

_____

_____

10. The boss asked Joe to sit down and be quiet. Joe refused. He was still looking for information about "the incident."

     _____

     _____

11. The CIA became interested in the case. The agency sent several agents. The agents were supposed to investigate.

     _____

     _____

12. Ellen didn't want to talk to the agents. Her boss had told her that her job was in jeopardy.

     _____

     _____

13. Ellen bought a bus ticket. She slipped out of the office.

     _____

     _____

14. The CIA may track her down. They will deal with her harshly.

     _____

     _____

15. Ellen is away. The boss is trying to manage the news media.

     _____

     _____

16. Ellen has offered her story to an independent film company. The film company is tentatively interested.

     _____

     _____

17. The box has been placed in the nation's most secure prison. The prison is located in a desert.

     _____

     _____

18. Some people know what was in the box. Those people are in danger.

     _____

     _____

Awkward but Interesting: Reversed Sentence Patterns

What wakes up an audience faster than a triple latte? The words *in conclusion.* Knowing that a speech is almost over gives the listener an extra burst of attention. Similarly, in writing, the end of a chapter or a paragraph — and even the end of an individual sentence — may be a high-interest spot. Yet most writers fail to take advantage of this phenomenon. Instead, they lull the reader with the usual subject-verb-object/complement pattern. Run your eyeballs over these two examples:

> The hungry bear ran through the trees, across a clearing, and toward our SUV.

> Through the trees, across a clearing, and toward our SUV ran the hungry bear.

Nothing is wrong with the first sample sentence, but isn't the second a nice change of pace? In the second, *the hungry bear* is a punch line. The sentence leads the reader through the bear's route before revealing the subject. Granted, you wouldn't want to reverse all your sentences. Doing so would simply create another pattern with the potential to bore your reader. But stick an occasional reversed sentence in your writing, and your reader will thank you.

Don't reverse sentences by lapsing into passive voice. Active voice is when the subject does the action *(Mary poked Peter);* passive is when the subject receives the action *(Peter was poked by Mary).* Passive voice isn't wrong. In fact, it comes in handy very occasionally when you don't want to say who did what *(The window was broken).* But passive is wordy and awkward. If you can stay active, do so.

These sentences are in the usual order. Hit reverse gear and reword. Aim for the same meaning expressed in a different order. To keep you awake, I tuck in a couple of passive-voice sentences. Change them to active voice (any order) for a better, stronger expression.

0. The paper deliverer tossed onto our lawn a sticky, soggy mess of a newspaper.

_____

_____

A. **A sticky, soggy mess of a newspaper the paper deliverer tossed onto our lawn.**

19. Duke, our favorite Pug, was soon sprinting from the kitchen, sliding through the living room, and making a bee-line for the lawn.

_____

_____

20. The locked front door was in Duke's way.

_____

_____

21. The newspaper and advertisements were not chewed by Duke.

_____

_____

22. Duke did place a few tooth marks and about a hundred scratches on the front door.

_____

_____

23. Puppy obedience school was unsuccessful for Duke.

_____

_____

24. The paper deliverer stood on the front porch listening to Duke's frantic efforts.

_____

_____

25. He was not a fan of dogs.

_____

_____

26. His left leg had seven dog-bite scars.

_____

_____

27. Duke was not to blame for the paper deliverer's tooth marks.

_____

_____

28. The mail carrier's scars, on the other hand, were inflicted by Duke.

_____

_____

Shedding and Eliminating Redundancy

Don't you hate listening to the same thing twice? I hate listening to the same thing twice. You probably hate listening . . . okay, I'm sure you get the point by now! Repetition is boring. You should avoid it in your writing, regardless of the form it takes — and it does take many forms, including doubled adjectives _(calm and serene),_ extra phrases _(six feet tall in height),_ or just plain saying the same thing two different ways _(in my opinion I think)._

Rewrite the following sentences, eliminating the extra words (if any) to avoid redundancy.

0. Anxious and extremely tense, Susannah approached the starting line where the race would begin.

_____

_____

A. **Extremely tense, Susannah approached the starting line.** I chose *extremely tense,* but you could cut those words and stay with *anxious.* Just don't use both *tense* and *anxious* because they say pretty much the same thing. The other cut (*where the race would begin*) is justified because that's what a *starting line* is.

29. Susannah's new and innovative idea for racing strategy was to cut away quickly from the crowd and separate herself.

_____

_____

30. I believe that in my view Susannah has a great chance of winning and finishing in first place.

_____

_____

31. The spikes that she installed and put in on her tire rims should easily and without much effort cut her opponents' tires.

_____

_____

32. Bethany thinks that Susannah scattered tacks and little nails over the left side of the course, where her chief and most important rival rides.

_____

_____

33. There are two sides to every story, of course; Susannah and Bethany have different ideas about what is fair and unfair in a motorcycle race.

_____

_____

34. A little tack can alter the outcome of the race in an important and significant way.

_____

_____

35. Susannah says that in future days to come she will win legally or not at all.

_____

_____

Calling All Overachievers: Extra Practice Honing Your Sentences

In Figure 19-1 is a short story excerpt that could use some major help. Revise it as you see fit, paying attention to varied sentence patterns, unnecessary words, and choppiness.

Figure 19-1:
Sample
short story
excerpt
with horrid
sentence
structures.

> Darla fainted. Darla was lying on the floor in a heap. Her legs were bent under her. She breathed in quick pants at a rapid rate. Henry came running as fast as he could. He neared Darla and gasped. "My angel," he said. His heart was beating. His cardiologist would be worried about the fast rate. Henry did not care. Henry cared only about Darla. She was the love of his life. She was unconscious. He said, "Angel Pie, you don't have to pawn your engagement ring." He knelt next to her.

Answers to Sentence Improvement Problems

1 **Despite the fact that Jesse is considering retirement, his mortgage holder thinks that Jesse should work at least 100 more years.** My answer begins with a prepositional phrase. You may also start with _Although Jesse is . . ._ or _Contrary to Jesse's desire to . . . ._

2 **Because Jesse's debt is quite large, the bank wants him to work hard.** The first time I show this sentence structure to my students, they often protest that "you can't begin a sentence with _because._" Yes, you can, as long as you have a complete thought in the sentence.

WARNING!

Take care not to dangle an introduction here. (See Chapter 15 for more information on danglers.) If you write something like _Wanting Jesse to work hard, Jesse's debt . . . ,_ you're saying that _the debt,_ not the bank, wants Jesse to work hard.

3 **In addition to his desire to drink martinis on a tropical island, Jesse also wants to keep his house.** I start here with a prepositional phrase, but a clause (_Even though Jesse wants to drink martinis on a tropical island_) would also be a good beginning, pairing nicely with the rest of the sentence (_Jesse also wants to keep his house_).

4 **Impractical in every way, the plan is especially unrealistic in letting Jesse drink martinis all day.** The introduction here is just another way to describe _plan,_ the subject of the main part of the sentence.

5 **Speaking to Jesse in a loud voice, the bank manager points out that he has $.02 in his savings account.** Here the bank manager is still speaking, but that thought is expressed by an introductory verb form now, not by a separate sentence.

6 **Angering easily, the bank manager admits that Jesse brings out the worst in her.** I added _admits_ so that _the bank manager_ is the subject of the sentence. A dangler (an error I explain in Chapter 15) would be created by leaving _Jesse_ as the subject and beginning with _angering_ or a similar expression. In such a sentence, _Jesse_ would be the one _angering easily_ — not the meaning you want to convey. Another possible correction: _Bringing out the worst in the bank manager, Jesse angered her easily._

7 **Even though he is an honest man, Jesse considered robbing the bank.** The first part of the sentence is a clause because it has a subject and a verb, but it depends upon the statement in the second part of the sentence to complete the thought.

8 **With martinis on a tropical island in her future, the bank manager eventually decided to rob the bank.** Here a nice set of prepositional phrases packs an opening punch.

9 **Joseph Shmo, who is a prize-winning reporter, asked the boss a number of questions.** You can also drop the _who is,_ leaving _a prize-winning reporter_ to do the job. (The shortened form is called an appositive, but you don't need to know that. You don't need to know what was in the box either.)

10 **The boss asked Joe to sit down and be quiet, but Joe, who was still looking for information, refused.** Here _who_ tacks the extra information about _Joe_ firmly to the rest of the sentence.

11 **The CIA, which was interested in the case, sent several agents who were supposed to investigate.** The pronoun _which_ stands in for the CIA and introduces extra information about that secretive agency.

12 **Ellen didn't want to talk to the agents because her boss had told her that her job was in jeopardy.** The new, combined sentence has a cause-and-effect structure introduced by the word _because._

13 **When she slipped out of the office, Ellen bought a bus ticket.** The word *when* ties the information about slipping out to the reason Ellen slipped out.

14 **If the CIA tracks her down, they will deal with her harshly.** Ignoring the CIA isn't nice. Writing choppy sentences isn't nice either! *If* expresses a possibility, as does the verb *may* in the original.

15 **While Ellen is away, the boss is trying to manage the news media.** A time expression works nicely here, tying Ellen's absence to the boss's press conference.

16 **Ellen has offered her story to an independent film company that is tentatively interested.** When you use *that* to introduce an idea, a comma is seldom necessary.

17 **The box has been placed in the nation's most secure prison, which is located in a desert.** When you use *which* to introduce an idea, a comma usually separates the *which* statement from the rest of the sentence. (Check out Chapter 5 for more information on comma use.)

18 **Whoever knows what was in the box is in danger.** Sounds like the plot of a new TV series, doesn't it? When you're tucking ideas into your sentences, don't forget *whatever* and *whoever* — very useful little words!

19 **Sprinting from the kitchen, sliding through the living room, and making a bee-line for the lawn was Duke, our favorite Pug.** By placing the subject, *Duke*, near the end, you gain drama.

20 **In Duke's way was the locked front door.** Not a big change, but placing the *locked front door* at the end is a way to emphasize the tragedy of the barrier that the eager dog can't surmount.

21 **Duke didn't chew the newspaper and advertisements.** The original sentence is passive, not usually a good choice. The correction is a straightforward, active voice, subject-verb-object order. You can also flip the standard order and place the object before the subject and verb.

22 **On the front door a few tooth marks and about a hundred scratches placed Duke.** The new order is dramatic, emphasizing *Duke*. It may sound awkward to your ear, however. That's the trade-off with reverse order sentences. You gain interest but startle (and perhaps disturb) your reader. Use this sort of sentence sparingly!

23 **Unsuccessful for Duke was puppy obedience school.** Leading with the description *unsuccessful* is a surprising, and therefore interesting, choice.

24 **On the front porch listening to Duke's frantic efforts stood the paper deliverer.** Leading with phrases *(on the front porch and listening to Duke's frantic efforts)* is unusual but effective.

25 **Not a fan of dogs was he.** This reverse-order sentence has a comic effect, highlighting *not a fan of dogs* by placing it in an unexpected position.

26 **Seven dog-bite scars had his left leg.** Like question 25, this reverse-order sentence focuses on *seven dog-bite scars*.

27 **Not to blame for the paper deliverer's tooth marks was Duke.** Leading with a negative *(not)* isn't something you'd want to do every day, but every seven days or so (just kidding — what I mean is on rare occasions), you can get a lot of attention with this pattern.

28 **On the other hand, Duke did inflict the mail carrier's scars.** The passive voice of the original is a real no-no. You do know, because the sentence tells you, who chomped on the mail carrier. Passive voice is therefore unnecessary and awkward.

29 **Susannah's new idea for racing strategy was to cut away quickly from the crowd.** You may cut *new* and leave *innovative,* but don't use both. Also, you may drop *to cut away quickly from the crowd* and leave *separate herself.* If that's your option, you may want to move *quickly* to the end of the sentence, just to retain the idea of speed.

30 **Susannah has a great chance of winning.** Why say *I believe* or *in my view?* If you're saying that Susannah has a chance, the listener or reader knows that's what you think. *Winning* and *finishing in first place* are the same; choose either one.

31 **The spikes that she installed on her tire rims should easily cut her opponents' tires.** More doubles: *installed* and *put in* match, as do *easily* and *without much effort.* Choose one of each, but not both.

32 **Bethany thinks that Susannah scattered tacks over the left side of the course, where her chief rival rides.** I imagine that a hardware specialist could explain the difference between *tacks* and *little nails,* but to the general reader, the distinction is irrelevant. Ditto for *chief* and *most important.*

33 **Susannah and Bethany have different ideas about what is fair in a motorcycle race.** The whole first part of the sentence is unnecessary. Of course differing points of view exist, and as the sentence goes on to specify, the general statement is a waste of words. Also, if the bikers can't agree on what's fair, by definition they also don't agree on what's unfair, so that part of the statement may also be cut.

34 **A little tack can alter the outcome of the race in an important way.** If you prefer, drop *important* and keep *significant.* Just don't use the two together.

35 **Susannah says that in the future she will win legally or not at all.** Is there a future in the past? Or somewhere else in time? Once you say *future,* you don't have to add *days to come.* (If you'd rather keep *days to come,* go for it and drop *future.*)

Darla fainted. **Lying on the floor in a heap, her legs bent under her,** [36]

she breathed in quick pants at a rapid rate. Henry came r Running as [37]

fast as he could **came Henry. Nearing Darla, he gasped, "My angel."** [38] [39]

His heart was beating **so fast that his cardiologist would worry.** Henry [40]

did not care. Henry cared only about Darla, the love of his life, now [41]

unconscious. **Kneeling next to her he said,** "Angel Pie, you don't have to [42]

pawn your engagement ring."

36 Three sentences — *Darla was lying on the floor in a heap, Her legs were bent under her,* and *She breathed in quick pants* — may be easily combined. The ideas in the first two sentences are turned into introductory elements, with the last of the three sentences as the main idea. If you add an introductory element with a verb form, be sure that the subject of the main section of the sentence is the person or thing doing the action or in the state of being mentioned in the introduction. Another possible combination: After Darla fainted, she was lying on the floor in a heap. With her legs under her, she breathed in quick pants.

37 The revision cuts repetition; *rapid* and *quick* are the same.

38 The sentence *Henry came running as fast as he could* has been reversed to create an interesting variation on the standard sentence pattern.

39 Two sentences — *He neared Darla and gasped. "My angel," he said.* — have been combined. The new version, with an introductory element *(Nearing Darla)*, is more concise.

40 A subordinate *(that his cardiologist would worry)* tucks an idea from one sentence into another. Another possibility: He neared Darla and gasped, "My angel."

41 The original story ends with several short, choppy sentences. The revision combines all but the last sentence.

42 The last two sentences of the original combine with an introductory verb form, *kneeling*. If you begin with *kneeling,* be sure that *he* or *Henry* is the subject of the main part of the sentence. You can also revise this section in this way: "Angel Pie, you don't have to pawn your engagement ring," he said as he knelt next to her.

Chapter 20

Steering Clear of Tricky Word Traps

*B*ecause little things mean a lot, as the saying goes, this chapter puts your writing under a microscope. The tiny errors that can sink you — a nonstandard expression, a faulty irregular verb, and the wrong word from a pair of similar words, for example — are in focus here. Peer through the lens and raise your writing to the highest level.

Separating Almost-Twins: Commonly Confused Words

Do you know any twins who resemble each other but have completely different personalities? One is a professional hang glider, perhaps, and the other a librarian. Then you understand that each half of a similar-looking pair may function in a vastly different way, and woe to the writer who sends one to do the other's job. This section divulges the ones that trip up most people.

> **Affect** usually expresses action: Mallory's tantrum did not *affect* her mother's decision to leave the candy aisle.

> **Effect** is most often used as a noun and means "result": One *effect* of Mallory's sweet tooth was a truly impressive dental bill.

Both *affect* and *effect* may be used in other ways, though much less frequently. *Affect* as a noun means "the way someone displays emotions." *Effect* as a verb means "to bring about a change in the face of opposition." In this chapter, though, I concentrate on the more common usage for each.

Got it? If you think you know how you're affected by the effect of these almost-twins, check out the next set of commonly confused words.

> **Farther** refers to distance: Mallory runs *farther* than anyone else when a candy bar is at stake.

> **Further** refers to just about everything but distance (intensity, degree, time, and so forth): When Mallory thought *further* about the matter, she decided that artificial sweetener was never a good choice.

Other pairs (or triplets) are quite different in appearance, but for some reason people mix them up:

> **Like** expresses similarity, but it may not be attached to a subject/verb combo: She jumps _like_ Mike.

> **As** expresses similarity too, but it's the one you want in front of a subject/verb: She jumps _as_ Mike does, but she gets paid less for her leaps.

> **Such as** introduces examples: Mallory's cupboard is stocked with sweets such as pie filling, pudding mix, and chocolate.

The last commonly confused words often go together, but they aren't interchangeable.

> **Imply** is "to hint": Mallory never actually asked for a gumdrop, but she strongly _implied_ that one would be welcome.

> **Infer** is "to figure something out that has been implied": Hearing Mallory's "Ode on a Gumdrop," I _inferred_ that the bag of candy would probably be empty after Mallory's visit.

Can you tell the following twins and triplets apart? Circle the best word or phrase in each set of parentheses.

_**Q.**_ Fueled by the caffeine in two double-lattes, Jake drove (farther/further) than anyone else.

_**A.**_ **Farther**. If you're dealing with distance, _farther_ is the one you want.

 1. The judge insisted on (farther/further) proof that the cop's speed gun was broken.

 2. I gave the judge tons of proof, (like/as/such as) a photo of my car, a statement from my girlfriend about how I always drive slowly, and a perfect-attendance award I earned in second grade.

 3. Waving my wallet vigorously, I (implied/inferred) that it was empty and paying the fine was out of the question.

 4. (Like/As) judges often do, Judge Crater stubbornly refused to hear my side of the story.

 5. "Don't go any (farther/further) with your testimony," he snarled.

 6. (Like/As) a statue, I shut up and sat as still as a stone.

 7. The judge, unfortunately, (implied/inferred) from my behavior that I was silently protesting his ruling.

 8. The (affect/effect) of this decision was disastrous.

 9. Nothing I said, when I started talking again, (affected/effected) the judge's ruling.

10. Financial setbacks (like/as/such as) speeding tickets completely wreck my budget.

11. I can't convince my romantic partner to spend (farther/further) time with me without reservations at an expensive restaurant.

12. High-priced food, in my experience, (affects/effects) the way a potential date reacts; if I plan a bowling evening, my date will (imply/infer) that I'm poor and dump me.

Comparing Quantities without Numbers

Lost in the fog of the history of English is the reason why different words are used to describe singulars and plurals when you're counting or measuring:

More than, many, and **fewer** work for plurals: *more than* nineteen witnesses, *many* problems, *fewer* than fifty coffee cups. These words work well with things you can count.

Less, much, and **over** take you into singular territory: *less* interest in the sport, *much* unrest, *over* an hour. These words are best with things you can measure but not count.

The word *over* is frequently misused in place of *more* or *more than*.

Amount is appropriate when the item you're discussing is singular: the *amount* of enthusiasm.

Number applies to plurals: the *number* of bowties.

Between is the word you want when you're talking about two people or things: I'm having trouble choosing *between* pistachio and chocolate chip.

Among is for groups of three or more: *Among* the twelve candidates for mayor, Shirley stands out.

Uncover your toes (in case you need to count higher than ten) and take a stab at this sentence. Circle the correct word in each set of parentheses.

Q. Just (between/among) you and me, do you think he needs a dye job?

A. **between**. *You* plus *me* equals two, and *between* is the word for couples. *Among* comes into play for three or more, as in *among the five of us*.

13. The boss sent (more than/over) 300 memos describing when and how we can order paper for the copy machine.

14. We employees, all 4,546 of us, discussed the memo (between/among) ourselves, and despite (many/much) difference of opinion, we eventually agreed on one thing.

15. We decided that e-mail uses (fewer/less) paper and is easier to ignore.

16. The boss's (many/much) memos scold us for the (number/amount) of paper we waste.

17. Recently, the boss's secretary collected (more than/over) 5,000 sheets of paper from our desks, all of them memos sent to us by the boss.

18. Surely it takes (fewer/less) energy to shelve the issue altogether.

19. (More than/over) a year ago the boss caught "shredding fever."

20. The (number/amount) of important material he shredded is impossible to determine.

21. Personally, in a contest (between/among) him and his dog, the dog would win the award for "Best Boss."

22. The dog would fire (fewer/less) employees.

23. With the dog in charge, the (amount/number) of barking would also decrease.

24. (Among/between) the other candidates for a replacement boss that I would consider are all the inhabitants of New York City.

Sorry to Bust Your Bubble, but Some Common Expressions Are Wrong

English *should of* been easier, I *cannot help but* think. *Being that* English is difficult to learn, I'm going to *try and* spend more time studying it. *Irregardless*, I'll still have time to fold origami, a hobby which I *can't hardly* resist because it does *not* have *no* stress attached to it.

By now I'm sure you've figured out that the italicized words in the preceding paragraph are all problematic. In proper English, they don't exist. If you're using any made-up expressions, it's time to remove them from your speech and writing and substitute the correct words, which you can see in Table 20-1.

Table 20-1	Correcting Made-Up Words
Wrong	*Right*
Should of Would of Could of	Should have, should've Would have, would've Could have, could've
Cannot help but	Cannot help [insert the *-ing* form of the verb]: *Cannot help wondering,* for example
Being that	Because
Try and	Try to
Irregardless	Regardless
Can't hardly	Can hardly

Here's your challenge: Rewrite the following sentences, substituting proper English for any nonstandard terms. I throw a few correct sentences into the mix, so when you find one, simply write "correct" in the blank.

0. I can't help but think that your questions about the final exam are extremely annoying.

_____

_____

A. I can't help thinking that your questions about the final exam are extremely annoying.
The expressions *can't help but* and *cannot help but* are double negatives. English, not always the most logical language in the universe, is logical in this instance: The two negatives (*not* and *but*) cancel each other and express a positive meaning. Thus the original sentence means that you can stop thinking this way if you want to do so.

25. Irregardless of the teacher's views on technology in the classroom, Mark sends an instant message to his brother.

_____

_____

26. Kevin doesn't answer immediately, being that he's in the middle of the sandbox.

_____

_____

27. "I'll try and answer Mark after snack," he thinks.

_____

_____

28. The teacher doesn't want no distraction from the peanut butter cookies she has prepared, so she confiscates Kevin's PDA, which sends and receives e-mail, keeps track of Kevin's play dates, and handles instant messages.

_____

_____

29. Kevin should of hidden his PDA until nap time.

_____

_____

30. Mark can't hardly believe some of the stories Kevin tells about kindergarten.

_____

_____

31. Mark remembers his own days in finger-paint land, which he should of treasured.

_____

_____

32. Because the third grade room is near the kindergarten, Mark could of walked out of the classroom and spoken directly to Kevin.

_____

_____

33. Kevin can't help thinking about his PDA, which now resides on the teacher's desk.

_____

_____

34. Being that the day is almost over, Kevin asks the teacher to return his PDA.

_____

_____

35. "Being in kindergarten is really annoying sometimes," Kevin thinks.

_____

_____

36. "I can't hardly wait until I'm in first grade," he remarks.

_____

_____

Verbs That Will Give You a Headache

Sit (not _set_) yourself down for some practice with four headache-inducing verbs. Afterward you can _lie_ (not _lay_) down for a rest.

To **lie** is "to rest or recline the body." (Yes, it also means that you aren't telling the truth, but that definition isn't a problem.) The past tense of _lie_ is _lay_. The form of the verb _lie_ that combines with _has, have,_ or _had_ is _lain_.

To **lay** is "to place something" or "to put." The past tense of _lay_ is _laid_. For _lay_, the form that combines with _has, have,_ or _had_ is _laid_.

To **sit** is "to bend your knees and put your bottom on some sort of surface." The past tense and the combo form are both _sat_.

To **set** is "to place, to put something somewhere." The past tense and combo forms are also _set_.

To tell the difference between these two pairs of verbs, think of _lie_ and _sit_ as actions that a person does to himself or herself: I _lie_ down, I _sit_ in the chair. _Lay_ and _set,_ on the other hand, are actions that a person does to something else: I _lay_ the check on the desk, I _set_ the vase down on the piano.

Don't set down your pen until you try the following questions. Circle the correct form of the verb in the parentheses.

Q. Yesterday Alice was so tired that she (lie/lay/lied/laid, lain) down for a nap even though her favorite soap was on television.

A. lay. The meaning in this sentence is "to rest or to recline," so the verb you want is _to lie,_ and the past tense of _to lie_ is _lay_.

37. In the soap, the main character (lies/lays) in bed, comatose.

38. In the world of soaps, the rule is that the doctor must (sit/set) by the bed every day with a look of concern and love on his or her face.

39. In yesterday's episode, the doctor (sit/sat/set) a bouquet of flowers on the nightstand.

40. When the nurse told the doctor to go home and (lie/lay) down, the doctor replied that she would "(sit/set) down for a while."

41. Last week the doctor (lay/laid) a wreath on the tomb of the unknown soldier.

42. The viewers think the wreath that (lies/lays) there is a sign that the soldier is really the doctor's long lost lover.

43. During sweeps week, the long lost lover will show up and (sit/set) next to the doctor in the cafeteria.

44. The final show will reveal that the long lost lover has (lain/laid) in a bed, comatose too.

45. While the doctor (sits/sets) there gobbling tuna salad, the lover will explain what happened to the evil twin and other soap mysteries.

Combining Rightfully Independent Words

A few pairs are often written — erroneously — as a single word: *a lot* (never *alot*) and *all right* (never *alright*). A couple of other pairs have both a single- and a double-word form, and confusing these pairs changes the meaning of your sentence:

✔ *Already* (by this time) and *all ready* (completely prepared)

✔ *Everyday* (ordinary) and *every day* (daily)

✔ *Sometime* (at an unspecified moment) and *some time* (a period of time)

Can you find the correct form in the following pairs? Circle your choices.

Q. Because Jennifer sneezes (alot/a lot), Abigail has (already/all ready) packed a dozen handkerchiefs.

A. **a lot, already**. The single-word form *alot* is never correct. In the second parentheses, the meaning you want is "by this time," so *already* is the one.

46. The sneezing will end (sometime/some time).

47. Jennifer has devoted (sometime/some time) to the study of the nose and its explosions.

48. She has discovered that most people sneeze at least once (everyday/every day).

49. Jennifer herself sneezes at least ten times a day, so she buys (alot/a lot) of tissues.

50. When Abigail arrived to take Jennifer to the airport, Jennifer was (already/all ready).

51. Jennifer carried her (everyday/every day) handkerchief, a blue cotton square.

52. Abigail packed a fresh outfit for (everyday/every day) of the trip.

53. "Come on (already/all ready)!" sighed Abigail with impatience.

54. "It will take us (sometime/some time) to get to the airport and through security," she added.

55. "(Alright!/All right!) I'm coming," yelled Jennifer.

Calling All Overachievers: Extra Practice with Tricky Words

In Figure 20-1 check out an obituary that (never, I assure you) appeared in a local paper. Whenever you encounter a misused word, correct the clunker. You should find ten mistakes.

Lloyd Demos Dies at 81: Specialized in Ancient Egypt

Lloyd Demos died yesterday as he was pursuing farther study in ancient Egyptian culture. Demos, who effected the lives of many residents of our town, had alot of varied interests. By the time he died he had all ready learned 12 languages, including ancient Egyptian, and spent some time everyday studying Egyptian grammar so that his writing would be alright. Demos had just set down to supper when the Grim Reaper appeared at his door. Irregardless, Demos insisted on finishing his mashed potatoes, though he was heard to say, "I would like to lay down for a while." Demos, who wrote over 50 books, will be fondly remembered.

Figure 20-1: Mock obituary filled with errors.

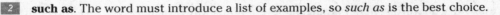

Answers to Tricky Word Problems

1   **further**. In this sentence you want a word that indicates a greater degree, so *further* fills the bill.

2   **such as**. The word must introduce a list of examples, so *such as* is the best choice.

If you introduce examples with *like*, you exclude those examples. In the preceding answer, *like* means that the speaker in the sentence did *not* provide a photo of his car, a statement from his girlfriend, or an attendance award. Instead he provided items that were similar to those on this list.

3   **implied**. The speaker in this sentence is hinting that his finances are in bad shape, and *to imply* is "to hint."

4   **As**. In front of a subject/verb combo, *as* is the only appropriate choice.

5   **further**. The verb *go* makes you think of distance (and *farther* is the word you want for distance), but testimony is not a road that can be measured. Instead, the judge is referring to time, and *further* does the job.

6   **Like**. The speaker resembles a statue, and *like* expresses similarity. Because no verb follows, *like* is better than *as*.

7   **inferred**. Picking up on subtle hints, the judge *inferred* that the speaker was annoyed with the speeding ticket.

8   **effect**. The sentence calls for a noun meaning *result*. Bingo: *effect* wins.

9   **affected**. Here you're looking for a verb that's the same as *influence*. *Affect* is that verb.

10   **such as**. The tickets are presented as an example of budget-wreckers, and *such as* introduces examples.

11   **further**. Once you're talking about time, *farther* isn't an option, because *farther* refers to distance.

12   **affects, infer**. Substitute the verb *influences* and the sentence makes sense. *Affect* is a verb meaning "influence." In the second part of the sentence, the date will "figure out," or *infer* the poverty.

13   **more than**. *Memos*, a plural, calls for *more than*.

14   **among, much**. Because more than two employees are talking, *among* is the one you want. *Between* works for couples, not mobs. In the second parentheses, *much* is the choice because *difference* is singular.

15   **less**. The word *paper* is singular, so *less* is appropriate.

16   **many, amount**. *Many* works for plurals, and *memos* is a plural word. In the second parentheses, the singular *paper* is the issue. *Number* works with plurals, but *amount* is for singular expressions.

17   **more than**. When you're talking about *sheets*, you're in plural land. Use *more than*.

18 **less**. It may take *fewer* employees to shelve the issue, but it takes *less* energy, because *energy* is singular.

19 **over**. One year calls for *over,* the term for singulars.

20 **amount**. The word *material* is singular, even though the term may refer to a ton of stuff, as in *the material in my file cabinet that I don't want to work on.* Singular takes *amount.*

21 **between**. In comparing two potential candidates for leadership awards, *between* is best.

22 **fewer**. *Employees* is a plural, so *fewer* does the job.

23 **amount**. Here you're talking about *barking* (yes, the boss barks too), so *amount* is needed for the singular term.

24 **Among**. If you're looking at *all the inhabitants of New York City,* you're talking about more than two people. Hence, *among.*

25 **Regardless of the teacher's views on technology in the classroom, Mark sends an instant message to his brother.** *Irregardless* is the Loch Ness Monster of formal English; it doesn't exist. Substitute *regardless.*

26 **Kevin doesn't answer immediately, because he is in the middle of the sandbox.** Another non-existent expression is *being that.* Use *because* or *as.*

27 **"I'll try to answer Mark after snack," he thinks.** The expression *try and* says that the speaker is going to do two things: *try* and *answer.* But the real meaning of the sentence is "try to answer."

28 **The teacher doesn't want any distraction from the peanut butter cookies she has prepared, so she confiscates Kevin's PDA, which sends and receives e-mail, keeps track of Kevin's play dates, and handles instant messages.** Double negatives are a no-no. Change *doesn't want no* to *doesn't want any.*

29 **Kevin should have hidden his PDA until nap time.** The expression *should of* sounds like *should've,* but *should've* is the contraction of *should have,* not *should of.*

30 **Mark can hardly believe some of the stories Kevin tells about kindergarten.** *Can't hardly* is a double negative, which reverses the intended meaning of the sentence. Go with *can hardly,* which means that Mark thinks Kevin is exaggerating.

31 **Mark remembers his own days in finger-paint land, which he should've treasured.** The contraction *should've* is the short form of *should have.*

32 **Because the third grade room is near the kindergarten, Mark could have walked out of the classroom and spoken directly to Kevin.** Either *could have* or *could've* is fine, but stay away from *could of.*

33 **correct**. The expression *can't help* is fine when it precedes the *-ing* form of the verb. Just don't place it with *but,* because then you'll have a double negative.

34 **Because the day is almost over, Kevin asks the teacher to return his PDA.** Delete *being that* wherever you find it; send in *because* instead.

35 **correct**. In this sentence *being* is fine because it's a verb, not a faulty substitute for *because*.

36 **"I can hardly wait until I'm in first grade," he remarks.** *Can't hardly,* a double negative, flips your meaning. *Can hardly* says that waiting is a tough task.

37 **lies**. The character, in suitably pale makeup, rests in bed, so *lies* is correct.

38 **sit**. The doctor isn't placing something else on the bed but instead making a lap. Go for *sit.*

39 **set**. To place something somewhere calls for the verb *set.*

40 **lie, sit**. Both of these spots call for personal body movements, not the placement of something else. *To lie* and *to sit* deal with plopping in bed, on the couch, or in a chair.

41 **laid**. Because the doctor placed the wreath, the verb of choice is *to lay,* and the past tense of *to lay* is *laid.*

42 **lies**. This one is a bit tricky. The doctor *lays* the wreath, but the wreath itself just *lies* (rests) there.

43 **sit**. The lover will pull out a chair and *sit* in it, not place an object somewhere.

44 **lain**. The lover has been stretched out in a bed, in the traditional soapy coma, so the verb must be a form of *lie.* The combo form of *lie* is *lain.*

45 **sits**. The doctor isn't placing something, just staying in a chair, eating. The verb is *to sit,* and the form that matches *doctor* is *sits.*

46 **sometime**. The sentence refers to a particular moment (knowing Jennifer, about an hour after the first achoo). *Sometime* means "at an unspecified time."

47 **some time**. You want to say "a period of time," which, handily enough, is the meaning of *some time.*

48 **every day**. Here you're going for "daily," so the two-word form does the job.

49 **a lot**. Never, never, never one word! Always two! No matter what you see printed on signs, awnings, and papers.

50 **all ready**. She had her briefcase, suitcase, computer case, and every other case *prepared.* Hence, *all ready.*

51 **everyday**. Her ordinary handkerchief (thus her *everyday* handkerchief) isn't as fancy as the silk number she carries when she's dressed up.

52 **every day**. The meaning implied here is "every single day."

53 **already**. Abigail means "by this time!"

54 **some time**. Because Jennifer never remembers to remove all her piercing jewelry, it does indeed take a period of time (*some time*) to go through the metal detector.

55 **All right!** I know, I know. You just opened a magazine and saw a headline with the "word" *alright* in it. Wrong. Wrong. Always wrong! It's two words.

Lloyd Demos Dies at 81: Specialized in Ancient Egypt

Lloyd Demos died yesterday as he was pursuing ~~farther~~ **further** study in
ancient Egyptian culture. Demos, who ~~effected~~ **affected** the lives of many
residents of our town, had ~~alot~~ **a lot** of varied interests. By the time he
died he had ~~all ready~~ **already** learned 12 languages, including ancient
Egyptian, and spent some time ~~everyday~~ **every day** studying Egyptian
grammar so that his writing would be ~~alright~~ **all right**. Demos had just
~~set~~ **sat** down to supper when the Grim Reaper appeared at his door.
~~Irregardless~~ **Regardless**, Demos insisted on finishing his mashed
potatoes, though he was heard to say, "I would like to ~~lay~~ **lie** down for a
while." Demos, who wrote ~~over~~ **more than** 50 books, will be fondly
remembered.

56 *Farther* refers to distance; *further* is for time, intensity, or duration.

57 *Effected* can be a verb, but as such it means "to be the sole agent of change." In this sentence "influenced" is the more likely meaning, so *affected* is the one you want.

58 *A lot* is always written as two words.

59 *All ready* as two words means "completely prepared," but in this sentence you want "by this time," which is the definition of *already*.

60 *Everyday* as one word means "ordinary." As two words, it means "daily," the one you want here.

61 *All right* is always two words, never one.

62 *Sat* is the past tense of *sit*, which is the verb you want for plopping your body in a chair. *Set* is to place something else somewhere else.

63 *Irregardless* doesn't exist, but *regardless* expresses the same idea.

64 *Lie* is to rest or recline; *lay* (in the present tense) is to put something down somewhere. Demos wants to rest, so *lie* is appropriate.

65 *Fifty books* is plural, so *more than* comes into play. *Over* is for singular terms.

Part VI
The Part of Tens

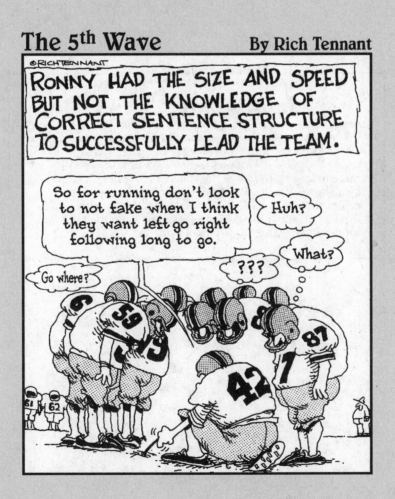

In this part . . .

The renowned Dummies Part of Tens gives you a list of "overcorrections," mistakes people make when they're trying to speak or write with extreme formality and not quite managing to follow the rules of grammar. This part also shows you the worst, avoid-at-all-cost, common errors that can sink your writing faster than a torpedo from a nuclear sub. No exercises here — just the best tips for improving your English. Read on.

Chapter 21

Ten Overcorrections

In This Chapter
▶ Avoiding overly formal or incorrect English
▶ Putting a stop to unnecessary changes

*E*nglish teachers recognize a certain tone of voice that comes into play the minute people learn that they're talking to a grammarian. All of a sudden the eyes glaze over, the chin lifts, and the grammar/style portion of the brain goes into overdrive. *Who* becomes *whom* for no reason at all. Verb tenses tangle up, and *had* is suddenly as common as shoulder pads at an '80s party. Sadly, what I call "overcorrection" is as bad an error as whatever mistake it's designed to avoid. If you want to identify these grammar and style potholes so that you can steer around them, read on.

Substituting "Whom" for "Who"

True, some uneducated people never utter the word *whom*, even when it's needed in a sentence. But throwing *whom* into every situation isn't a good idea either. Sentences requiring *whom* are actually quite rare. In fact, you need *whom* only when the sentence calls for an object of some sort. (Check out Chapter 10 for more information on *who* and *whom*.)

Objects receive the action of the verb, as in *Whom did you call?* In this sentence, *whom* receives the action of the verb *did call*. (*You,* in case you were wondering, is the subject.) The problem with *whom* is that when it does show up, it's often in a sentence containing other thoughts, so you have to sort out the various threads. One common error: *Whom shall I say is calling?* Sounds nice, right? But it's wrong. Untangling shows you why: *I shall say whom is calling. Whom is calling?* Nope. *Who is calling.*

Inserting Unnecessary "Had's"

As a helping verb, *had* is very good (hangs out in all the best clubs, does community service without a court order, and so on). But it shouldn't be overused. *Had* places an action in the past before another action in the past, as in this sentence: *Archie had already shaved when the aerosol can exploded.* On a timeline, the *shaving* precedes the *exploding*, and both precede the present moment. Bingo. The *shaving* part of the sentence gets the *had*. The overcorrection comes when people sprinkle *had's* all over, without rhyme or reason: *Archie had already shaved when the aerosol can had exploded.*

Throwing in "Have" at Random

Another helping verb, *have,* shows up where it has no business, I suspect because it makes the sentence sound more complicated and therefore somehow more "advanced." Like last year's style at a fashionable club, an unnecessary *have* stands out, but not in a good way. The *have* error I hear the most is *Nice to have met you.* Oh really? The *have* places the meeting in the past, before another, present action. So *nice to have met you* implies some sort of deadline, as in *nice to have met you before our wedding* or *nice to have met you before it was time for me to clip your toenails.* The better expression is *nice to meet you* (now, in the present, as we talk).

Sending "I" to Do a "Me" Job

Me sounds childlike, doesn't it? It conjures up memories of "Me Tarzan!" and similar statements. But *I* isn't the personal pronoun for every sentence. *I* is a subject pronoun, so it belongs in a subject spot — or after a linking verb — and nowhere else. An error that pops up frequently is *I* as the object of a preposition: *between you and I* or *except you and I.* Penalty box! The correct phrases are *between you and me* and *except you and me.*

Speaking or Writing Passively

The government, in my humble opinion, is to blame for this particular overcorrection. Official forms tend to throw passive verbs all over the place, perhaps because passive voice allows the writer to omit the subject — the doer, and therefore the one responsible — for the action. How much safer it must feel to write *the taxes were tripled yesterday* rather than *I tripled your taxes yesterday; now please vote for me.* But passive voice comes across as stilted. Unless you need it (perhaps because you truly don't know who did the action or because the subject isn't the point of the sentence), opt for active voice.

Making Sentence Structure Too Complicated

Hey, I can handle complications. I live in New York, where buying an apartment involves a two- or three-inch pile of official forms, each of which must be signed in triplicate. But complicated sentences (which abound in the pile of forms I just mentioned) don't make your writing look more mature. They just make your writing awkward. Stay away from sentences like *It was this treaty that ended the war* and substitute *This treaty ended the war.* Run from *That which he discovered yesterday is the invention which will make his fortune* and toward *The invention he discovered yesterday will make his fortune.*

Letting Descriptions Dangle

Description is good, especially when you're agreeing to a blind date with someone you've never met. (Think of the sentence *Howie is pleasantly plump,* in which *pleasantly plump* tells you something important about *Howie.*) Descriptions containing verb forms are good too, because they give you even more information: *Howie, howling at the moon as he does every evening, is happy to double date.* The description *howling at the moon as he does every evening* is certainly an eye-opener, giving you a lot of information about *Howie.* Descriptions in the beginning of a sentence are especially good, because they vary the usual, boring sentence pattern: *Running with his friend Wolfie, Howie often stays out all night.* The description *running with his friend Wolfie* tells you something about *Howie* that you probably should know.

But — and this is a big but — don't overuse the introductory description, or you'll simply create a new, but immediately boring, sentence pattern. Also, be sure that the introductory description applies to the subject — the first person mentioned in the sentence. If not, you have a dangler, a truly big no-no.

Becoming Allergic to "They" and "Their"

For some writers, the pronouns *they* and *their* seem to be radioactive. Because many writers make the mistake of pairing the plural *their* with something singular (say, *a person* or *everybody*), overcorrectors do the opposite. Even when a plural is justified, these writers send in *he or she* and similar phrases. Bad idea! Plurals (*the guys, three grapefruits, both, several, a few,* and so on) match with other plurals (*they* and *their*). So don't write *The kids blew off his or her homework and blamed the dog.* Instead, keep the plurals together: *The kids blew off their homework and blamed the dog.*

Being Semi-Attached to Semicolons

Semicolons (the dot on top of the comma) link two complete sentences. They also separate items in a list, when at least one of the listed items contains a comma already. But that's it for the semicolon. It isn't a fancy comma or a weak colon. It's a semicolon and proud to be one. (National Semicolon Day is next week.) Why am I talking about semicolons? Because too many people throw them around like dog treats at a kennel. Don't; throw them around. Oops. I mean *Don't throw them around.*

Not Knowing When Enough Is Enough

I'm a writing teacher, and as much as anyone else in the field, I'm guilty of asking for more, more, and did I mention I want to see more detail? So when some poor kid hands me a paper about an apple, I'm there with my red pen (teachers' revenge color), writing *What color is the apple? How many seeds does it have?* In the real world, however, I'm not particularly interested in reading 15 sentences about an apple when all I want to know is who threw it at my head when I was returning graded essays. The cure for underexplaining isn't overexplaining. The best path is to provide interesting and relevant details and nothing more. And if your readers wander around wondering how many seeds were in that apple, that's their problem.

Chapter 22

Ten Errors to Avoid at All Cost

What did you forget? Your lunch? A parachute? I ask these questions to point out that some mistakes are worse than others. If the plane is going down, I personally am willing to forgo the peanut butter and jelly, but not that handy little life-saving device.

Your writing can crash also, especially if you err in a few specific ways. Ten ways, actually, which I explain here. Everyone makes mistakes, but this chapter shows you how to avoid the big ones.

Writing Incomplete Sentences

Unless, of course, you want to make a style point. I pause to acknowledge that the preceding sentence is incomplete. That's my attempt at irony and also my way of pointing out that sometimes breaking the rules is a good thing. In a forest of complete sentences, an occasional incomplete statement calls attention to an important point. However, a forest of incomplete sentences is *not* a style; it's just poor English and calls into question whether you know how to fashion a complete sentence. That's a bad impression to give your reader. Be sure that each of your sentences has a subject-verb pair, an endmark, and a complete thought. (For more information on complete sentences, take a look at Chapter 4.)

Letting Sentences Run On and On

A run-on sentence is actually two or more sentences stuck together without any legal "glue" — a word such as *and* or a semicolon. The worst form of run-on is what grammarians call a *comma splice*, in which a comma attempts (and fails) to attach one complete sentence to another. Be especially careful with words that resemble legal joiners (*consequently, however, therefore, nevertheless,* and so forth). Use them for the meaning, but not for glue. (Chapter 4 explains run-ons in greater detail.)

Forgetting to Capitalize "I"

Nothing screams louder than a sentence like *Do you realize that i am yours forever?* I'm not even going to discuss *i M yours 4ever.* If you write this way, fine. I wish you a happy life. Ditto if you put a little circle on top of the *i* instead of a dot. You and I will have to agree to go our separate ways. But even if you don't go that far, you risk alienating the reader by breaking so basic a rule. The personal pronoun *I* is always capped. Period.

Being Stingy with Quotation Marks

Whether you're writing for school, work, or personal reasons, honesty requires you to credit your sources. Lifting someone else's words, dropping them into your own writing, and omitting the quotation marks is as dishonest as passing the teller a note demanding *all the money*. In school such practices earn "F" grades; in work or public life, you may be sued. The solution is simple. If it's not yours, credit the source, as I have in this example, in which I cite a nonexistent author: *As Martin Sherman writes, "Plagiarism is a fatal wound to the body of knowledge."*

Using Pronouns Incorrectly

Pronouns — noun substitutes such as *he, they, all, other, neither,* and the like — are governed by more rules than the citizens of a fanatical tyrant. Even if you don't know every fine point, you should never neglect the basics: Pronouns should replace one and only one noun, and that noun should be clearly identifiable. Don't use an object pronoun in a subject-pronoun spot. Singular pronouns should replace singular nouns, and plurals match with plurals. (Check out Chapters 3 and 10 for details on these issues.)

Placing New Words in the Wrong Context

New words seep into your vocabulary gradually. First, they begin to look familiar when they show up in something you're reading. Later, you recognize them as old friends. Later still, you feel comfortable using them in your own sentences. Don't skip any of these stages! Every teacher, including me, has received papers from someone who memorized the "100 words most likely to show up on standardized tests" and who is determined to get as much mileage out of them as possible. The problem is that the nuances of a word's meaning are hard to grasp from a list or a couple of encounters. Let me assure you that premature use of vocabulary can be *really* embarrassing. You may find yourself, as one of my students did, writing about "New York City's government *suppository* of documents." (**Hint:** A *suppository* is a way of getting medicine into the body without a needle or a spoon. Look it up.)

Letting Slang Seep into Your Speech

It ain't that slang is a total bomb. In fact, slang can be bad — the real bee's knees. But if you don't have the 411, you may miss the boat.

That paragraph contains a mixture of slang from several different eras. You may have recognized one of the slang expressions and missed another. Therein lies the problem. Slang changes fast, so fast that no one can possibly keep up. If your reader understands that *bad* in the sentence above is slang for "good," fine. But the reader who grasps that concept may not realize that *bee's knees* is a term for the latest, best fashion. By the way, *411* means "information." *Ain't* is a corruption of "isn't," and *total bomb* conveys "failure." Bottom line: A writer who uses slang risks confusion. Also, slang sounds informal; if you want to impress a boss or a teacher, it's not the best vocabulary to employ.

Forgetting to Proofread

Even if you finished the paper or project only ten minutes before you have to cram it into the mailbox, take the time to proofread your work. Yo maye ffind tat som latters are nut where they sould be, not to mentione. punctuation,

Relying on Computer Checks for Grammar and Spelling

You can't cash them in, but computer checks are popular anyway, and you should remember to glance at them as you write. (I'm referring to the red and green lines that show up on the screen to alert you to a possible mistake.) I have to admit that sometimes they actually help, but they're not 100 percent accurate. First of all, plenty of eras slip through. (See what I mean? That last sentence should read *plenty of errors.*) Secondly, the computer often identifies a mistake when the sentence is actually correct. I get little wavy lines lots of times, and as you have figured out by now, I'm prefect. Er . . . perfect.

Repeating Yourself

In conclusion, at the end of this chapter, I would like to state and declare that saying the same thing more than once repetitively is a real drag, an annoyance, and a pain. Don't — do not — repeat, because repetition isn't a fun or enjoyable way to pass the time. Repetition will send your reader away fast and quickly, not to mention rapidly. Shall I reiterate the point? Once is enough.

Appendix

Grabbing Grammar Goofs

· ·

*H*ow sharp are your eyes? This appendix is the grammatical equivalent of an optometrist's chart. If you can see it with 20/20 vision, you'll spot 30 mistakes in each of the four exercises. Of course, after you spot the errors, your mission is to correct them. The errors may involve faulty structure or word choice, punctuation, capitalization, and anything else the *English Grammar Workbook For Dummies* covers.

Exercise One

Sneak a peek at the college catalogue (from a university that exists only in my mind) in Figure A-1. This course description has many faults — 30, by my count. Your count may differ slightly depending on how you group your answers. Don't worry about numbers — your mission is to search and destroy the mistakes.

6901 World Domination (3 credits): Professor Peck, Mr. Lapham, Ms. Austin. One two-hour lecture period per week is required. Three periods of fieldwork per week is also required.

This course on world domination and dictatorship involve both lecture and that they put into practice what students will learn. A student will report to their faculty advisors once a month. Everyone must keep a journal of revolutions started, governments overthrown, and peasants' oppressed. Readings include Karl and Groucho Marx's masterful essay, "Laughing All The Way to The Throne", and Chairman Mayo's autobiography, *Hold the Bacon*. This is sure to interest students who's career plans are to be an emperor; tsar; dictator; or reality-show winner. By the time the course concludes, students have gathered all necessary information about what it takes to rule the world. We will be discussing topics like propaganda, media manipulation, and telegenic coronation clothes (including crown-jewel selection). Working in the field, spy networks will be set up, this will count as a quarter of the grade. The students's task is to outmaneuver everyone in the course by becoming the first to conquer a hostile country that is required for graduation. Exams also emphasizes real practical skills, and theoretical ideas. Students only write two papers.

Admission to this course and it's sequel (Universal Domination) are by permission of the Department of Politically Science Irregardless of age or class rank, applicants should be as motivated than the average freshman and should try and visit the departmental office for an interview.

Figure A-1:
A scary sample course description that needs some work (in more ways than one).

Exercise Two

The letter from a made-up publisher, in Figure A-2, is full of errors. Try your hand at correcting all 30.

Higgen Publishing Company

459 elm Avenue

Bronxton, VT 05599

October 31, 2006

Mr. Chester Slonton

33 Warwickville Road

Alaistair, CA 90990

Dear Mr. Slonton:

Thank you for sending us your novel, "The Lily Droops at Dawn." To read over 1,000 pages about a love affair between plants is a very unique experience. In your talented hands, both of the plants becomes characters that are well-rounded and of great interest to the reader. Before Mr. Higgen, whom you know is our founder, commits to publishing this masterpiece, I must ask for some real minor changes.

Most of the editors, including Mr. Higgen, was confused about the names. You are absolutely right in stating that each of the lovers are in the lily family, scientifically they have similar characteristics. Calling the lovers Lila and Lyle would not of been a problem if the characters were distinguished from one another in personality or habits or appearance. Unfortunately, your main characters resembles each other in petal color and height. True, one of the lilies is said to be smartest, but the reader doesnt know which.

A second problem are the love scenes. You mention in your cover letter that you can make them more lengthier. Mr. Higgen feels, and I agree, that you write vivid; nevertheless, we think you could cut them alot without losing the reader's attention. After all, once a person has read one flower proposal, he or she has essentially read them all.

Finally, the ending needs work. When the lily droops, the book ended. Are you comfortable with a tiny change. Market research shows that books with happy endings appeal to the readers, whoever he or she may be. These volumes sell good. Instead of drooping, perhaps the lily could spread it's petals and welcome the dawn. Or become a rose.

Higgen Publishing would like this novel for their fall list. I hope that you are open to the changes I had outlined in this letter. I cannot help but mention that Higgen Publishing is probably the only publisher with experience in plant romance volumes I look forward to having talked with you about the editing process.

Sincerely,

Cynthia Higgen

Figure A-2:
A sample letter from a publisher (with a lot of mistakes, so you know it must be fake).

Exercise Three

Try your hand at editing the newspaper article in Figure A-3. You should find 30 errors, including some in the quoted material. (If you're quoting someone who makes a grammar error, you may usually leave the error in the quotation in order to convey someone's style or personality. For the purposes of this exercise, however, correct every mistake.)

Hold the Tights: a Former Television Star Plays Shakespeare

Silver, the actor that played a talking horse on the Emmy-winning series *Mr. Said* is now starring in the Royal Theater production of "Hamlet." The handsome blond recently agreed to discuss his approach to acting. It were never about talking, in Silvers' view. As he had munched oats and sipped delicately from a water pail, the colt explained that he learned to talk at the age of one. Him talking was not fulfilling enough, only acting met his need for recognition.

"I started by reciting monologues for whomever would listen," he said. Then one day I got a call from a Hollywood agent offering me the part of Mr. Said." Tossing his mane in the air, Silver continued, "I plays that role for nine seasons. You get typecast. Nobody want to take a chance on your dramatic ability if they can find someone else for the role." He added, "Sitting by the phone one day, it rang, and my agent told me that I had a audition." That audition resulted in him getting the part. Silver is the only horse that have ever played Hamlet, as far as he knows.

The actor has all ready began rehearsals. His costume includes a traditionally velvet coat but no tights. "Between you and I," he whispered, "the tights snag on my fur." Director Ed Walketers asked Silver to consider shaving, and he also tried several types of material for the tights. Even Silver's wife got involved in this key costuming decision. "No one tried harder than her to find tights I could wear," Silver said. Nothing was suitable for this extremely unique situation.

Silver is equally as involved with the role itself. "I relate to Hamlet's problems," he explained. "Us horses often find it hard to take action and being decisive." The role is also exhausting; Silver lays down for a quickly nap everyday before going onstage as Hamlet.

Figure A-3:
A sample newspaper article with a plethora of errors.

Exercise Four

Don't you hate computer manuals? The one in Figure A-4 is even worse than the usual techno-babble because it contains 30 mistakes. Correct them!

Installing You're New Widget Wheel

To install the widget wheel, a computer should first be turned off, then follow these simple steps.

Important: If you have an A4019 or a newest model, please discard this manual. You must have sent for manual number 218B, or, in the case of a computer that previously has a widget, for manual number 330B. Being that your computer is not covered in this manual, discard it. Faulty directions have been responsible for explosions and that software crashed.

1. Unpack the widget wheel which looks like a sharks tooth.

2. Unpack the two disk poles. Grasp the disk pole that is more circular. Lining up the teeth with the teeth on the widget. *Note*: Teeth should be brushed everyday with a WidgetBrush. see enclosed order form for more information.

3. After the teeth are tight clenched, a person should insert the widget disk into slot C. However, if the widget disk has a blue strip, in which case it should be inserted into slot D. Don't mix up the slots as the computer will catch fire. Neither of these slots are open when the computer is standing upright. Sit the computer on its side before beginning this step.

4. Turn on the computer. If the screen is blank call the service specialist at 914-555-5039. If the screen blinks rapid from red to green (or from blue to yellow in model 2W4T), run further from the screen. This means the widget was installed improper; the computer is all together unusable.

5. You are almost ready to enjoy your new widget!! Place a hand on the mouse that is not wearing any rings, including wedding rings. Depending upon the model number, either press firmly or softly. Some widgets can work good no matter what the pressure.

Figure A-4:
The world's biggest headache inducer: A sample of a poorly written computer manual.

Answers to Exercise One

In the following figure the errors from the original course description are boldfaced and crossed out, with a possible correction following each one, as well as an occasional addition of a missing word or mark. All corrections are boldfaced and underlined. Check the corresponding numbered explanations that follow the revised course description.

6901 World Domination (3 credits): Professor Peck, Mr. Lapham, Ms. Austin. One two-hour lecture period per week is required. Three periods of fieldwork per week ~~is~~ **are** also required. [1]

This course on world domination and dictatorship ~~involve~~ **involves** both lecture and ~~that they put into practice~~ **practical application of** what students ~~will~~ **learn**. [2] [3] [4]

~~A student~~ **Students** will report to their faculty advisors once a month. Everyone must keep a [5] journal of revolutions started, governments overthrown, and peasants**'** oppressed. Readings [6] include Karl and Groucho Marx's masterful essay, "Laughing All ~~T~~**t**he Way to ~~T~~**t**he Throne,"**,** and [7] [8] Chairman Mayo's autobiography, *Hold the Bacon*. This **reading list** is sure to interest students [9] ~~who's~~ **whose** career plans are to be an emperor**,** tsar**,** dictator**,** or reality-show winner. By the [10] [11] time the course concludes, students **will have** gathered all necessary information about what it [12] takes to rule the world. We will be discussing topics ~~like~~ **such as** propaganda, media [13] manipulation, and telegenic coronation clothes (including crown-jewel selection). Working in the field, ~~spy networks will be set up~~ **students will set up spy networks;** [14] [15] ~~this~~ **fieldwork** will count as a quarter of the grade. The ~~students's~~ **students'** task [16] [17] **that is required for graduation** is to outmaneuver everyone **else** in the course by becoming [19] [18] the first to conquer a hostile country ~~that is required for graduation~~. Exams also [21] ~~emphasizes~~ **emphasize** ~~real~~ **really** practical skills**,** and theoretical ideas. Students [20] [22] ~~only~~ write **only** two papers. [23]

Admission to this course and it**'**s sequel (Universal Domination) ~~are~~ **is** by permission of the [24] [25] Department of ~~Politically~~ **Political** Science. ~~Irregardless~~ **Regardless** of age or class rank, [26] [28] applicants should be as motivated ~~than~~ **as** the average freshman and should try ~~and~~ **to** visit the [29] [30] departmental office for an interview.

[27]

1 The subject is *three periods,* a plural, so the verb *(are)* must also be plural.

2 The subject *course* is singular, so the verb *(involves)* must also be singular.

3 To keep the sentence parallel, the noun *lecture* should be coupled with another noun, not with a subject/verb combo.

4 The *practical application* is simultaneous to the learning, so future tense isn't what you want. Go for present *(learn)*.

5 The paragraph refers to *students* (plural), so a shift in one spot to singular is inappropriate. Also, *a student* should never pair with *their,* because singulars and plurals don't match.

6 The original sentence includes the possessive *peasants'* for no valid reason. The possessive form should be linked to a noun, but here it precedes a verb form *(oppressed)*.

7 In titles, articles (such as *the* in this title) shouldn't be capitalized.

8 When a comma follows quoted material, the comma is placed inside the closing quotation mark.

9 In the original sentence the pronoun *this* is vague. Insert the clarifying expression, *reading list*.

10 The contraction *who's* means "who is," but the sentence calls for the possessive *whose*.

11 Items in a series are separated by semicolons only when one or more of the items contain a comma. In this series, no item contains a comma, so semicolons aren't necessary.

12 A future deadline *(by the time the course concludes)* calls for future perfect tense *(will have gathered)*.

13 *Like* excludes the items listed and refers to items that are similar. In this sentence the listed items are examples and should be preceded by *such as*.

14 The original sentence contains a dangler, *working in the field.* An introductory element containing a verb form must refer to the subject, and *spy networks* aren't *working in the field.* Reword the sentence so that the *students* are *working in the field*.

15 Two complete sentences may not be joined by a comma. Substitute a semicolon or make two sentences.

16 The pronoun *this* is too vague all by itself. Substitute a noun *(fieldwork)* to clarify the meaning.

17 To create a possessive form for a plural ending in the letter *s,* just add an apostrophe, not an extra *s*.

18 The student is *in* the course and so must be compared to everyone *else*.

19 In the original, this misplaced description seems to say that *a country* is required for graduation, not the *task*. Descriptions should be close to the word they describe.

20 The plural subject, *exams,* requires a plural verb, *emphasize*.

21 The description *practical* should be intensified by an adverb *(really)*, not by an adjective *(real)*.

22 If you unite two complete sentences with the word *and,* a comma precedes the *and*. If you unite two of anything else (in this sentence, two nouns — *skills* and *ideas*), no comma precedes the *and*.

23 The descriptive word *only* should precede the word being compared — in this case, *only two* as compared to *three* or *four* or whatever the professor assigns.

24 Possessive pronouns have no apostrophes.

25 *Admission* is singular and takes a singular verb, *is*.

26 The adjective *Political* describes the noun *Science*. *Politically* is an adverb and may describe only verbs *(speaking politically)* or other descriptions *(politically inexperienced)*.

27 A statement should end with a period, which is missing in the original.

28 *Irregardless* isn't standard English. Substitute *regardless*.

29 *As* and *than* don't belong in the same comparison. An *as* comparison is for equal items and a *than* comparison for unequal items.

30 *Try and* implies two actions, but the sentence refers to one that should be attempted. The proper expression is *try to*.

Answers to Exercise Two

In the following figure the errors from the original letter are boldfaced and crossed out, with a possible correction following each one, as well as an occasional addition of a missing word or mark. All corrections are boldfaced and underlined. Check the corresponding numbered explanations that follow the revised letter.

Higgen Publishing Company

31 459 ~~elm~~ **Elm** Avenue

Bronxton, VT 05599

October 31, 2006

Mr. Chester Slonton

33 Warwickville Road

Alaistair, CA 90990

Dear Mr. Slonton:

Thank you for sending us your novel, **"~~The Lily Droops at Dawn."~~** *The Lily Droops at Dawn.* **32**

33 To read ~~over~~ **more than** 1,000 pages about a love affair between plants is a ~~very~~ unique **34**

experience. In your talented hands, both of the plants ~~becomes~~ **become** characters that are **35**

well-rounded and ~~of great interest~~ **interesting** to the reader. Before Mr. Higgen, ~~whom~~ **who** **37**

36 you know is our founder, commits to publishing this masterpiece, I must ask for some

~~real~~ **really** minor changes.

38 Most of the editors, including Mr. Higgen, ~~was~~ **were** confused about the names. You are

39 absolutely right in stating that each of the lovers ~~are~~ **is** in the lily family**;** scientifically they have **41**

40 similar characteristics. Calling the lovers Lila and Lyle would not ~~of~~ **have** been a problem if the **42**

characters were distinguished from one another in personality or habits or appearance.

Unfortunately, your main characters ~~resembles~~ **resemble** each other in petal color and height. **43**

True, one of the lilies is said to be ~~smartest~~ **smarter**, but the reader doesn't know which. **45**

44

46 A second problem ~~are~~ **is** the love scenes. You mention in your cover letter that you can make

them ~~more~~ lengthier. Mr. Higgen feels, and I agree, that you write ~~vivid~~ **vividly**; nevertheless, **48**

47 we think you could cut them ~~alot~~ **a lot** without losing the reader's attention. After all, once a

49 person has read one flower proposal, he or she has essentially read them all.

Finally, the ending needs work. When the lily droops, the book ~~ended~~ **ends**. Are you **50**

comfortable with a tiny change**/?** Market research shows that books with happy endings appeal

51 to the readers, whoever ~~he or she~~ **they** may be. These volumes sell ~~good~~ **well**. Instead of **53**

52 drooping, perhaps the lily could spread it**'**s petals and welcome the ~~dawn. Or~~ **dawn or** become **55**

54 a rose.

Higgen Publishing would like this novel for ~~their~~ **its** fall list. I hope that you are open to the **56**

changes I ~~had~~ outlined in this letter. I cannot help ~~but mention~~ **mentioning** that Higgen **58**

57 Publishing is probably the only publisher with experience in plant romance volumes**.** I look **59**

forward to ~~having talked~~ **talking** with you about the editing process.

60

Sincerely,

Cynthia Higgen

31 Proper names are capitalized.

32 The title of a full-length work (in this case, a novel) is italicized or underlined, not enclosed in quotation marks.

33 *Over* precedes a singular word, and *more than* precedes a plural.

34 *Unique* is an absolute, so no degrees of uniqueness (*very unique, a little unique,* and so on) exist.

35 *Both* is plural and should be matched with the plural verb *become*.

36 The original sentence isn't parallel because it pairs the simple description *well rounded* with the phrase *of great interest.* The correction changes the phrase to a simple description, *interesting.*

37 The pronoun *who* is needed to act as a subject for the verb *is*.

38 *Real* is an adjective and appropriate for descriptions of people, places, things, or ideas. The adverb *really* intensifies the description *minor*.

39 *Most of the editors* is a plural subject and requires a plural verb, *were*.

40 *Each of the lovers* is a singular subject and requires a singular verb, *is*.

41 A comma may not join two complete sentences. Use a semicolon instead.

42 *Would of* doesn't exist in standard English. The proper expression is *would have,* here changed to the negative *would not have.*

43 The plural subject *characters* needs the plural verb *resemble*.

44 *Smartest* is for the extreme in groups of three or more. Because only two lilies are compared, *smarter* is correct.

45 The contraction *doesn't* contains an apostrophe.

46 The singular subject *problem* takes the singular verb *is*.

47 Double comparisons aren't correct. Use *lengthier* or *more lengthy*.

48 The verb *write* may be described by the adverb *vividly* but not by the adjective *vivid*.

49 The expression *a lot* is always written as two words.

50 The present-tense verb *ends* works best with the rest of the sentence, which contains the present-tense verb *droops*.

51 This sentence, a question, calls for a question mark instead of a period.

52 The plural pronoun *they* refers to *readers*.

53 *Good* is an adjective, but the sentence calls for the adverb *well* to describe the verb *sell*.

54 A possessive pronoun, such as *its,* never includes an apostrophe.

55 The expression *or become a rose* is a fragment and may not stand as a separate sentence.

56 A company is singular, so the matching pronoun is *its*.

57 The helping verb *had* is used only to place one action in the past before another past action.

58 *Cannot help but mention* is a double negative.

59 Every sentence needs an endmark. This statement calls for a period.

60 *Having talked* implies a deadline, and the sentence doesn't support such a meaning.

Answers to Exercise Three

In the following figure the errors from the original article are boldfaced and crossed out, with a possible correction following each one, as well as an occasional addition of a missing word or mark. All corrections are boldfaced and underlined. Check the corresponding numbered explanations that follow the revised article.

61 Hold the Tights: ~~a~~ **A** Former Television Star Plays Shakespeare

Silver, the actor that played a talking horse on the Emmy-winning series *Mr. Said*__,__ is now **62**

starring in the Royal Theater production of ~~"Hamlet."~~ *__Hamlet__*. The handsome blond recently **63**

64 agreed to discuss his approach to acting. It ~~were~~ **was** never about talking, in ~~Silvers'~~ **Silver's** **65**

66 view. As he ~~had~~ munched oats and sipped delicately from a water pail, the colt explained that

67 he learned to talk at the age of one. ~~Him~~ **His** talking was not fulfilling enough__;__ only acting met **68**

his need for recognition.

69 "I started by reciting monologues for ~~whomever~~ **whoever** would listen," he said. **"**Then one day **70**

I got a call from a Hollywood agent offering me the part of Mr. Said." Tossing his mane in the air,

Silver continued, "I ~~plays~~ **played** that role for nine seasons. You get typecast. Nobody

71

72 ~~want~~ **wants** to take a chance on your dramatic ability if ~~they~~ **he or she** can find someone else **73**

for the role." He added, "Sitting by the phone one day, ~~it rang~~ **I heard the phone ring**, and my **74**

agent told me that I had ~~a~~ **an** audition." That audition resulted in ~~him~~ **his** getting the part. Silver

75 **76**

77 is the only horse that ~~have~~ **has** ever played Hamlet, as far as he knows.

78 The actor has ~~all ready~~ **already** ~~began~~ **begun** rehearsals. His costume includes a **79**

80 ~~traditionally~~ **traditional** velvet coat but no tights. "Between you and ~~I~~ **me**," he whispered, "the **81**

tights snag on my fur." Director Ed Walketers asked Silver to consider shaving, and ~~he~~ **Silver** **82**

also tried several types of material for the tights. Even Silver's wife got involved in this key

costuming decision. "No one tried harder than ~~her~~ **she** to find tights I could wear," Silver said. **83**

84 Nothing was suitable for this ~~extremely~~ **unique** situation.

85 Silver is equally ~~as~~ involved with the role itself. "I relate to Hamlet's problems," he explained.

86 ~~"Us~~ **We** horses often find it hard to take action and ~~being~~ **to be** decisive." The role is also **87**

88 exhausting; Silver ~~lays~~ **lies** down for a ~~quickly~~ **quick** nap ~~everyday~~ **every day** before going **90**

onstage as Hamlet.

89

61 The first word of a title and a subtitle should always be capitalized.

62 *Silver* identifies the horse being discussed. The original sentence has a comma at the beginning of the long, descriptive expression (*the actor who played a talking horse on the Emmy-winning series* Mr. Said) but none at the end. The second comma is necessary because the information supplied is extra, not essential to the meaning of the sentence. It should be set off from the rest of the sentence by a pair of commas.

63 The title of a full-length work (in this sentence, a play) should be in italics or underlined.

64 The singular *it* pairs with the singular verb *was*.

65 A singular possessive is formed by the addition of an apostrophe and the letter *s*.

66 The helping verb *had* places one past action before another past action, but in this sentence the actions take place at the same time. Drop the *had*.

67 The possessive pronoun *his* should precede an *-ing* form of a verb that is being used as a noun (in this sentence, *talking*).

68 Two complete sentences shouldn't be joined by a comma. Use a semicolon instead.

69 The subject pronoun *whoever* is needed as the subject of the verb *would listen*. The preposition *for* may have confused you because normally an object follows a preposition. However, in this sentence the entire expression *(whoever would listen)* is the object of the preposition, not just the pronoun.

70 A quotation mark belongs at the beginning and the end of the quotation.

71 The past tense verb matches the meaning of the sentence.

72 The pronoun *nobody* is singular and requires a singular verb, *wants*.

73 Only singular pronouns (in this sentence, *he or she*) can refer to the singular pronoun *nobody*.

74 In the original sentence, *it* (the phone) is sitting by the phone — illogical! Reword in some way so that the speaker is sitting by the phone. Another possible correction: Add a subject/verb combo to the beginning of the sentence so that it reads *When I was sitting by the phone*.

75 The article *an* precedes vowel sounds, such as the *au* in *audition*.

76 The possessive pronoun *his* should precede the *-ing* form of a verb that is being used as a noun (in this sentence, *getting*).

77 Because *only one horse* is the meaning of the pronoun *that*, the verb paired with *that* is singular. *Has* is singular, and *have* is plural.

78 The single word *already* means "before this time," the meaning required by the sentence.

79 *Begun* is the combination form of *to begin* and here is paired with *has*.

80 The adjective *traditional* describes the noun *coat*.

81 *Between* is a preposition and thus takes an object. The pronoun *me* is an object.

82 Two males appear in the sentence *(Silver* and *Ed),* so the pronoun *he* is unclear. Substitute a noun.

83 The missing word in the original is *did,* as in *than she did. Her* is inappropriate as the subject of the implied verb *did.*

84 *Unique* is an absolute and can't be compared, so the *extremely* must be deleted.

85 The comparison *equally* should not be followed by *as.*

86 *We* is the subject pronoun needed here. *Us* is for objects.

87 To keep the sentence parallel, *to be* should be paired with *to take action.* Another alternative is to change *to take action* to *acting.*

88 *To lay* is "to place something else somewhere." *To lie* is "to rest or to recline," the meaning here.

89 The noun *nap* must be described by an adjective *(quick),* not an adverb *(quickly).*

90 The single word *everyday* means "ordinary." In this sentence you need the two-word form, which means "each day."

Answers to Exercise Four

In the following figure the errors from the original manual are boldfaced and crossed out, with a possible correction following each one, as well as an occasional addition of a missing word or mark. All corrections are boldfaced and underlined. Check the corresponding numbered explanations that follow the revised manual.

91

Installing ~~You're~~ **Your** New Widget Wheel

92

To install the widget wheel, ~~a computer should first be turned off~~ **first turn the computer**

93

off/and then follow these simple steps.

94

Important: If you have an A4019 or a ~~newest~~ **newer** model, please discard this manual. You

95

must ~~have sent~~ **send** for manual number 218B, or, in the case of a computer that previously

96

~~has~~ **had** a widget, for manual number 330B. ~~Being that~~ **Because** your computer is not covered

97

98

in this manual, discard ~~it~~ **the manual**. Faulty directions have been responsible for explosions

99

and ~~that software crashed~~ **software crashes**.

100

1. Unpack the widget wheel**,** which looks like a shark's tooth.

101

102

2. Unpack the two disk poles. Grasp the disk pole that is more **nearly** circular. ~~Lining~~ **Line** up

103

the teeth with the teeth on the widget. *Note:* Teeth should be brushed ~~everyday~~ **every day**

104

105

with a WidgetBrush. ~~s~~**S**ee enclosed order form for more information.

106

3. After the teeth are ~~tight~~ **tightly** clenched, ~~a person should~~ insert the widget disk into slot C.

107

However, if the widget disk has a blue strip**,** ~~in which case it should be inserted into slot D~~

108

insert the widget into slot D. Don't mix up the slots as the computer will catch fire. Neither

109

of these slots ~~are~~ **is** open when the computer is standing upright. ~~Sit~~ **Set** the computer on its

110

side before beginning this step.

111

4. Turn on the computer. If the screen is blank**,** call the service specialist at 914-555-5039. If the

screen blinks ~~rapid~~ **rapidly** from red to green (or from blue to yellow in model 2W4T), run

112

113

~~further~~ **farther** from the screen. ~~This~~ **Blinking** means the widget was installed

114

~~improper~~ **improperly**; the computer is ~~all together~~ **altogether** unusable.

115

116

5. You are almost ready to enjoy your new widget! Place a hand **that is not wearing any**

117

rings, including wedding rings, on the mouse ~~that is not wearing any rings, including~~

118

~~wedding rings~~. Depending upon the model number, ~~either~~ press **either** firmly or softly.

119

Some widgets can work ~~good~~ **well** no matter what the pressure.

120

91 The contraction *you're* means "you are." In this sentence you want the possessive pronoun *your*.

92 An introductory verb form *(to install the Widget Wheel)* must refer to the subject, but the subject in the original sentence is *a computer*. Reword the sentence so that the subject is the person who is installing — the understood *you*.

93 The adverb *then* is not capable of uniting two complete sentences on its own. Delete the comma and insert *and*.

94 The *-est* comparison singles out one extreme from a group of three or more. In this sentence you're talking about a comparison between two things only — model A4019 and the group of everything *newer*. (The group counts as one thing because the items in the group aren't discussed as individuals.)

95 The verb *send* is in present tense and addresses what the installer must do now, not what the installer must have done previously. The present perfect tense *(have sent)* implies a connection with the past.

96 The word *previously* tips you off to the fact that you're talking about past tense, so *had* works better than *has*.

97 The expression *being that* is not standard; use *because* instead.

98 The pronoun *it* must have a clear meaning, but the original sentence provides two possible alternatives, *computer* and *manual*. The correction clarifies the meaning of *it*.

99 Two terms linked by *and* need a similar grammatical identity in order to keep the sentence parallel. The original sentence joins a noun *(explosions)* with a clause *(that software crashed)*. The correction links two nouns, *explosions* and *crashes*.

100 A description beginning with *which* is usually set off by a comma from the word it describes.

101 The tooth belongs to the shark, so you need the possessive *shark's*.

102 *Circular* is an absolute. It may be approached but not compared. The disk pole may be *circular* or *more nearly circular*.

103 The original sentence is a fragment; it has no complete thought. The correction has a subject (the understood *you*) and a verb *(line)* and a complete thought.

104 *Everyday* means "ordinary." *Every day* means "daily."

105 A sentence always begins with a capital letter.

106 *Tightly* is an adverb, needed to describe the verb *clenched*.

107 *A person* is a new expression in this piece, which has been addressing *you* either directly or by implication. For consistency, change *a person* to *you* understood.

108 The original is a fragment, not a complete sentence. The reworded version has a complete thought.

109 The pronoun *neither* is singular and takes the singular verb *is*.

110 *Sit* is what the subject does by bending knees and plopping onto a chair. *Set* means that you're placing something else into some position.

111 An introductory expression with a verb is usually set off by a comma from the main idea of the sentence. Insert a comma after *blank*.

112 The adverb *rapidly* is needed to describe the action *blink*.

113 *Farther* is for distance, and *further* is for time or intensity. Here you need the distance word.

114 The pronoun *this* is too vague. Go for the specific term, *blinking*.

115 The adverb *improperly* is needed to describe the action *installed*.

116 *All together* means "as one." *Altogether* means "completely," the definition that fits this sentence.

117 Don't double up on endmarks. One per sentence does the job.

118 The description is in the wrong place in the original sentence. Place it after *hands,* the word being described.

119 The duo *either/or* should link words or expressions with the same grammatical identity. In the original sentence, a verb-description combo is linked to a description. Move *either* so that two descriptions are linked.

120 The adverb *well* is needed to describe the verb *can work*.

Index

BUSINESS, CAREERS & PERSONAL FINANCE

0-7645-5307-0

0-7645-5331-3 *†

Also available:

- Accounting For Dummies †
  0-7645-5314-3
- Business Plans Kit For Dummies †
  0-7645-5365-8
- Cover Letters For Dummies
  0-7645-5224-4
- Frugal Living For Dummies
  0-7645-5403-4
- Leadership For Dummies
  0-7645-5176-0
- Managing For Dummies
  0-7645-1771-6

- Marketing For Dummies
  0-7645-5600-2
- Personal Finance For Dummies *
  0-7645-2590-5
- Project Management For Dummies
  0-7645-5283-X
- Resumes For Dummies †
  0-7645-5471-9
- Selling For Dummies
  0-7645-5363-1
- Small Business Kit For Dummies *†
  0-7645-5093-4

HOME & BUSINESS COMPUTER BASICS

0-7645-4074-2

0-7645-3758-X

Also available:

- ACT! 6 For Dummies
  0-7645-2645-6
- iLife '04 All-in-One Desk Reference
  For Dummies
  0-7645-7347-0
- iPAQ For Dummies
  0-7645-6769-1
- Mac OS X Panther Timesaving
  Techniques For Dummies
  0-7645-5812-9
- Macs For Dummies
  0-7645-5656-8
- Microsoft Money 2004 For Dummies
  0-7645-4195-1

- Office 2003 All-in-One Desk Reference
  For Dummies
  0-7645-3883-7
- Outlook 2003 For Dummies
  0-7645-3759-8
- PCs For Dummies
  0-7645-4074-2
- TiVo For Dummies
  0-7645-6923-6
- Upgrading and Fixing PCs For Dummies
  0-7645-1665-5
- Windows XP Timesaving Techniques
  For Dummies
  0-7645-3748-2

FOOD, HOME, GARDEN, HOBBIES, MUSIC & PETS

0-7645-5295-3

0-7645-5232-5

Also available:

- Bass Guitar For Dummies
  0-7645-2487-9
- Diabetes Cookbook For Dummies
  0-7645-5230-9
- Gardening For Dummies *
  0-7645-5130-2
- Guitar For Dummies
  0-7645-5106-X
- Holiday Decorating For Dummies
  0-7645-2570-0
- Home Improvement All-in-One
  For Dummies
  0-7645-5680-0

- Knitting For Dummies
  0-7645-5395-X
- Piano For Dummies
  0-7645-5105-1
- Puppies For Dummies
  0-7645-5255-4
- Scrapbooking For Dummies
  0-7645-7208-3
- Senior Dogs For Dummies
  0-7645-5818-8
- Singing For Dummies
  0-7645-2475-5
- 30-Minute Meals For Dummies
  0-7645-2589-1

INTERNET & DIGITAL MEDIA

0-7645-1664-7

0-7645-6924-4

Also available:

- 2005 Online Shopping Directory
  For Dummies
  0-7645-7495-7
- CD & DVD Recording For Dummies
  0-7645-5956-7
- eBay For Dummies
  0-7645-5654-1
- Fighting Spam For Dummies
  0-7645-5965-6
- Genealogy Online For Dummies
  0-7645-5964-8
- Google For Dummies
  0-7645-4420-9

- Home Recording For Musicians
  For Dummies
  0-7645-1634-5
- The Internet For Dummies
  0-7645-4173-0
- iPod & iTunes For Dummies
  0-7645-7772-7
- Preventing Identity Theft For Dummies
  0-7645-7336-5
- Pro Tools All-in-One Desk Reference
  For Dummies
  0-7645-5714-9
- Roxio Easy Media Creator For Dummies
  0-7645-7131-1

* Separate Canadian edition also available
† Separate U.K. edition also available

Available wherever books are sold. For more information or to order direct: U.S. customers visit www.dummies.com or call 1-877-762-2974.
U.K. customers visit www.wileyeurope.com or call 0800 243407. Canadian customers visit www.wiley.ca or call 1-800-567-4797.

SPORTS, FITNESS, PARENTING, RELIGION & SPIRITUALITY

0-7645-5146-9

0-7645-5418-2

Also available:

- Adoption For Dummies
  0-7645-5488-3
- Basketball For Dummies
  0-7645-5248-1
- The Bible For Dummies
  0-7645-5296-1
- Buddhism For Dummies
  0-7645-5359-3
- Catholicism For Dummies
  0-7645-5391-7
- Hockey For Dummies
  0-7645-5228-7

- Judaism For Dummies
  0-7645-5299-6
- Martial Arts For Dummies
  0-7645-5358-5
- Pilates For Dummies
  0-7645-5397-6
- Religion For Dummies
  0-7645-5264-3
- Teaching Kids to Read For Dummies
  0-7645-4043-2
- Weight Training For Dummies
  0-7645-5168-X
- Yoga For Dummies
  0-7645-5117-5

TRAVEL

0-7645-5438-7

0-7645-5453-0

Also available:

- Alaska For Dummies
  0-7645-1761-9
- Arizona For Dummies
  0-7645-6938-4
- Cancún and the Yucatán For Dummies
  0-7645-2437-2
- Cruise Vacations For Dummies
  0-7645-6941-4
- Europe For Dummies
  0-7645-5456-5
- Ireland For Dummies
  0-7645-5455-7

- Las Vegas For Dummies
  0-7645-5448-4
- London For Dummies
  0-7645-4277-X
- New York City For Dummies
  0-7645-6945-7
- Paris For Dummies
  0-7645-5494-8
- RV Vacations For Dummies
  0-7645-5443-3
- Walt Disney World & Orlando For Dummies
  0-7645-6943-0

GRAPHICS, DESIGN & WEB DEVELOPMENT

0-7645-4345-8

0-7645-5589-8

Also available:

- Adobe Acrobat 6 PDF For Dummies
  0-7645-3760-1
- Building a Web Site For Dummies
  0-7645-7144-3
- Dreamweaver MX 2004 For Dummies
  0-7645-4342-3
- FrontPage 2003 For Dummies
  0-7645-3882-9
- HTML 4 For Dummies
  0-7645-1995-6
- Illustrator cs For Dummies
  0-7645-4084-X

- Macromedia Flash MX 2004 For Dummies
  0-7645-4358-X
- Photoshop 7 All-in-One Desk Reference
  For Dummies
  0-7645-1667-1
- Photoshop cs Timesaving Techniques
  For Dummies
  0-7645-6782-9
- PHP 5 For Dummies
  0-7645-4166-8
- PowerPoint 2003 For Dummies
  0-7645-3908-6
- QuarkXPress 6 For Dummies
  0-7645-2593-X

NETWORKING, SECURITY, PROGRAMMING & DATABASES

0-7645-6852-3

0-7645-5784-X

Also available:

- A+ Certification For Dummies
  0-7645-4187-0
- Access 2003 All-in-One Desk Reference
  For Dummies
  0-7645-3988-4
- Beginning Programming For Dummies
  0-7645-4997-9
- C For Dummies
  0-7645-7068-4
- Firewalls For Dummies
  0-7645-4048-3
- Home Networking For Dummies
  0-7645-42796

- Network Security For Dummies
  0-7645-1679-5
- Networking For Dummies
  0-7645-1677-9
- TCP/IP For Dummies
  0-7645-1760-0
- VBA For Dummies
  0-7645-3989-2
- Wireless All In-One Desk Reference
  For Dummies
  0-7645-7496-5
- Wireless Home Networking For Dummies
  0-7645-3910-8

English Grammar Workbook For Dummies®

Punctuating Sentences Correctly

I cover all the punctuation marks in this book, but here are some quick tips for when and how to use the marks that most often trip people up:

Comma:

- ✔ To set apart the name of a person being addressed
- ✔ After an introductory expression
- ✔ To separate extra, nonessential statements from the rest of the sentence

Semicolon:

- ✔ To join two complete sentences without using *and, but,* and similar words
- ✔ To separate items in a list when at least one item contains a comma

Colon:

- ✔ Following the *Dear Sir or Madam* line in a business letter
- ✔ To introduce a long quotation or a list

Dash:

- ✔ To separate and emphasize an extra comment in a sentence
- ✔ To show a range

Apostrophe:

- ✔ To show possession (*Herman's* hermit, the *girls'* gym class)
- ✔ To substitute for missing numerals (*'07*)
- ✔ To substitute for missing letters in contractions (*Isn't, what's,* and *he's,* for example)

Hyphens:

- ✔ Divide words or syllables at the end of a line
- ✔ Link two descriptions of one word (*second-string quarterback*)
- ✔ Attach prefixes to capitalized words (*anti-Communist*)

Adding Variety to Sentences

Add interest to your writing with these tricks:

- ✔ **Start with a description.** *(Dangling over the cliff, Martha considered her options.)*
- ✔ **Combine sentences by inserting one idea into another.** *(Martha, who hated heights, looked at the ground.)*
- ✔ **Occasionally reverse the usual subject-verb order.** *(On the valley floor thumped Martha.)*
- ✔ **Cut unnecessary words.** *(The mountain was 3000 feet high in altitude.)*
- ✔ **Look for strong verbs.** (*Strolled* or *rushed* instead of *went,* for example)

Commonly Confused Words

Affect: Generally a verb meaning "to influence"
Effect: Usually a noun meaning "result"

Good: Describes a person, place, thing, or idea
Well: Describes an action

Lie: As a verb, "to rest or recline"
Lay: As a verb, "to place in a certain position"

Its: Shows possession
It's: Contraction of "it is"

There: Indicates a position or place
Their: Shows possession
They're: Contraction of "they are"

Like: As a preposition, means "similar to"
As: Precedes a subject/verb statement

Because: Introduces a reason
Since: Makes a statement about time

If: Indicates a possibility
Whether: Introduces two choices ("whether or not")

That: Preceding a subject/verb statement, usually introduces essential information and *isn't* preceded by a comma
Which: Preceding a subject/verb statement, indicates extra information and *is* preceded by a comma

Between: For two choices
Among: For a group of three or more

Farther: Use for distance
Further: Use for time or intensity

Different from: The correct expression!
Different than: Not correct in standard English

Healthy: Refers to physical or mental well-being
Healthful: Refers to habits or food that contribute to good health

Comprise: To consist of; to be composed of. For example, "The United Nations *comprises* more than 100 countries."
Compose: To make up something. For example, "The United Nations *is composed of* more than 100 countries."

Who's: A contraction meaning "who is."
Whose: A possessive pronoun (belonging to *who*).

English Grammar Workbook For Dummies®

Cheat Sheet

The Anatomy of a Complete Sentence

For a sentence to be complete, it must have all of the following:

- At least one subject/verb pair
- A complete, coherent thought
- An endmark (period, question mark, or exclamation point)

Descriptions that Are Incomparable

Words that express absolute states can't be compared. Take the following, for example:

- **Unique** (not *really unique* or *very unique*).
- **Round** (never *rounder* or *roundest*).
- **Perfect** (not *more perfect* or *extremely perfect*).
- **True** (stay away from *most true*).
- **Dead** (*deader* or *deadest*? I don't think so.)

Tricky Singular/Plural Situations

A lot of the time, it's pretty obvious whether a noun is singular or plural. Some words, however, aren't so clear, making the task of determining whether you should use a singular or plural verb with them tough. Follow these guidelines:

- *Each* and *every* create a singular subject, no matter what they precede, and therefore take a singular verb.
- Pronouns containing *-body, -thing,* and *-one* (such as *everybody, anything,* and *someone*) are singular and can't pair with *their* (a plural).
- Companies are singular; they take a singular verb and pronoun (*it*, not *they* or *their)*.
- In sentences that contain *neither/nor* or *either/or*, match the verb to the closest subject.

What to Capitalize

- Proper names
- The first word in a sentence
- Titles before and attached to names
- Titles used as substitutes for names
- The first word and all other important words in a title or subtitle. (See Chapter 9 for the nuances of headline-style titles and sentence-style titles.)
- Each letter in an acronym
- Some abbreviations. (See Chapter 9 for details.)

What to Lowercase

- Years in school (*senior, junior,* and so forth)
- School subjects, except for languages (*history, science,* and *algebra,* for example)
- Titles not attached to or used as names
- Directions (*north, south, inward, up,* and so on)
- General terms for geographical features (*canyon, river, mountain,* and the like)
- Scholarly degrees

Possessive Rules

To use possessive nouns and pronouns properly, follow these rules:

- Make a possessive noun by adding an apostrophe and the letter *s* to a singular noun.
- Tack an apostrophe to a plural noun that ends in the letter *s* to create a possessive.
- To show possession, add an apostrophe and the letter *s* to a plural noun that doesn't end in the letter *s*.
- Possessive pronouns (*my, his, theirs, whose,* and so forth) never contain apostrophes.
- Place a possessive noun or pronoun in front of an *-ing* verb form used as a noun (*my* swimming, *Arthur's* dancing, and the like).

Copyright © 2006 Wiley Publishing, Inc.
All rights reserved.
Item 9932-1
For more information about Wiley Publishing, call 1-800-762-2974.

For Dummies: Bestselling Book Series for Beginners